Broken Truths

Nigeria's Elusive Quest for National Cohesion

Adonis & Abbey Publishers Ltd
24 Old Queen Street, London SW1H 9HP United Kingdom
Website: http://www.adonis-abbey.com
E-mail Address: editor@adonis-abbey.com

Website: http://www.adonis-abbey.com
E-mail Address: editor@adonis-abbey.com

Nigeria:
No. 39 Jimmy Carter Street, Suites C3 – C6 J-Plus Plaza Asokoro, Abuja, Nigeria
Tel: +234 (0) 7058078841/08052035034

British Library Cataloguing-in-Publication Data
A catalogue record for this book is available from the British Library

ISBN: 9781913976118

Broken Truths

Nigeria's Elusive Quest for National Cohesion

Matthew Hassan Kukah

ADONIS & ABBEY
PUBLISHERS LTD

Broken Truths is an essential reading for anyone wishing to understand Nigeria's current identity crisis and to find ways to help resolve it. Bishop Kukah brings both solid academic analysis alongside four decades of experience building bridges across Nigeria's religious and ethnic divides to his candid assessment.... Drawing on politics, history, religion, and tradition, Bishop Kukah delivers lectures that show remarkable consistency in diagnosing Nigeria's fundamental governance problems, as well as a prophetic knack for revealing what has come to pass: a divided society struggling for its ethical soul, with many opportunities for change but saddled with leaders unwilling to embrace a vision of broad-based public good.

Darren Kew, Ph.D.
Associate Professor, University of Massachusetts, Boston
Executive Director, Center for Peace, Democracy, and Development

---

In this *tour de force*, made up of a collection of convocation Lectures at universities across Nigeria's vast and diverse geopolitical zones, Bishop Kukah confirms and reestablishes his solid and inimitable reputation as an incisive and thoughtful, if also provocative public intellectual. He forcefully and passionately speaks truth not only to power but also to the generality of Nigerians about their political and social responsibility to keep faith with the country's founding fathers' and mothers' vision of a federal Nigeria, anchored on the pursuit of "Unity in Diversity."
...*Broken Truths: Nigeria's Elusive Quest for National Cohesion* takes on significance in mapping the way to resolve the crisis in meaningful, dispassionate, and public-interest ways

Bishop Kukah's narration in this collection, simple, straightforward, captivating, didactic, and optimistic, is a story of a mixture of hope, sin, and redemption, set in a cross-national and global comparative mould. It refreshingly makes the case that, beyond the fetishism of our particular identities, the way forward is to respect and recognize our various identities, which add up to our common universality. This is the enduring and powerful message of *Broken Truths: Nigeria's Elusive Quest for National Cohesion.*

L. Adele Jinadu, *Professor of Political Science & Non-Resident Senior Fellow of the Centre for Democracy & Development Past President African Association of Political Science, Past Vice President, International Political Science Association*

Bishop Kukah has been at the forefront of public life in Nigeria for many decades. This book not only gives a comprehensive overview of the many problems facing Nigeria but importantly it offers solutions for how the country can get out of the quagmire it is currently facing. It is a call to action to young Nigerians, to chart a new course for their country and should be essential reading for all those invested in Nigeria's future.

Idayat Hassan, *Director, Centre for Democracy and Development, Abuja*

Bishop Kukah is at his best when addressing university audiences as the context frees his imagination to explore the intellectual depths of our national problems and how to solve them. The essays in this compendium explore two problems – the fracture caused by the manipulation of ethno-religious divides and consistent failure of leadership. The result is the inability to engage the path of correction which would involve accepting the plural nature of our society, managing our diversity effectively and building national cohesion. His language is brutally honest, hurting many sensibilities, but then the core message is that broken truths can only amplify, not solve our problems.

Professor Jibrin Ibrahim, *Senior Fellow, Centre for Democracy and Development, Abuja*

Brilliantly, clearly, insistently and almost stridently, Bishop Kukah in these collection of convocation lectures in Nigerian universities, makes his arguments for active and honest citizenship and committed and transformative leadership with the vision, determination and openness to engage our plural identities as Nigerians and tackle our most difficult governance and developments as peoples united by common irreversible destinies. Bishop Kukah as he usually does in a profoundly humane way makes the call for action that recognizes the integrity of our individual and collective spiritual and political selves.

Tade Akin Aina, *Scholar, Poet and Researcher, Head of Research, Mastercard Foundation, Kigali, Rwanda, Toronto, Canada.*

Table of Contents

Dedication

The Collection is dedicated to all the Members of the Academic community who believe in the power of Ideas to change societies. To all those Universities that opened their doors to me and those invitations I am still to attend to and all the Students in our institutions of learning, hold the dream because we will all change our country sooner than later.

Foreword

Even to an audience of readers who are getting to know or hear from one of the most revered persons in Africa, Bishop Matthew Hassan Kukah, for the first time in their intellectual inquiry, spotting his intellectual ingenuity is the least they can do as they listen to his captivating words and the constructive arguments he weaves together in all fora. However, for anyone familiar with the fecundity of his intellectual productions, this book would strengthen their academic bond created and sustained by a culture of originality that the man has built for himself since coming to the public limelight. The essentialism of Bishop Kukah's intellectual trajectory as far as Nigeria's and, by extension, African (socio-) political discourse is concerned, is underscored by a couple of things that are yet again provided in substantial quantity in this instructive exploration. When the Bishop speaks, he creates his audience, and even the enforcement of a wrong set of the audience does not bother his awareness that his message must meet the target people–his own audience. Bishop Kukah writes for the ones within whose capacity lies the ability to transform the society–the youth–and irrespective of the age-group of audiences before him, he has a way of making his messages evaporate that spatial confinement to meet his targets.

Furthermore, Bishop Kukah comfortably merges spiritual resourcefulness with cultural and political thoughts, which has helped him see the basic requirements that propel a nation into greatness when they undertake them and understand the framework of the many civilizations that have attained enviable development through it. Anyone unfamiliar with how he achieved this in his previous academic engagement is given another golden opportunity to grab this knowledge in this work he has premiered. The African writer is guilty of complicity because he writes to get personal endorsement and development by painting his people in a bad light. Consider, for example, that one of the issues addressed in this work is the place of identity construction enhanced by writers, and this is the first stage of development that a person must reach to attain a geometrical height in their desire for self-discovery, self-realization, and growth.

To this extent, this book challenges creative writers on whose shoulders lie the responsibility of showcasing Africa to the world.

However, after realizing that his target audience in the book is the youths (Nigerian youths and African youths in general), readers can reaffirm that he has his audience in mind, even when circumstantial audiences are given to him. Although he is aware that the political class is the primary culprits of this scourge, he does not carry his message to them, obviously because he is aware that their heart is sealed and may be immune to common universal morals.

All the intellectual unfoldings in this book are a cornucopia of the lectures he delivered at different universities in the country, stressing implicitly that the roles of university institutions as a laboratory of critical reasoning and constructive ideas production cannot be underplayed by the government's unserious or lackadaisical attitudes to education. Universities are ivory towers where ideas are developed to redeem the people's condemnable history and rejuvenate the energy that would give them the audacity to ask for their greatness. People do this in different ways, one of which is by the conscious application of theoretical and philosophical ideas absorbed in their seeking knowledge so that their future would be recreated in ways that would generally have an enduring impact on them. This way, Bishop Kukah has always said, is the most effective way to use education as an instrument.

If Nigeria is an attentive student, all the materials needed for its transformation are given at zero cost in this book by the sagacious Bishop Kukah. The book provides an excellent overview of Nigeria's problems. Among other things, it identifies that the foundation for the deterioration of the country is caused by the systematic division orchestrated by its leaders and the political merchants whose primary, and by far the most important, aspiration on Nigeria is not how they would facilitate its geometric acceleration in political, economic, social, cultural spheres, but how they would make gains off the country's woes. The author laments this idea as it is considered highly acidic to the growth of the country. He asserts that having such corrupt ambition against the country has sterilized all sense of moral rectitude and drained every energy capable of instigating them into actions that would bring any iota of good tidings to the country. Without mincing words, the solution to this otherwise complex condition is offered. The fact that people can identify terrorism, hooliganism, political mercantilism, and other dangerous enemies of the nation's growth means that the identifier has successfully done the preliminary job.

The job of offering solutions to the myriad of challenges facilitated by the factors identified is the actual definition of problem-solving. Bishop Kukah knows, and so do the perpetrators of the evil, that the proliferation of terrorist activities would wreak maximum discord on the bond that ties the country together. Unlike them, however, he knows that the devastating consequences could be enduring and, in the most extreme cases, plant a generational seed of mistrust, distrust, and mutual suspicion. In this case, the innocent future generations who are uninvolved in the perpetuation of the crises would be the ones suffering from the pangs of violence that their ancestors (living today) have caused them.

This book would reveal that underneath the author's avoidance of the political class and his embracement of the academic society to talk to a group of people who would be launched into the different institutions of the Nigerian society is a conclusion that the hearts of the evil perpetrators are sealed. In addition, it demonstrates that it would be more profitable to plant the seed of moral rectitude into the ones who are still innocent and whose hearts are still tender to accommodate critical reasoning. The progression of Bishop Kukah's intellectual charity to the different Nigerian universities, as exemplified in this book, would show the observant reader that the author understands that part of the raging consequences of irresponsible leadership is its encouragement of divisive politics, ethnocentric narratives, and obsessive tribal loyalty, all of which would be eternally dangerous to the oneness of the country.

Meanwhile, it does not require the intelligence of Albert Einstein to understand this, especially when one is familiar with the political project of the country, Nigeria. However, despite one's intelligence, what is challenging to get is the ability to understand how all these weaken the identity infrastructure of the country and how yet again they remain sources of their moral and psychological paralysis. This author effortlessly marshals his arguments, emphasizing that the country is fractured by the form of politics its leaders play or resolve to play, regardless of its proven insensitivity to the nation's good health. However, players at the political ring or in the corridors of power may be intellectually deficient in recognizing that their actions are anti-democratic and against commonsense; the country cannot be protected from the imminent damnation that hangs in the balance as a result of their ignorance.

Again, when a nation sustains an injury due to the overlapping ignorance or uncharismatic attitudes of its leaders, it is difficult to find solutions within them. And this is where countries or other forms of human identity are characteristically different from others. An injury sustained by an individual would be dressed on them, and the proper antidote would be administered accordingly. However, the situation is different when the injury is inflicted on a nation. For it to be effectively attended to, the innocent ones coming behind would be the ones to receive the antidote, for they would serve as the flesh to replace the older ones when the older ones become obsolete. This is precisely the crusade that Bishop Kukah embarks on through his delivery of critical thinking simulating lectures across various universities in the country.

Nigeria is bleeding both literally and literarily, and it requires an extraordinary boldness from its intellectuals, who, in this case, are the medical experts, to tend to its open wounds, confront the injury, and apply the necessary cure to it. This is another reason this foresighted individual gave various lectures on how the country can first heal from its wound and be poised to take preventive measures against similar occurrences in the future. This lies with the emerging generation, and they need to be told right from their (under)graduate level of study what responsibility lies ahead of them if Nigeria is to become their dream country.

At this rate, one would clearly understand what Bishop Kukah's agenda has been all along. For the most part, this outstanding individual is concerned about leadership in the country. He understands that those in tertiary institutions would dominate the leadership positions, obviously because they would occupy the various aspects of the country's institutions. Whether they function as presidents, senators, governors, chairmen, or councillors in their various political geography, what is essential is that they would lead with what they have in their heads. Therefore, the straightforward formula of garbage in, garbage out would be inevitably applied, which means that if their skulls are empty of ideas, they would not be far from being a burden to the system. Quality leadership would be substituted for empty grandstanding, efficient policies would be replaced by empty rhetoric, and purposeful nation-building would be replaced by blatant patrimonialism, which would exacerbate the nation's problems, which can be highly devastating When such is noted, it becomes the duty of the foresighted ones to offer lasting solutions to the problems, and that is what Bishop Kukah has done in this book you are holding. He puts it rather more poignantly, and you do not need to take my word for it. Read the book.

I predict that, just like me, every reader of this book would be struck by one symbolic idea that the basis for the evangelization of revolutionary thinking is the awareness that the Nigerian case or situation is significant. Powerful not because the country is a combination of heterogeneous identities but because symbolic historical experiences define and make it unique. It is important not to get carried away with the notion that the various inter-ethnic hostilities that have characterized Nigeria post-independence, which is peculiar to previously colonized geographies, are why the country is different politically. Having approached elastic limits through various altercations and contentions, the country has retraced its national steps and, in the process, replanted the nationalist spirit into the hearts of the heady ones, which is the foundation of my conclusion that Nigeria is significant. Although many people have proposed that various ethnic groups in the country should foreclose ethnic sentiments as the basis for building a solid and formidable civilization, I do not subscribe to this irascible conclusion, and my reading of this book shows that the author and I hold identical ground on this conclusion.

A people's cultural identity is their primary legacy to which they are introduced before they are exposed to the political identity that binds them. The fact that they thus are bound to others by this creed, however, does not invalidate their ethnic identity, but there is the vast possibility that they may be consciously nurtured to embrace a nation of plural identities to which they would pledge their moral loyalty in nurturing. This would create a sense of respect for themselves and others, bearing in mind that they owe others a similar amount of sincerity in their business of building the country. When they attain this level of consciousness, they would understand that their dedication to the country's development is necessary because it would determine their collective survival and enhance their national respect and place them within the appropriate place on the map of modernity. It explains the persistence of this ingenious individual to reiterate the need for the consolidation of the different cultural ideas in the country for collective purposes. Notably, it is soothing that he highlights the various ways

These can be achieved in this book.

This book would be of interdisciplinary importance because it allows readers from a wide range of academic backgrounds to draw ideas that correspond to their theoretical modelling and gives them pointers to develop more ideas from what he has provided here. The political message for the country's generality is latent and evident in the different instances he draws in the book. Meanwhile, the student populace is allowed to look at the country from different perspectives and challenge themselves on the numerous ways by which they can be of assistance to its rejuvenation. Historians who care to consolidate their knowledge about the factors that shape the history of a country will also benefit from the book because they would find sufficient materials that would improve on what the knowledge they have already, challenge them where necessary, and also shed light on otherwise dark areas of their scholarship, especially about the nation.

What remains paramount in this work is the encouragement to rebuild a nation that has remained destabilized because those saddled with the responsibility of constructing a good one has different ambitions. They are distracted by these very ambitions that they end up causing more problems for the country to solve than they met. Undoubtedly, this book will boost your understanding of the country. It is a journey worth taking.

Toyin Falola,
University Distinguished Professor
Jacob and Sanger Mossiker Chair in the Humanities
The University of Texas at Austin

———

Introduction

Over the years, I have found myself being drawn to the University Community for both pastoral and academic reasons. Pastorally, I have served briefly, formally and informally as Chaplain in a few Universities in Nigeria and in the UK in the course of my studies abroad. At a second level, I have participated in the academic life of Universities in the course of my public speaking engagements spanning the better part of well over forty years. I have served at the highest levels of policy formulation and implementation in a few Universities in Nigeria in the following capacities: Vice Chairman, Board of Trustees, American University, Yola, 2012-2020, Pro Chancellor & Chairman, Governing Council, Nasarawa State University, 2014-2018, Chairman, BOT, Nok University, Kachia, 2021- Pro Chancellor & Chairman, Governing Council, Veritas Catholic University, 2022-. I have received Honorary Doctorate Degrees from private and government owned Universities across the country. With all sense of modesty, I can claim to be more than a spectator in the arena of academia.

In all of these I have come into close contact with the management dynamics of our Universities. In a sense, I have come to appreciate the huge gaps and changes that have happened in the University system in Nigeria over the years. I have seen the ebb and flow of academic life from the early days of the first universities to the crises that were heightened around the 80s. Today, the Nigerian University has become a theatre of miniature wars waged against the backdrop of conflict of interests between the academic and non-academic staff on the one hand and the government on the other. The interests of students who are the reason why the institutions exist have often been sidelined in the course of these turf wars.

The average Nigerian my age will have more than a fair idea of what it was to be a student in what we can call the first generation universities such as the University of Ibadan, Ibadan, University of Nigeria, Nsukka, Ahmadu Bello University, Zaria. They were followed in the late 70s and 80s by such other Universities as those of Benin, Ife, Calabar, and Lagos. Then, from the return of Democracy in 1999 onwards, State Governments and individuals began to establish both State and Private Universities across the country. The last ten or so years have seen what can best be described as a boom as the total numbers have now soared to well over 120 universities across Nigeria.

Years of military coups and counter coups gradually took a toll on

University education. The military, obsessed with their command structure saw academic freedom as a threat to the power of the state. With no reflexes for debates, negotiations and consensus building, the military dictators soon came on a collision course with the University system. University lecturers, anxious to defend both their academic freedom and welfare were insistent on a creating a conducive environment for research and teaching. In 1978, the Lecturers set up an umbrella for negotiating with both the university management and the federal government known as the Association of Staff Union of Universities, ASUU to replace the former Nigerian Association of University Teachers in 1965.

The federal government responded by charging ASUU with the insubordination for; **teaching what they were not paid to teach!** The tensions would later break the university walls, leading to arrests, sacking or dismissals of academic staff. Senior academic staff woke up to a *season of migration* in their hundreds and later, thousands leading to the loss of substantial manpower. We watched as the migrations became a deluge. Today, it is the miracle of the indefatigable spirit of Nigeria that despite it all, hundreds, thousands of new entrants have ensured that the wheels of academic learning continued to turn in Nigeria. Warts and all, the Nigerian University has displayed the greatest resilience.

In a way, my involvement with civil society in the struggle against military rule ensured that I found myself drawn to the arena of politics within the Universities through ASUU. I shared in their passion and was friend to some of the most distinguished members of their family. I had felt persuaded by the moral force of the likes of Claude Ake, Bala Usman, Festus Iyayi, George and his brother, Mike Kwanashie, Eskor Toyo, Bade Onimode, and the younger generation of scholars such as Attahiru Jega, Jibrin Jibo and many others too numerous to mention. We may have had ideological differences but Nigeria is too broken for the seeds of any ideology to even germinate. It has been simply a matter of life and death for the ordinary citizen.

In the later years of my life, most especially from the last twenty or so years, my engagements with the University have taken a slightly different tone, moving from the culture of **aluta** to the Boardroom. Perhaps this may have come with circumspection of age, but, somehow, my focus and beliefs have remained the same: the university must be the incubator holding the visions and values of what must constitute a good society.

In the course of the last twenty years, I have been a recipient of Honorary Doctorate Degrees from universities such as Ebonyi State University, Abakaliki, Afe Babalola University, Ekiti, American University, Yola, Achievers University, Owo. I found myself being invited to deliver Convocation lectures from north to south. I have managed to juggle my time and accepted most of the invitations. Some, I just could not accommodate on my schedule or we just deferred to another day in future. All of these have simply humbled me because they are not honours one can take lightly in a complex society such as ours.

Nigerians have witnessed a steady decline in the quality of teaching and the loss of motivation and morale in Nigerian universities. Funding education generally has remained a source of serious controversy. However, one has also watched as our Universities have gradually descended into ethno-religious enclaves where ethnicity, religious bigotry, regionalism, petty jealousies have distracted the academic community from providing our nation with an intellectual roadmap for national development. Being introduced as a university teacher elicits at best a yawn especially as citizens have gradually moved to worship the gods of scandalous opportunism, corruption and malfeasance that have engulfed the country. I have remained an optimist: without a good university system, we have no future.

Thus, the book in your hands, **Broken Tongues,** is a first volume that aims at bringing some of my Convocation Lectures to the larger public. The reader will appreciate that there is a slightly different style to these lectures as can be seen in their length. I can understand if the reader considers them to be too long. However, the setting of the Convocation Lecture that I became familiar with was often different from what obtains in other places where such lectures are inserted in the programme of Convocation ceremonies. All the Lectures I delivered were stand- alone events and I was often told to speak for one hour or any time of my choice.

It is these settings that allowed me to introduce themes that I often believed needed to become part of debate and discussions within or without the Institution. I am not good at reading my text word for word before the camera or my audiences. As such, my idea has often been to present a menu that would be consumed by the staff and students well afterwards. I am unable to measure how effective this style has been, but

Introduction

my idea has always been to encourage more seminars or debates around these issues.

I am simply putting the reader on advance notice as to the length of these Lectures. In many instances, my lectures have been printed by the Universities on the eve of the presentations, but distributions have naturally been within a small part of the academic community. Over the years, I have come under pressure from a wide section of the Nigerian population asking for permission to publish my articles, papers and lectures. A good number have offered to do so at their own personal expenses. I have been surprise by the number of people who tell me that they have created a section of my writings in their personal homes or libraries. I am therefore hopeful that by putting out this first set of academic Essays, I will satisfy the interests of those who have, to use their own words, craved for my writings to be in permanent print.

In 2005, the Indian born renowned philosopher, economist, and Nobel prize winner, Professor Amartya Sen published a book titled, **The Argumentative Indian**. Essentially, the book of Essays draws from the Indian tradition of debates and argument and sees the tradition of arguments as being necessary for the enhancement of Democracy. I am persuaded by the argument of Sen and that is the reason why I have found these lectures a very important outlet for the generation of ideas for the public good. In the process of these interventions in public debate, I agree that by challenging the state's power structures which are often not aligned to the common good, I am, like the famous South African writer, Donald Woods, titled his autobiography, **asking for trouble**. However, in my humble view, I am convinced that **asking for trouble** is the greatest service a public intellectual can offer to his society because it points at a more noble vision for the society. Intelligent argumentation, with no malicious intent can be a source of repentance, renewal and rejuvenation for a fractured society.

The reader will see that the Lectures are not laden with footnotes and so on. I have tried to use a language that is quite accessible to both the academician and students. The strength of any argument is not to be measured by those who agree with us, but how well the point being made draws attention to larger issues and stirs further debates and clarifications. I am hopeful that this collection will help to generate more ideas as we seek to build a better society. The reader will forgive the fact that in a few of the Lectures, some quotations have been repeated in more than one lecture. This speaks to the importance of the relevant quotations or references to me. I am not unaware that my thoughts are not original, but perhaps calling attention to our situation will help to heal the brokenness of our nation.

Finally, I want to thank my good friend Professor Toyin Falola who not only read through all the drafts but made very useful comments and wrote the Foreword. I am thankful to Sr. Kathleen McGarvey, OLA, who read many of these draft Lectures when they were first written and often made some challenging observations. I thank my publisher, Professor Jideofor Adibe and his team at Adonis & Abbey Publishers. Professor Adibe proved to be a core professional with a keen eye and a pretty hard task master. He made some useful observations and comments. To you, the reader, for holding this book in your hands, I am thankful and hope that it contributes to given some direction in our struggle to fix this great country.

On 24th February, 2022, a shocked world woke up to the news of Russian invasion of Ukraine. There are no moral claims of ridding the world of weapons of mass destruction or an evil dictator. I feel a sense of vindication in my decision to include the final chapter, The Just War Theory and the Iraq War which was written for a different audience outside Nigeria. I had always felt that the issues in the paper required further debates and clarification amidst the violence unleashed by religious extremists constantly making dubious moral claims for their evil. I hope the reader finds it useful and that we all learn that human stupidity and the arrogance of power will remain with us for some time.

CHAPTER ONE

Nigeria & the Future of Africa

My conclusion in this Lecture is that despite our fractured history, Nigeria has a date with destiny. Tragic as our collective failures have been, it is my firm belief that even the best of our critics has done very little to deepen our understanding of how and why we are the way we are. Most of our commentators have focused their analysis on describing the nature of our woes. Consequently, a blanket of self-doubt and pity has been spread over us no thanks to those who ought to have shown the way. Whereas other nations have adopted storytelling, the construction of myths, and the invention and construction of identity to define their roles and place in history, we have turned our own stories and myths into instruments for self-laceration and cultural suicide.

The Nigerians writers, artists and historians have not helped us in our understanding of ourselves. Our novelists focus more on our failures, while our artists create the impression that all there is to life in Nigeria is drugs, witchcraft, demonism, and blood. Our historians have focused on our divisions, behaving as if our occasional misunderstanding and clashes, whether they be based on religion or ethnicity, are anything different from what is happening elsewhere. Binyavanga Wainaina, the late Kenyan writer, has offered a satirical piece of advice for those who are writing about Africa especially those with an eye on a big literary prize. He says:

> Among your characters you must always include The Starving African, who wanders the refugee camp nearly naked, and waits for the benevolence of the West. Her children have flies on their eyelids and pot bellies, and her breasts are flat and empty. She must look utterly helpless. She can have no past, no history; such diversions ruin the dramatic moment. Moans are good. She must never say anything about herself in the dialogue except to speak of her (unspeakable) suffering... Avoid having the African characters laugh, or struggle to educate their kids, or just make do in mundane circumstances. Have them illuminate

something about Europe or America in Africa. African characters should be colourful, exotic, larger than life—but empty inside, with no dialogue, no conflicts or resolutions in their stories, no depth or quirks to confuse the cause... Describe, in detail, naked breasts (young, old, conservative, recently raped, big, small) or mutilated genitals, or enhanced genitals. Or any kind of genitals. And dead bodies. Or, better, naked dead bodies. And especially rotting naked dead bodies. Remember, any work you submit in which people look filthy and miserable will be referred to as the 'real Africa', and you want that on your dust jacket. Do not feel queasy about this: you are trying to help them to get aid from the West. The biggest taboo in writing about Africa is to describe or show dead or suffering white people."[1]

This is the stuff of Nobel Prizes and other international awards that drive African writings more than the patriotic urge to paint our countries in their positive image. Almost every nation's history today is the result of mythical construction, redefinition and repackaging by their scholars. Whether it be Conrad, Rudyard Kipling, or a Mungo Park, their stories shaped the way their people saw us and still see us. Sadly, we have still not found our way out of this deliberately constructed prison.

America's greatness today has been constructed on the foundation of carefully constructed myths of origin and alleged *manifest destiny.* Whether presented as a *city on a hill,* or their land as *God's own country*, the founding fathers of modern United States of America have succeeded by manufacturing an identity of greatness and invincibility. A deliberate and very careful reconstruction of history has redefined the way the rest of the world perceives the modern United States of America. Today, the United States, a former British colony, has turned its former colonizer into a glorified outpost. The United Kingdom now defines its future in relation to whether or not they are on the right side of the United States. It was to avoid causing harm to this relationship that Tony Blair, the former British Prime Minister, followed Bush to war blind folded.

To assert its independence, the Americans altered the vocabulary of the English language, and in most areas of their lives, from the cinema,

---

[1] www.granta.com/extracts/2615 -

sports, and literature, they managed to put paid to the overbearing role of British colonialism and taste. They have changed Soccer and Cricket to American Football and Baseball, they have changed the way that the rest of the world sees their role in the history of slavery. They have managed to ensure that their memories and ours about the Indians are distorted or tailored to suit their ideology. Indeed, Keith Richburg, in his controversial book, *Out of America: A Black Man Confronts Africa*, ends his story by thanking God that his ancestors were taken out of Africa and in the process, he was saved from the tragedy that is Africa today.

China, hitherto, a back-water country which was conquered by Japan, today stands on the pinnacle of world greatness. Today, it is clear that the whole of the 21st century belongs to China. They turned their back on the so called programme of modernization offered by the rampaging, terrorizing western colonisers who were then poised to overrun and subjugate the world. India, Malaysia, Indonesia or Singapore have achieved monumental and unstoppable growth largely by seeking their identity by looking inwards. This is why the likes of Lee Kwan Yew and Mohammed Mahathir have attributed their success to their *Asian values* which became the plank for their development and growth. African scholars and patriots spoke of and dreamt of an African Renaissance, but all that has paled into a whimper, now drowned by the sad noise generated by our blind mimicking of other values. Let me not bore you, but I will return to these themes later.

My concern in this Lecture is to address the complex problems that our nation faces, compared with the dreams and visions of others, and ask if, indeed, this nation has a future or if it is doomed to failure as the cynics among us want us to believe. Categorically, my conclusion is that a great future awaits our nation. But for that to happen, we need to create new myths, move away from the distorted pictures that have emerged from the writing of some of our respected artists who present only the worst of our nation.

By defaming our nation and swearing by the truths of international do-gooders couched as international aid, Non-Governmental Agencies and institutions of charity do the same, without decoding their agenda. We are of course winning international recognition and awards by painting the images that reinforce already existing western prejudices. Today, one major reason why Nigerians believe their nation is corrupt is because *Transparency International* says so, Human Rights Watch is the one to determine the level of our human rights violations. The only story that Nigerians will swear by is the one they heard from the *British Broadcasting Corporation (BBC), Cable News Network, CNN* and so on. We all foolishly assume that these organisations have no agenda and we fail to believe how much they are tied to both big capital and their governments. Lou Dobbs has published a very curious book titled, *War on the Middle Class: How the Government, Big Business, and Special Interest Groups Are Waging War on the American Dream and How to Fight Back*. It is the story of how big business has held America to ransom and how this influence is used to frustrate the ordinary working American. It reads like a book on a developing nation!

I wish to argue that the future of Africa and black people is intrinsically bound to the future of Nigeria. I also wish to argue that imbibing the democratic ethos and institutionalizing democratic processes and culture will create a climate of freedom, thus enabling the energies of our people to blossom for the attainment of greatness. I will therefore divide this paper into four sections and a conclusion. Section 1 will briefly review the historical processes that have led us to where we are today and show how these forces have constrained our progress. Section 2 will identify democracy as the key to laying the foundation to national cohesion and integration and briefly explore Nigeria's hazardous journey. Section 3 will locate the place of Nigeria in the struggle for African renewal. By way of Conclusion, I will seek to identify what we need to do and why our institutions of higher learning must be repositioned to help our nation rise beyond the sad past that makes us belief that we are somehow *children of a lesser god*. I also wish to argue that a new institution like **Benson Idahosa University** is well placed to provide a combination of intellectual and moral education as a tool for development of the new African as a person of faith and belief in his/her God-given capabilities.

1. Decoding the Nigerian Mosaic: Who are We and What are We?

Nigerians have pooh-poohed the idea that their country was named by the mistress of Lord Lugard after the River Niger. We have continued to dredge up and recycle old tales about why we have not progressed, and we have based them on some accidents of history. These arguments range from the ravages of slavery and colonialism to the decision to bring together groups of varying and complex cultural outlooks. For example, we are often told that our inability to unite is because Nigeria is not a nation by deliberate choice and that our unity was contrived. This is anchored on a popular mantra which says that Nigeria is a *mere geographical expression*. Although this expression has been attributed to the late Chief Obafemi Awolowo and has become part of the sacred texts for explaining why we are not making much progress, it is clear upon further reflection that this is not fully correct. Not only does this view predate the late sage, it was never really original to him and he may have actually borrowed it from Churchill, the former British Prime Minister who also seems to have borrowed the idea from someone else.

The notion of a *mere geographical expression* was apparently first used in 1814 by Prince Clemens Metternich, a key player in the Congress of Vienna and who used the concept to deny any serious concessions to Italy. The Congress lasted between November 1, 1814 and June 8, 1815. It was called after the defeat of Napoleon to help deal with the issues of new boundaries within Europe. Prince Metternich was a bitter enemy of both democracy and freedom. Subsequently, in 1928, one Edward Lewis warned that if the United States did not sit up, it would, like Italy become a *mere geographical expression*. Churchill subsequently warned that Britain ran the risk of irrelevance by being a *mere geographical expression!* Perhaps it is from here that Chief Awolowo may have borrowed the notion and applied it to Nigeria. So, those who use this expression to argue against the possibility of Nigeria's attainment of greatness, need to come up with new ideas because we are in good company. An understanding of this is important because it should help us appreciate the fact that there is no shortcut to greatness. Every nation has had to go through the tortuous hills and valleys of history. Overcoming these obstacles has been the key to survival.

Secondly, I do not feel that even the best of us have really and truly come to appreciate the peculiar nature of Nigeria's story. Perhaps, it is important for us to restate what we are ***Not***, rather than focus too much on recycled stereotypes that have become our identity, purporting to define who we are. Sad as these stereotypes may be, they are partly the result of deliberately skewed scholarship which has luxuriated in celebrating our nation's failures. Whatever anyone may say about Nigeria and Nigerians, we are not like any other black nation in the world. Indeed, when one closely examines this country, its peculiar mix or complexity, we cannot but appreciate the fact that this nation occupies a special place in God's plans. Indeed, it does seem that outsiders do appreciate this distinctiveness of Nigeria far more than we do. As I said, Nigerians must appreciate what we are *Not*.

We are black, but there is something about the Nigerian as a black person. We are not like the black *African Americans*, descendants of our Africans carried away by slavery to the United States of America. We are not black people who are descendants of black slaves from the Caribbean islands that are predominantly in the United States and the United Kingdom. We are also not like the descendants of black slaves who have settled in the Caribbean islands from Haiti to idyllic Barbados. These carry the burden of identity and some remain bitter about their lack of black purity. Within Africa, we are not like blacks in South Africa, Kenya, Tanzania or Zambia who have swaths of white and Indian populations descended from different European or Asian nations. These have become part of the texture of their blackness. We do not have to be strangers on our beaches like they are in Kenya or South Africa. The concentration of blackness in Nigeria approximates what, to borrow the title of a book by a black British writer, we might call, *some kind of black.*

Even the texture of our religious mix is exceptional. Our Muslim population is not like any other anywhere in the whole world. Ours are not like the Muslims in India and Pakistan who sought separation and are still caught in that web. Rather than seek separation, our founding fathers put up a strong defense and called on one another to avoid the *Pakistanisation* of Nigeria in the wake of independence. From 1967-70, our Muslims fought a three-year civil war to keep our predominantly Christian Igbo brothers and sisters in the tent of one Nigeria. In 1990, when a group of predominantly Christian soldiers staged a relatively successful coup and proceeded to excise the Northern states on the grounds of religion, Christian soldiers and civilians rose stoutly against the proposition. That was what killed that coup!

Today, few Nigerians appreciate the fact that we have been conspired against from the very beginning of our history. Records emerging from British colonial archives show that a stable Nigeria was not in the mind of the British before independence. Two years or so ago, TELL Magazine ran an interview with a British colonial officer who confessed that there had been conspiracy to abort the dreams of a united Nigeria right from the beginning and that the country was programmed to self-destruct. Mr. Charles Sharp, the former Managing Director of the New Nigerian Newspaper, published an astonishing article which seems to have drawn no interest from our government Intelligence agencies. As the story went, Mr. Sharp said that on a trip to the United States he had run into an old *Central Intelligence Agency (CIA)* agent who had been stationed in Kaduna. He had run the CIA outpost in Kaduna-South in the 60s, a location which curiously now bears the name Television perhaps because the local people associated his masts with those of Television station in those days. He said he met this gentleman (now in retirement) somewhere with tones of old tapes of his dirty job in Nigeria. The CIA man admitted that he had been responsible for running a false story which he claimed he picked from a broadcast outside Nigeria to the effect that many Northerners had been killed in the South, a development that triggered off the killings in Northern Nigeria. When asked to verify the source of the news, the old CIA man, removed from the nation he had betrayed and now awaiting his final days in retirement, said bluntly that there had been no substance to the story and that the CIA had made up the story. Nigeria fought a war that was externally propelled, survived and is still standing.

Similarly, it is interesting that the source of Nigeria's purported admission into the *Organization of African Conference (OIC),* did not come from Nigeria, but it was the result of a well-choreographed manipulation of information by a foreign news agency which again seemed determined to succeed in its attempt to send Nigeria into war. And, as those who were around can recall, the events of the time nearly threw our nation into another civil war.

In the hey days of Abacha, the Americans contrived a false story that Nigerian airwaves were not safe. It turned out later that there was no scientific basis for the story other than the need to keep Nigeria on a leash. Again, during the Abacha era, a group of Nigerians sold a dummy that the country had an outbreak of cholera when the nation had a chance to host the Youth World Cup. There was no truth in the story, but the main objective was to sow further confusion in the name of fighting General Abacha. The event was taken to Qatar! Finally, Thomas Gordon's book, *Gideon's Spies: The Secret History of MOSSAD,* tells the story of Israeli intelligence. But of interest is the story of how a key Israeli intelligence Officer faked a Canadian passport, approached and had audience with the then Head of State, Major General Buhari, and from there took up the challenge of sending Alhaji Dikko back to Nigeria in a crate!

It is now possible for one to appreciate the context of the anecdotal story credited to Mr. Boutros Ghali, the former Secretary General of the United Nations. On being asked where he would love to retire to, he mentioned three countries: Egypt, the United States and Nigeria. His reasons for choosing Nigeria were curious and significant. He said he wanted Egypt because that is where he was born, the United States of America because that is where he rose to the pinnacle of his career and finally, Nigeria. On being asked why, he stated that although he had never been to the country, it was clearly one place he would love to visit just to see how and why a country that has been so conspired against by the international community is still standing despite all the threats against its stability. It is hard to know whether Nigerians would react differently if they knew or accept this theory or if the sense of self-denigration has become so deep that we would just write this off as a cop out.

However, in his own wisdom, God has endowed to this special kind of black, a wealth of resources, human and natural, to achieve greatness. Our inability to escape the trap set by our enemies is what has kept us down. Through the sponsorship of coups and the injection of the virus of volatility, those who have conspired against us have ensured that our nation has remained permanently on the boil. It seems that now, circumstances have changed, ushering new opportunities for us. The challenge now is whether we shall take it with both hands. To be sure, every opportunity has danger lurking on the side. And, in transiting to greatness, nations have often either collapsed or managed to stabilize. We survived colonial rule, we survive the land mines insulated into the landscape of the new polity. We have survived the military, we have survived flawed elections, and so on. The real challenge now is how to develop the mechanisms for coping with the new opportunities and come to terms with the fact that there are no shortcuts to greatness.

In an excellent study titled, *The J Curve, A New Way to Understand Why Nations Rise and Fall,* Ian Bremmer, President of Eurasia Group, a Political Risk Consultancy, has imported an Economic theory and used it to develop some excellent arguments regarding the nature of the rise and fall of nations. Simply put, his J Curve theory suggests that all nations are on the J curve, the stability of nations merely depends on whether nations stay or move to the right or left, the top or the bottom of the J Curve. This is what constitutes nation building. He argues that those nations on the left of the curve, those he calls *closed societies* (characterized by lack of democracy and freedom, like North Korea, Cuba, and Zimbabwe) ironically do possess relative peace and stability. Those on the right side of the curve characterized by openness and democracy are often subjected to pressure, tensions, volatility and, to some extent, chaos.

Ian Bremmer further identifies the following as important ways and means of identifying growth in a nation:

- Openness to competition,
- Access to international markets,
- Public provision of incentives for investment and export,
- High level of literacy and schooling,
- Successful land reforms,
- Social opportunities
- Political and civic rights: right to shout, criticize, protest, demonstrate.
- International support[2]

Post authoritarian regimes lend themselves to different outcomes and the most important and significant is the possibility of sliding back to chaos. From the Exodus story, we know that human nature, faced with challenges of breaking new frontiers of uncertainty tend to want to go back to yesterday's vomit. We recall the story of how quickly the people of Israel forgot the hardships of making bricks without straws, the humiliation of slavery, how they forgot very quickly all the miracles worked by God through Moses. Faced with early discomfort, they confronted Moses and said: Why did we not die in Yahweh's hands in the land of Egypt, when we were able to sit down to pans of meat and could eat bread to our heart's content?[3].

---

[2] Ian Bremmer: The J Curve: A New Way To Understand Why Nations Rise and Fall (Simon & Schuster. New York. 2006)

[3] Exodus 16: 3

In the study referred to above, Bremmer takes a look at South Africa and Yugoslavia and poses the question: why did South Africa successfully overcome its difficulties and manage to navigate from authoritarian rule to civilian rule while Yugoslavia slid into chaos? He argues that the success of South Africa was based on three major developments. Firstly, changes in South Africa occurred at a time that the world had great expectations and consequently, the international community lent the country its support. Secondly, the collapse of Communism offered no rival to the triumph of the liberal economics of the western nations. Finally, there was the personality cult that was built around Mr. Nelson Mandela. Perhaps, a far more important fact that has been ignored by Dr Bremmer is the role of both the international and internal anti-apartheid movement in making South Africa ungovernable under apartheid. But, added to all these was the total commitment of both black and white people to overcome the limits of race, ethnicity and other shades of differences and to all assemble under the moral rainbow umbrella hoisted by the likes of Archbishop Desmond Tutu and the moral voices in South Africa.

Yugoslavia on the other hand collapsed because the six federal republics that had been compulsorily herded into one country (Serbia, Croatia, Bosnia-Herzegovina, Slovenia, Macedonia and Montenegro) were led by demagogues who took advantage of the frustrations on the ground. These groups were made up of Orthodox Christians (Macedonia, Serbia and Montenegro), Catholics (Croatia and Slovenia) and Muslims (Serbia and Kosovo). The fall of Communism created new forms of nationalism, throwing up ethnic chauvinists such as Slobodan Milosevic. Fires of anger and hate were stoked, and the Serbs were presented as the most threatened race circled by enemies everywhere. As we know, civil war broke out, the country disintegrated, Milosevic was whisked to the World Court, died during his trial, and has since been buried along with the old Yugoslavia.

From the experience of the two countries, we can see that whereas the people of South Africa were committed to putting ethnicity behind them and forging a new nation, the people of Yugoslavia on the other hand opted to resuscitate ethnic rivalries and sought to establish ethnic based supremacy. These tendencies cut away at the heart of national unity and thus prepared the way for the tragic war that led to the collapse of this nation. Unlike South Africa, the western nations showed no interest in the war in Balkans as the Serbs sparked off what turned to be one of the ugliest ethno-religious wars in modern history. With Tito gone, they did not have even a Fredrick de Klerk or a Mandela, two men who proved how significant brave individuals can change history. To appreciate the lessons from these nations, we need to briefly retrace our own steps, identify some of the similarities if any, and then proceed to explain how and why Nigeria must tread very carefully.

2. The Difficult birth of Nigeria's Democracy

Many Africans will consider the notion of a conspiracy against Africa and the black race as a cop out. However, on closer examination, the evidence seems to me to be astonishing. Ignoring this theme is in part due to the dubious belief by the elites that all we need to do is struggle to catch up with the rest of the world. This of course is a reinforcement of the ideology of slavery and colonialism which was the historically most aggressive step ever taken to eliminate, depopulate and decapitate the hopes of an entire race. A popular idea in the western mind was the marketing of colonialism as a *civilizing mission* which was meant to bring us into the orbit of modernity. But, when we see the conditions of slaves in Europe and America then as now, one would wonder how we could have ever come to imagine that the *civilizing mission* was anything but a devil's deal. For, if that were the case, then perhaps the slaves would not have ended up in conditions which have been well captured by history. For, if we follow this logic, then we could have concluded that these slaves would have gone straight into some of the universities in Europe and America, become equipped with the tools of their modernization and shipped back home. But, we know better even without reading the trials and travails of Booker Washington in his biography, *Up From Slavery*, or the monumental tour de force of Alex Haley, Roots. We may remember the outpouring of raw emotions that followed the showing of that film many years ago.

Even at home, to get the *civilizers* out of our land when we wanted out land back, was a struggle paid for with blood and sweat. Apart from the wars of resistance that were waged across the African continent when the white man first invaded, almost one hundred years later, these wars had to persist for the Africans to secure the space to reestablish control of their land. So, again, if the civilizing mission were about opening routes for us into the new world, then we would not have had to lay down our lives to secure independence. A casual look at the stories of independence struggles today will yield staggering results. Sadly, this is not a project that African scholars are taking seriously. For, only this year, Ghana's celebration of its 50th anniversary of independence which would have given us a chance to restate and question some of our assumptions concerning these relations did not manage to rise up to the occasion. Strange enough, even Kwame Nkrumah, without whom the story of the African struggle would not have been the same, was talked about merely in whispers.

Today, the history of almost all African countries is still coloured by the ravages of our colonial past. Some of the bitterness and the distortions will remain with us for a long time unless and until some serious effort is made to place these events in proper context. Let us take a few examples.

After some nearly one hundred years of engagement ranging from slavery, illegitimate and legitimate trade, missionary activities and a range of other forms of engagement, colonialists spread across Africa began a process of unwinding this unholy gridlock on the throat of our continent. The period of colonialism had been marked by all forms of brutality, sheer wickedness, negation of our collective humanity and an uneven partnership that left Africa and Africans severely wounded. Thanks to the imagination of the African, some of our brave men and women began some process of seeking freedom and a better life for themselves and subsequently for their countries.

The stories of our struggles for freedom are stories of confrontations and conflicts, wars against oppression marked by bloodshed, imprisonment, treachery, and blackmail. Clearly, the colonialists had no intention of restoring any serious form of dignity to the black person. Wherever and whenever a black man showed signs of seeking what today we might call human rights, they risked death, exile, or imprisonment. The fight for freedom was as ferocious as the fight for the continuation of domination. Wherever the colonialists found that the pressures for freedom were getting too much, they opted for plan B, which meant the recruitment of men and women that they considered loyal to their rule. Let us take two examples.

By the 40s, the British and other colonialist nations were still not in the mood to grant freedom to colonized people that were of non-European descent. Thus, when Winston Churchill and President Roosevelt drew up the Atlantic Charter supporting the rights of peoples to choose their own governments, these freedoms were meant only for the conquered peoples of Europe! It was Roosevelt who, pained by the misery that he witnessed in some British and French colonies he visited, pushed both the British and the French against their will to open up the gates of freedom. The result is that, contrary to the popular view that the French or the British granted independence to our peoples, colonizing states surrendered both to internal and external pressures. When it became clear that independence had to be granted, the colonialists began to prepare a soft landing spaces for themselves. Where they did not spark civil wars, they embarked on a programme of systematic divisions, stoking the embers of inter clan and inter-tribal wars and thus setting the pace for a volatile continent. Thus, from Algeria, Morocco, the Congo, Ghana, Kenya, Nigeria, to modern day Zimbabwe, what we have are stories of blood and tears. The elimination or intimidation of recalcitrant patriots from Patrice Lumumba, Ben Bella, Nkrumah, Jomo Kenyatta, Nnamdi Azikiwe, and a host of others spread across nations and continents were all part of these games. Where these patriots were not killed outright, they were either imprisoned or exiled. Unable to contain them, Churchill had a penchant for diminishing anti colonialists if he could not deny them power or eliminate them outright. In places like Burma, Hitler referred to the father of Ms Aung San Su Kyi, the foremost leader of the Burmese people then, as a *traitor rebel leader*[4]. Similarly, Andrew W Cordier who worked for the United Nations from its inception in 1961 until 1961, in a correspondence with his friend and college mentor Dr V.F. Schwalm, was quoted to have to have asserted that "Nkrumah is the Mussolini of Africa while Lumumba is its little Hitler[5].."

Over the Suez Canal, both the United Kingdom and the United States combined to deal with the transgressions of Egypt for daring to question their right to occupy this strip of water. When Nasser took over the Canal, he loudly proclaimed: 'Today, in the name of the people, I am taking over the Company. Tonight, our Egyptian canal will be run by the Egyptians'. Britain reacted with panic and hysteria, and declared

---

[4] Matthew Kukah: Burma: *A Revolution Deferred.* 30/10/07

[5] Cited in Carole J.L. Collins, 'The Cold War Comes to Africa: Cordier and the 1960 Congo Crisis', *Journal of International Affairs , Summer 1993, Vol. 47, No. 1, (Summer 1993), p.259*

that, 'We would not tolerate having Nasser's thumb on our windpipe'. The Suez debacle, according to Martin Meredith, slowed down British interest in colonies and, with it, retreat from Empire gathered momentum[6]

3. Nigeria's Struggle with Democracy

Given the tortuous nature of our political terrain and the difficulties that we have had with democracy, it is, to my mind, a miracle that we are still standing as a nation. With six military coups, not to talk of the very many failed ones, endless bloodletting as a result of communal and so called religious crises along with a civil war, one would think that Nigeria should, by now have given up on the idea of staying together. We have tried 11 elections (1951, 1954, 1959, 1964, 1979, 1983, 1998, 2003, 20070) seven Constitutional initiatives (1927-2006), and some would say we still have not succeeded yet. So, why are we still on this road?

In my view, we do not have a choice. The road to democracy is the road that we must all travel. Given our historical and cultural variations, in the end, how we shape it, how we configure it is another matter altogether. But our dreams must remain irreversible, because, as I believe, it is the absence of democracy that has thwarted our growth.

First of all, we must appreciate the fact that despite the difficulties, the essential ingredients of democracy are beginning to take shape in our society. Such characteristics of democracy as *free speech, open and robust debate, subordination of the military to civilian rule, mass participation, freedom to organize, free expression, free organization, protection of liberties, legal remedies, property rights, security and certainty of processes, access and distribution of news and information, unfettered right of participation, participation of women in the process.* All these are the signs of the return of democracy. Indeed, we must concede that this opening of the political space is the greatest reason for our hope because with openness comes the enrichment of the quality of debate, discussion, and consensus. Under a dictatorship, we might have had full stomachs, a strong national economy, but like Chile, we would

---

[6] Martin Meredith: The Fate of Africa: A History of Fifty Years of Independence. (Public Affairs. New York. 2005) p43

have been denied free speech, have our rights violated and so on. Or, like North Korea, we could suffer both dictatorship, hunger and still be denied free speech. To be sure, our rights have been violated even in this democracy, but we must not forget that previously, under the military, we had no means of seeking redress at all.

Professor Amartya Sen has posited three values of democracy: *intrinsic, instrumentalist* and *constructive*. The *Intrinsic* value of democracy lies in the impulse of freedom and all the ingredients of democracy reside in the hearts of each an everyone of us. A second value of democracy is its *instrumentalist* in the sense that each and every one of us has a utilitarian disposition, seeking always a means of maximizing our benefits by using whatever gives us that opportunity. Therefore, properly applied, it could and should become an instrument for growth and development both of ideas and the national agenda. Democracy is *constructive* in the sense that through the platform of robust debates, we can articulate our views and contribute to shaping public policy. To that extent, democracy can be said to be a universal norm, not in its practice but in its impulse in the heart of each and every one of us. It is universal not in the sense that we all see it in the same way, but essentially in the sense that once its benefits are experienced by us, we would naturally appreciate them. This explains why, when it is threatened or taken away, individuals and groups who have experienced it want to fight hard to get it back. The same must be said of us now. So, what are the challenges that lie ahead today? By way of Conclusion, it is to these that we shall now turn.

4. Summary and Conclusion

The business of our nation is still an unfinished business. There are many who will argue that we have a *Nigerian state* but we do not have a *nation*. And I believe that they are right when we consider the ingredients that make up a nation. But, again, we can ask, and so what? A nation is an aggregate of evolutionary processes that arise from chains of interactions between the various blood-related members of the community. A nation is founded on commonality of identity, blood relationship and culture. This is because, as we see from its derivation, nation derives from the Latin word, *nascere*, to be born. The former Republican Presidential candidate and front-line Republican, Mr. Patrick Buchanan, has also argued that: *A nation is organic, a nation is alive, a nation has a beating heart. A Constitution does not create a nation. A nation writes a Constitution that is already the birth certificate of the nation already born in the hearts of its people.*[7]

He has further argued that: *Patriotism is the soul of a nation. It is what keeps a nation alive. When patriotism dies, when a nation loses the love and loyalty of its people, the nation dies and begins to decompose*[8].

Buchanan conflates three major themes here: the nexus between Constitutionalism, Patriotism and their interface with the making of a nation. The relation of all is so closely connected that they all clearly feed on one another. We must appreciate that Nigeria is still a *work in progress.* As I have noted, we have fumbled and stumbled in many areas and we have foolishly allowed too many opportunities to slip by. We have come from a rough road and we should thank God that we have come so far. However, there is the need for us to rethink certain assumptions about ourselves and our condition. There are, a lot of things that Nigerians must rid themselves of if we are to make some appreciable progress.

First of all, Nigeria must appreciate its significance, role and place in the world in general and for the African in particular. Nigeria needs to appreciate where the African is coming from, where we have been and where we are now so as to prepare for where we might be in future. Despite slavery, the African has always sought for freedom. From the revolts of the Black Jacobins in Haiti to the dreams of Marcus Garvey, the sentiments and emotions for the black man/woman has been the need to *return home.* Perhaps with hindsight, it is easy to say that the great Marcus Garvey may have been naïve in conceptualizing *home,* but his cry for return to Africa was indeed a metaphor for explaining the need for the African everywhere in the world to have a *home* to look up to.

Clearly, our surge is irreversible and no matter what happens, I believe Africa is on the threshold of hope. On the issue of human and natural resources, look at the picture today: **Africa** has a current population of 800 million and by 2050, it is expected to climb to 2billion. Nigeria's 140 million could climb to almost 300 million while

---

[7] Patrick Buchanan: State of Emergency: The Third World Invasion and Conquest of America.(New York: Simon and Shuster. 2006)141

[8] Patrick Buchanan: State of Emergency, op cit. p139

smaller nations like Uganda and Somalia could climb from 23 and 50 million to 100 and 200 million respectively by 2050. It is easy to say that our populations are a liability due to increasing poverty and wars. However, now that democracy has become to a great extent, irreversible in Africa, we can clearly assume that in another ten to twenty years, Nigeria will definitely regain its rightful place as one of the leading nations in the world. The dream of being one of the leading economies in the world by the year 2020 is not an illusion and we should make it our collective mantra as we go along.

With new discoveries of resources on the continent and the increase in school enrolments, it is clear that an optimistic future lies ahead despite all the obstacles. Properly framed, these possibilities should make Africa turn away from war and focus more on internal cohesion, regional and continental unity. We have the human resources in the numbers.

Now look at our oil and mineral resources. **South Africa** has 88% of the world's Platinum, 80% of Manganese, 30% of Titanium, 40% of Gold. **Guinea** has a third of the world's Bauxite while **Botswana** and **Zimbabwe** have 25% of world Diamonds and Zimbabwe 12% of the world's Chromium. **Nigeria, Angola, Equatorial Guinea** have 3.4, 5.3, 6.4 billion barrels of oil in reserve. **Sudan, Ghana** have just discovered Oil and beyond oil, the list will continue to increase as time goes on. The United States and the Chinese dependence on our oil will increase. What the continent needs rather urgently is for the various African intellectuals and scientists to rally round their governments and continent. And, again, here, with the number of our experts in the Diaspora and such noble ventures like the Technical Aids Corps among others, we can begin to rally our intellectual property for the development of our nations. Nigeria must lead the way. It has hopefully turned the corner as far as democracy is concerned. If it manages to pull through the difficulties of the next few years and can get its hands around the issues of corruption, we should become the true leader of Africa.

From the World Trade Organization, the spinoff from globalization will continue to hurt the economies of many African nations. Most of the policies against us are deliberate and the international community will continue to keep shifting the goal posts. My thesis is that we have been conspired against, lied against, sinned against, and survived. They said we were sub-humans and used it to justify our enslavement. They haunted us and called our habitat the *Dark Continent.* They claimed we had no religion and that we could not be children of the same God. We have come through it all. They say that we are corrupt, we are dying of hunger, we have no industries and no infrastructure. We are a nation of scammers and con men and women. This is what they want the world to know about us. And, true or false, we have made their job easy, very easy indeed. There is no running away from the shame.

Today, how can you explain the fact that the Nigerian elite has stolen a total of four hundred billion dollars ($400b) and that most of this money or all of it is in foreign banks? Sad as it may be, this brings out clearly the complicity of the West against us by their alliances with the lowest and most corrupt specie of our race. When it is convenient, they can let a few little flies hang dry to show us that they are fighting corruption. Let us not be deceived. This battle will be won or lost by us and us alone if we are determined. China, Russia, Cuba, Libya, North Korea, Venezuela are all showing examples of how we can say No and work at our own pace. These nations may be defiant in democracy and other values, but they have some dignity. The British have shown that corruption in Nigeria is not the same as corruption in Saudi Arabia.

The President has recently called for both a *Marshall Plan for Africa* and a new Berlin Conference. This clash of metaphors is astonishing as it shows some sort of naivety on the part of the President's speech writers. First of all, why would anyone be agitating for a Marshall Plan when we have not fought a war and our conditions are so totally different? A Marshall Plan may sound exciting, but this blind photocopying of ideas is precisely the problem that we face as Africans. The idea is totally out of context. Another Berlin Conference? Well, the 1885 Berlin Conference was hatched by Europeans to steal and appropriate our lands. Whose lands will a second Berlin Conference steal and appropriate and, is it to be organized by Europeans or Africans? By making the calls in Berlin, was the President implying that the Conference takes place in Europe and should the Marshall plan be drawn up by the White House in the United States? I would have been happy if this speech had been made in Cape Coast, Ghana or Goree Island, Senegal and if the President conceived of a Mandela Plan for Africa or something of that nature. Clearly, the concepts were wrongly thought out and I fear they form our obsession with untested assumptions. For good or for bad, we already have a NEPAD agenda which, with its flaws, is a work in progress. Refining and fine tuning it should be our dream not the importation of supremacist ideologies that have outlived their usefulness.

Finally, it is clear that the world respects only the strong. This is the story of China, North Korea, or Russia today. The Niger-Delta has now become, not a habitat where decent human beings live, but a vortex of terror, war, and violence. Yet, statistically, the level of violence in the Niger-Delta in one year is far less than what happens in Brooklyn in a month! Contriving and creating worse case scenarios is part of the mind games that are being played. We have been said to be a violent nation and yet visitors here have told a different story. If you follow the progress of Nigeria from stories in the European media, you will not believe that anyone has a new car or that there are Universities and hospitals here. These worse case scenarios have been used as excuses. They laid the foundation for the invasion of Afghanistan and now the destruction of Iraq. They also have provided the blueprint for the way the world now sees Zimbabwe.

Right now, the Americans seem determined to find Al-Qaeda and the Talibans in our midst. Despite lack of any convincing evidence, the urge to *seek and find* them remains. At some point when the United States gets fed up, it will, as it did with Iraq, insist that there is evidence of threat to international security. Next thing is that we shall be told that since we have not worked hard enough, the Marines will help us find them. For, how do we explain the laughable fact that the evidence against those who have been arrested and are standing trial for terrorism is one Kalashnikov and some bags of fertilizer?

We have traveled on a long road marked with pain and suffering. But the resistance of our people has been strong, and we are still standing. Everyone seems to envy China today. Though their stories stretch a bit further, I believe we cannot envy them without looking at their past which is characterized by resilience, patriotism, determination, and sacrifice. Let us for take an example of what has come to be known in the history of China as the *Long Trek*.

On October 16th, 1934, the Chinese Communist troops numbering 100, 000 set out on a 6,000-mile trek from Kiangsi in the South. The Communists were fleeing from Chiang Kai- shek and the Kuomintang, the Nationalist Army. Some 90,000 men and women died during the trek which came to be known as the Long March. It galvanized the people and was precursor to the victory of the Communist Party in

1949. It took some thirty years for the Communist Party to throw up people like Deng Hi-siaoping, the founder of modern day China who based his philosophy on the aphorism that: *It does not matter if a cat is black or white as long as it catches mice.* That country has built on the conflicting legacies of the Mao Ze Dongs, Deng and hundreds of other leaders. There may have been conflicting methods, but the greatness of China was always on the horizon whether it is through the eyes of the Long Trek, the China Wall, or Tiananmen Square. We need to build on legacies and not seek to throw away the baby, the bath water, and the tub. There are many similar stories that can be reproduced regarding most nations which we all seem to envy today.

In Conclusion, the attempts to paint a negative picture of Africa will not end. After they softened up Mandela, they released him and built a wall of divinity around him. That has turned him into a totem of perfection. He managed to save South Africa from disintegration. He was presented as the quintessential leader that Africa should have. Well, maybe. I am of the view that Mr. Mandela, one of the greatest human beings of the last century has had his time. But Africa requires some *fixing, panel beating* and *mending.* The Mandela mystique must be complimented by a leadership that aims at fixing things, making Africa work and making the black person stand erect today.

In this way, the Mo Ibrahim award for Leadership is a major contribution to that world. It is a noble gesture, but it is not about to make African leaders more accountable as such. Mo Ibrahim needs to be commended for taking the initiative. However, I am afraid that Africa does not need to fear bad leaders, nor should we spend too much time looking for the right leaders. What Africa needs is a bit more. The environment has changed and I believe that bad leaders are gradually going to become an endangered species and an aberration if we can generate and sustain a new generation of young talented Africans here and in the Diaspora and get them to take their minds away from the negative images of Africa and become part of the building process.

There is need therefore for us to broaden our perception and interpretation of Leadership. Indeed, as we can see with the style presented to us by Alhaji Musa Yar'adua, even the leaders themselves are gradually beginning to become more conscious of the fact that their legitimacy depends on their capacity and ability to deliver the ingredients of good leadership. Now we hear of *Servant-Leaders* who are *Chief Servants,* and so on. It is too early for us to say whether the Mo Ibrahim vision will make a significant change or whether indeed, Servant Leadership necessarily has a future beyond the sentiments of a honeymoon. But it is only a concerted people, determined to reject their own oppression that can drive out bad leadership. We have done it before as a people, from Algeria, Haiti, Kenya, to South Africa and Zimbabwe. We can do it again only this time, the enemy is within.

In leading Africa, Nigeria must choose its options and strategies wisely. In its march towards restoring the dignity of the black man/woman, we may do well to keep in mind that the journey demands sacrifices and vision. We must learn from the mistakes of the past. Today, the best is still an ocean away, but the worst is well behind the mountains. From the moral foundations of **Benson Idahosa University**, we can produce the men and the women with the moral fibre to make Africa the home of humanity. After all, it will only be a *home coming* for all races since this has been the home of *Homo sapiens* for over 200,000 years[9]. May God show us the way and give us the grace to follow it. God bless you all.

Convocation Lecture, Benson Idahosa University, Benin City, December 13th, 2007

---

[9] For an illuminating and perhaps humbling admission of these realities, see Chris Mihill: *We Are All Africans, No Bones About It.* Guardian Weekly, July 20th, 1997, p23.

CHAPTER TWO

After The Insurgency: Some Thoughts on National Cohesion

1. Introduction

On December 26th, 1944, a commanding officer with the Japanese army named Major Yoshimi Taniguchi gave the following order to his soldiers, among whom was one Hiroo Onada: "You are absolutely forbidden to die by your own hand. It may take three years, it may take five, but whatever happens, we'll come back for you. Until then, so long as you have one soldier, you are to continue to lead him. You may have to live on coconuts. If that's the case, live on coconuts! Under no circumstances are you [to] give up your life voluntarily."

The assignment of Onada and his colleagues was to get behind enemy lines and make life miserable for the enemies of Japan, and in the process gather intelligence for their country. Onada himself had trained in the prestigious Nakago Intelligence School in Japan as an Imperial intelligence officer. He specialized in intelligence gathering and guerrilla warfare. Unfortunately, Lubang, the island they were sent to protect, was overrun on February 28th, 1945 by the Allied forces. Most of the soldiers fled or surrendered but Lt. Onada and his men split into groups and headed into the jungle to continue the fight as ordered. He and three of his colleagues formed one group. Unfortunately, the other three were killed while Onada, an expert at jungle tactics, survived.

He remained in the jungle for 29 years in obedience to the spirit and letter of the instructions given to him by his commanding officer. Even when he was persuaded to come out in 1974, his former commanding officer had to fly to the island to persuade him that the war was really over. "I was ordered to conduct a guerrilla warfare and not die", he said in defence of his beliefs. Thus, he firmly believed in the philosophy of fighting on to death, propelled by love of country and obeying the last orders. "I had to follow my orders because I am a soldier", he said.

Indeed, amidst the heroic celebrations of his return, he discovered a new Japan that was no longer in accord with his convictions and migrated to Brazil, where he lived until his death at the age of 91.

He was a man of great convictions, and even though we may consider him misguided, this story is important for what it says to us about commitment. He was quoted as saying: "If you have some thorns in your back, somebody needs to pull them out for you. We need buddies. The sense of belonging is born in the family and later includes friends, neighbors, community, and country. That is why the idea of a nation is really important".

This story should help us appreciate the complex issues surrounding motives for war and how difficult it is to speak of an end to war when the combatants are convinced of their cause and are driven by deep passion. So, when we speak of the end of any insurgency or war, it is important that we understand the nature of the events that led to the conflict in the first place. We need to define the actors, their philosophy, sponsors, and ideology. Wars could end by surrender or outright defeat of one side by the other. Either way, sometimes not everyone accepts outright defeat.

There are often individuals or groups who surrender only as a temporary tactic in the face of impending defeat. They are prepared to fight to the death and do not contemplate defeat as an option. They may retreat to regroup, re-organize, re-strategize and seek more support for their cause. Sometimes though, this claim of "fighting with the last drop of our blood" may be the last kick of a dying horse.[1] In the final analysis, closure and a real end to insurgency or war can depend on a multiplicity of factors. Whether a war ends by negotiation or outright defeat of the opponent, the future depends on what the victor does with the price of his or her victory and what steps are taken to assuage injured feelings or fasten national integration. If wounds are not nursed and new narratives are not constructed, the grief and the pain of loss could turn into a creed while we await the fire next time.

In our case here, Nigerians have been praying for an end to the insurgency. But what signs will be in the skies to show us that the insurgency is over? Is it when the guns go silent and victory has been

---

[1] In the case of the Nigerian Civil War, just before he fled to Abidjan and Col. Effiong surrendered to the federal troops during the Biafran War, Col. Ojukwu's swan song was actually a boast to the effect that even the grass of Biafra would rise up to fight to the end!

declared by the Joint Task Forces (JTF)? Is it after Mallam Ibrahim Shekau has been captured or killed in battle and his body shown to us? What if another leader steps forward? How will we know where arms have been stored and what arms have been retrieved? As the Bible says, is it likely that this devil could go away temporarily only to come back accompanied by other devils more deadly than him, only to wreck more havoc (Mt. 12: 45). The challenge for us is to figure out how to avoid this.

I want to argue in this Lecture that there is a correlation between the persistence today of a violent interpretation of Islam found in northern Nigeria and the grief of the conquest of the Sokoto caliphate in 1903. I believe that in this regard, the unresolved issues surrounding what Professor Adeleye aptly referred to as "the dilemma of the Waziri"[2] constitute a reservoir from where extremists have continued to draw some form of inspiration, to continue this war to reclaim what was lost to those they refer to as unbelievers. I will also look at the background of insurgency and trace the emergence of today's Boko Haram within a culture of resistance. I will address some lessons to be learnt from the threats we experience today, and will draw some light from methods used to end terror in other countries. I will conclude with some recommendations for the way forward towards reconciliation and the construction of a new order in our country.

2. The unresolved dilemma of the Waziri

The raw material for this drama can be gleaned from the famous speech which Lord Lugard, the then High Commissioner, delivered on March 21st, 1903, to the rump of the Caliphate. In that speech, Lord Lugard asserted the finality of the conquest and asserted the unambiguous transfer of power from the Caliphate to the British authorities. He said: 'All things which I have said the Fulani by conquest took the right to do, now pass to the British. Every Sultan and Emir and the Principal officers of the state will be appointed by the High Commissioner

---

[2] R. A. Adeleye, "The Dilemma of the Wazir: The Place of Risalat al-Wazir'ila ahl al'ilm wa 't-tadablur in the History of the Conquest of the Sokoto Caliphate," *Journal of the Historical Society of Nigeria* iv, 2 (June 1968).

throughout all the country…. The government will, in turn, hold the rights in land which the Fulani took by conquest from the people. The government holds the right of taxation, and will tell the Emirs and Chiefs what taxes that they may levy…. the government will have the right to all minerals. All men are pleased to worship God as they please. Mosques and places of worship will be treated by respect by us"[3].

Lord Lugard concluded that from then onwards, all Emirs were to swear their oath of allegiance in the name of Allah and the prophet to the colonial state.[4]

After the defeat and following the exit of Sultan Attahiru, the burden of deciding the future for Islam rested in the hands of Muhammadu Buhari, the Waziri. In summary, three options were open to the rump of the Caliphate. There were those who, like Onada above, believed that they would fight to the end and never surrender to the new conquerors. They believed that the Caliphate could still be reclaimed, and this is largely the lost glory that is being contested. Secondly, there were those who believed that some kind of cohabitation might be diplomatically worked out so that the religion could survive. Thirdly, there were those who believed that the new order should be supported, and ways to ensure a better future should be explored.

The Waziri, after advice from the scholars, decided to work out a modus vivendi with the colonial state. In his wisdom, he argued that since Lugard the conqueror had stated that all Muslims would be free to pray, pay Zakat and observe the Ramadan, there was no need for Hijra or continued fighting. Since the Caliphate had been founded as a home for Islam, the Waziri displayed some real diplomatic sagacity in this decision.

Amidst this dilemma, the Waziri received counsel to cooperate with the colonial state. According to a judge in Gwandu, "the world is a house of distress…The Christians do not impede religion and the rites of Islam established in our land. Their goal is seeking for territory and the over lordship in worldly matters. As regards Islam, they do not hinder anyone from it, from Futa to here…This is our particular kind of friendship with them at present. We show regard to them with the

---

[3] Fredrick Lugard, *Second Address to the Sultan, Waziri and Elders of Sokoto* (March 21st, 1903).
[4] Further on, the Emirs were also to refrain from lip service and deceit.

tongue and have intercourse with them in the affairs of the world, but never love them in our heart nor adopt their religion".[5] From then till now, the battle over the perception of the role of Islam and the State has merely been shaped by circumstances, but the key issues have not changed. The feeling that this loss can be redressed and that we can return to these glory days resides deep down.

This is not the place for us to go into the details of this phase of protest. However, the significance of this reference lies in the fact that it helps us understand the origins of violence in Northern Islam. But we need to make one passing remark as to how and why all this relates to the tensions between Islam and Christianity today.

It is curious to note that so many Muslim scholars writing on the history of northern Nigeria have continued to associate the colonial state with Christianity, although this distortion of history has been driven by ideology. Marxism historians fell into this gully of falsehood by arguing that somehow, colonialism and missionary activities were closely intertwined. Of course, except in the case of the Anglican Church which was part of the British establishment, other churches had a different experience with the colonial state. Indeed, given that the missionaries in the North were predominantly Irish, the tension between the Irish and the English (Catholics and Protestants) played itself out in most encounters, not ignoring the fact that the British concern principally was with exploitation of the resources of Nigeria and not religious pursuits, as the Gwandu judge above articulated very well.

Today, even among otherwise serious Muslim scholars, historians and writers, one reads of such expressions as, "Christian invaders", or the "massacre of Muslim personality and identity in the north by the Christians".[6] Scholars like Professor Ali Mazrui have been at the forefront of this misleading distortion of colonial history.[7] Against this backdrop, it is easy to see how suspicion, anxiety, and fears still persist

---

[5] T. Hodgkin, *Nigerian Perspectives* (London, 1975), 393.

[6] Auwalu Anwar, "From Maitatsine Revolts to Boko Haram: Examining the Socio-Economic Circumstances of Religious Crisis in Northern Nigeria," Paper Presented at a One Day Workshop organized by Media Practitioners in the Country on May 9th, 2013, pg. 6/7.

[7] His documentary, *The Africans: A Triple Heritage,* in 1986, started some of this misrepresentation. Professor Mazrui makes the same observations in a paper, "African Islam and Comprehensive Religion: Between Revivalism and Expansion," in *Islam in Africa: Proceedings of the Islam in Africa Conference,* Nur Alkali, Adamu Adamu et al. (Eds) (Spectrum Books: Ibadan, 1993), 247-265.

because Muslims grow up to believe that Christianity is a continuation of the colonial project. If we take this mindset, we can understand why ordinary Muslims treat Christians the way they do, how and why in the North we hear of people being threatened with death if they contemplate converting to Christianity. Against this backdrop, we can argue that Christians continue to suffer a double jeopardy: we have suffered from colonialism as a people, and now we continue to suffer from being considered to be associated with colonialists. This is why in the moment of crises, some Muslim youth have no qualms burning down churches or attacking Christians, seeing them as representatives of a foreign religion and interests. You can now understand why, a war in Afghanistan, some cartoons in Denmark, a beauty contest in Nigeria, are enough to provoke attack against churches in many states in northern Nigeria in pursuit of this blind and distorted logic that equates the West with Christianity.

The frustration, especially for those from the Middle Belt, lies in the fact that whereas some Muslims continue to see Christians as collaborators with the conquerors of their empire, the same colonialists, in collaboration with the rump of the conquered Caliphate, applied the ideology of feudalism and perpetrated the subjugation of the same communities through cultural hegemony and taxation. It is therefore no accident that the Plateau, the focus and the melting pot of missionary presence, has today become the theatre and the boiling pot of the tensions between Christians and Muslims. I make these points to help us understand that even if the insurgency is more deadly now, and certainly is not to be simplified as a Muslim versus Christian problem, the roots of all this hatred were sown many years ago. Let us now turn our attention to the Boko Haram insurgency itself.

3. Definitions and background of Insurgency

Insurgency has been defined as: "A protracted political-military activity directed towards completely or partially controlling the resources of a country through the use of irregular military forces and illegal political organizations".[8] The objective of insurgents is to threaten, subvert, or

---

[8] *A Guide to the Analysis of Insurgency*, (SCOPE NOTE, January 5th, 2009), 2.

weaken the government of the day. It often manages to control a particular area that serves as a base, and seeks greater expansion and consolidation with a view to staking its claim for territorial control. Their eventual objective, no matter how farfetched it may seem, is to take over the machinery of government and create a new government in the image and likeness of its ideology. Thus, an insurgency's aims and objectives can include:

- Limit the ability of the government and enhance their capability to provide public services. They often do this by sabotage of public utilities such as destruction of oil installations, sources of power and transportation, poisoning water supply, and so on.
- Obtaining the support of neutral but critical segments of the population (Media, Academia, Security agencies, other leaders).
- Increase its own visibility and publicity at the expense of government.
- Destruction of the confidence of government in its legitimacy.
- Neutralise the coercive power of the government (attacking or sacking Police or Military formations).[9]

Given what is before us, we can pose the question: Is it possible to identify an insurgency before it manifests itself? In other words, are there symptoms that a vigilant society can detect or identify? If so, what institutions bear the responsibility? The federal government, state governments, individuals, security agencies, or the media? The answers to these questions are hypothetical and contingent on other factors. For example, how seriously do ordinary citizens feel about their country and one another? What is the relationship between the ordinary citizens and the security agencies such as the police? Are there channels of communication that can be used, and if so, by whom?

So, on the whole, it really depends on the mechanisms that a government has in place to feel the pulse, ease, and encourage communication with its agencies. It also depends on how a government seeks to measure the expressions of dissatisfaction among the populace and its willingness to accept critical appraisal of policies. It depends on the kind of protection that whistle blowers can expect. A government

---

[9] Ibid., 4.

that is averse to criticism or sees everything in the frame of Friend or Foe risks alienation and the inability to hear the wails and the pain and suffering of citizens, and prefers the whispers of its orchestra of praise singers. A government needs to constantly monitor public opinion, have the right listening devices, and closely examine what the media is saying; what women groups, students and youth are saying; and what labour, civil society, or even the opposition political parties are saying.

So to answer the question, yes, it is possible to identify the symptoms of insurgency. However, for this to happen, the government must have Think tanks, academicians and retired men and women in the security services whom it can call upon at short notice or engage over a period of time for research and analysis.

Insurgencies do not happen overnight. The methods of recruitment, development of philosophy, spreading, and so on, take time and require planning and funding. Some of the pointers to the mobilization for insurgency are:

- Sudden departure of large numbers of young and skilled people (for training and indoctrination). Some centres or locations are known because they become popular destinations (as in the case of Yemen where Mutallab ended up, or Peshawar in Pakistan where Osama Bin Laden held sway).
- Defection of a noticeable number of members from existing parties to more radical ones.
- Increase in the stridency of ideological proselytization in rural areas.
- Increase in the number of foreign visitors or returnees from foreign travels.
- Increase in the smuggling or theft of small arms.
- Increase in robberies, kidnappings, and ransom demands.
- Presence of armed and strange people in rural areas.
- Mass circulation of cheap propaganda material.
- Establishment and registration of many charity organizations.

It is not just enough to see these strange things. The real issue is what to do with the information one has with the assurance that the information will be properly put to use. In most cases, our people have lost confidence, first in the government and its institutions such as the police force and other agencies. So, the first thing is for the federal and state government to develop witness protection and whistle blowing mechanisms that can encourage ordinary people to alert government agencies.

Sadly, there is a chasm between the people and security agencies, one borne out of their personal experiences. Ordinary people literally fear the police and the word security is very much dreaded, given the myth of secrecy and conspiracies around the concept. Ordinary citizens fear the policemen as individuals and groups, and dread the prospect of being asked to write a police report! They fear that you could incriminate yourself and there are fears that criminal gangs have infiltrated the police, and one's patriotism could endanger one's life. I have made a case for the need for more confidence building mechanisms to improve relations between the police and ordinary citizens. Reporting crime can be made easier and a more friendly atmosphere created by agents of the state.

4. The emergence of Boko Haram

What is Boko Haram today has been the subject of a lot of misunderstanding, misrepresentation, distortion, and half-truths. There has been very little academic attempt to really understand the origins and philosophy or ideology of the movement. It seems that Nigerians have been so saddened by the tragedy inflicted on the country by the viciousness and devilish wickedness of the movement that no one has cared to seek explanation. In discussions, whenever I have tried to make a case for our trying to even understand this devil, many people simply wonder, "Are you in sympathy with them?". Yet, I believe that even the devil needs to be understood if at all we are to avoid him. Similarly, I argue that if we assume that Boko Haram is evil and then proceed to simply look for where to hang a dog with a bad name, we will be mistaken because more dogs will still line up to commit the same crime.

The name 'Boko haram'

The first thing to say is that we have decided to call Boko Haram by a name that is of our own making and contrivance. Although the group is now called Boko Haram, I have argued elsewhere that from the point of view of nomenclature and grammar, Boko and Haram are two nouns, and there is no adjective to qualify any of the nouns. A little explanation of the origins of the words we are using might be of help here.

It is interesting that even within the Muslim community there are conflicting notions as to what the word *Boko* itself really means. It crept into the vocabulary right from the beginning of the incursions of the colonial state and the Western educational system. *Boko* was often used in relation to a second noun, *Ilimi*, meaning education. Thus, the full expression, *Ilimin Boko*, was used to derogatorily refer to Western education as distinct from what the Muslim community understood as the only form of education, namely, *Ilimin Islamiyya*, that is, Islamic education. While *Ilimin Islamiyya* was a form of catechesis focusing on teachings of the Holy Quran, its recitation and memory exercises were often the entry point for children into the faith of Islam. Its language of instruction was Arabic.

Ilimin Boko, on the other hand, was considered inferior and suspect because it did not teach about the Quran or Islam. Its teachers (white people), alphabets, and language of instruction (English) were all very strange, and their language was seemingly incomprehensible. In any case, white people and their incomprehensible ways were often associated with witchcraft, *Boka*. Then as now, the etymology of the word *Boko* remains suspect. For example, some people say that *Boko* is a corruption of *Boka*, which means sorcery or witchcraft. According to this school of thought, the word was used to convey the notion that Western education was as derogatory as sorcery or witchcraft and was therefore to be avoided. Since its harbinger was the enemy, it was naturally considered with suspicion as a means of destroying Islam in the way the colonial state had destroyed the Islamic polity.

Another school of thought says that *Boko* had always been used to refer to a counterfeit or fake. In traditional Islamic society, there was the concept of what was known during marriage ceremonies as *Amaryar Boko*. *Amarya* itself means a new bride. As the story goes, during a traditional wedding, hiding the bride from public view was an important part of the ceremonies. During a wedding, therefore, it was often common for a procession to be led by an *Amaryan boko* (a fake bride), who would be dressed as the real bride but merely to serve as a decoy. Thus, the excitement arose from getting the crowd to follow the fake bride while the surprise appearance of the real bride would be the climax of the ceremony! It can be argued that just as white Christian missionaries used the words *pagan* and *witchcraft* interchangeably to refer to African beliefs and culture, the coinage of the word *Boko* was meant to convey the same contempt for the new but strange and suspicious education by the white people within the Muslim community.

Thus, when both the missionaries and the colonial state started a programme of education, the Muslim ruling classes remained restrained and suspicious of the intentions. They decided to experiment by sending the children of the slaves and lower classes within their communities. It took a while before the ruling classes sensed the value of education as a tool of modernization and subsequently but gradually began to send their own children to school. When the first generation of Muslim elites decided to send their children to school, these children were often the subject of derision among their own mates and friends. Those children who believed they had remained faithful to Islam by holding on to *Ilimin Islamiyya*, derided their friends who sought *Ilimin Boko* by singing derogatory songs against them whenever the latter set out to school. One of those verses went something like this: "Yan makarantan boko, Ba karatu, ba sallah. Ba'a biyar hanya Allah. Sai yawan zagin Mallam". The translation of this song is: "Children of Western schools, You don't study, you don't pray, You don't follow God's path, You only abuse your teachers".[10]

Time has not eroded this deep suspicion because under the claim that education is on the concurrent list of the Constitution, we have no clear national programme of education with a standardized syllabus. Thus, with over 95% of Muslim youth in school using Arabic and Hausa as their foundation, and with the Northern elite unable to make a good case for English, this ignorance and prejudice has persisted. Another Federal Government decision which reinforced this climate of anxiety and prejudice among young Muslims was the takeover of schools and the constant reference to missionaries as an extension of foreign occupation.

Thus, for even the elites in the Northern states, the takeover of schools has been seen as a strategy that slowed down the influence of Christianity in Nigeria. Indeed, in one of his sermons, Yusuf was quoted as blaming missionary education for providing the necessary learning tools for the pursuit of the goals of the modern state.[11] In my knowledge of the North, I cannot think of one single school or public institution

---

[10] A good part of the information here is gleaned from an article written by Mahmud Jega.

[11] Ahmad Martada, *Boko Haram in Nigeria: Its Beginnings, Principles and Activities in Nigeria*, trans. Albdul Haq al Shanti (Bayero University, 2012), 4.

that has been built by Muslims, providing education that is open to people of all faiths, as Christians have done. As I noted above, and as the songs of the young men implied, the only education that many ordinary Muslims understand is the _Islamiyya_ school and the fact that education must necessarily be tied to the Holy Quran and the faith.

Let me turn attention now to a reflection on a culture of resistance from which people like Yusuf must have found inspiration. As I have indicated above, from the collapse of the Caliphate, efforts at reclaiming its lost glory or the values it supposedly espoused have been the driving force of many of those who history records today as fanatics and enemies of the state. They are often in conflict with the Emirate system or the traditional ruling classes, whom they accuse of aligning with and profiting from the state and, by extension, endangering the religion.

This is clearly seen in the Mahdist revolts. The idea of the Mahdi is a millenarian concept in Islam, albeit controversial. To the extent that his coming is tied to what we would today call end times, there have been many claimants to that mantle over Islamic history. As we know, periods of uncertainty, war, fear, oppression, and occupation often present this image as a response. The interpretations and views of the Mahdi among, for example, Sunnis and the Shi'ites, differ but this should not occupy our attention for now. What is important is the appropriation of this concept and how it has shaped revolts against the state in various parts of the world.

Towards the end of the nineteenth century, the Mahdist protests in Sudan and Egypt were the viable platform for resisting foreign occupation. The British takeover and absolute control of the Suez Canal around 1869 as a passageway to India saw the revival of slavery, taxation, and the oppression of the people. Madhism was therefore as much a struggle for freedom against foreign occupation and injustice as it was a moral struggle for the reclaiming of Islamic identity. The war of 1892, which saw the death of over 10,000 Mahdist soldiers and led to the capture of Khartoum, may have given Lord Herbert Kitchener the title of Lord, but its impact would resonate to some parts of what is today, northern Nigeria. By the time the British conquered the Sokoto caliphate, Madhism, as a form of protest against colonialism, was already an attractive option and metaphor, thanks to historical memories of the injustice of the colonial occupation.

In 1904, the Mahdist revolts started when a local Chief in Satiru, a community in the then Sokoto province, proclaimed himself Mahdi and went on to name his son, Prophet Isa, or Jesus. He was arrested and died in detention and his son went on to proclaim his father the Mahdi, but then announced himself Annabi Isa (Prophet Jesus). He and others lost their lives in the violence, but the struggle went on.[12]

The climax however came in January 1906, when the British government sent a detachment of soldiers to bring the situation under control. Their leaders, two white officers, Hillary and Blackwood, were killed in the cause of the battle against the rebels. In reaction, the British ordered a punitive expedition which went on a revenge mission. Mahmud Jega, a journalist, has given a succinct account: "The British got the Sultan Attahiru II to come to their aid against the Satirawa. A dozen district heads from all over Sokoto Emirate mobilized hundreds of horsemen and joined the colonial army in an attack on Satiru. Every adult male member of the Satiru community, about 2,000 of them, was killed in the punitive expedition to avenge Hillary's death. The captured women and children were dispersed all over the emirate. The village was then razed to the ground; Sultan Attahiru placed a curse on it, and today a forest reserve occupies the spot where Satiru once stood".[13] I will come back to this again, but for now, let us return to Boko Haram.

5. Asking some questions: Role of Memory, Injury and Bitterness

Most of the discussion about Boko Haram has focused on its emergence in the last three or so years. However, I believe it is important for us to look at a few questions and seek to find answers for them. For example, what are the immediate reasons that led to the emergence of Boko Haram? Was it an offshoot of some other movements? What was original about the group? Was there something in their teaching that should have alerted us of some impending doom? Why did Borno and Yobe become their location of choice? What conditions favoured their growth and spread? Why did Boko Haram choose the state and its security agencies, Christianity and Christians, and Western education as targets for the expression of its violent campaign? Where did their

---

[12] Anwar Auwalu, *The Maitatsine Revolts and Boko Haram*, 13.

[13] Mahmud Jega, *Of Alago, Baga and Satiru*, Daily Trust, May 21,2013; plus communication with the author.

venom come from? Where were they tutored in the hatred that they would later deploy? Who were their teachers and sources of inspiration?

Yusuf and the Gardawa

To appreciate the answers to these questions, we need to address the issues of where Yusuf came from. Clearly, his movement was an offshoot of what has come to be known as the Gardawa (sing, Gardi).[14] Their emergence has been traced to the collapse in the status of the ulama, which is largely based on the ability of the institution of state to incorporate them into the loop of power. The Gardawa, hitherto seen as the lowest dregs of society and, in the words of Dr. Anwar Auwalu, who has studied this subject, are noted for: "lacking in proper understanding of the basic principles of Islam, overzealous and intolerant and ignorant of the Arabic language".[15] The Gardawa often provided security for the schools, Tsangaya, and were considered to be nothing more than mere appendages. However, they filled the vacuum left by the ulama by assuming leadership, mobilizing followers, and embarking on simple preaching methods largely in the open air.[16]

Despite there being many before him, Muhammad Marwa stands out as the most famous of the Gardawa preachers. The story of his revolt is very well known and bears no repetition here. However, a few consistent strands can be gleaned. First, is the antagonism against the state, its agents, and institutions. Second, is the contempt for worldly goods and their attack on corruption in high places. Notwithstanding all this, it was not uncommon to find public officials, especially politicians, befriending these preachers often due to their charisma and ability to work a crowd. In particular, they were often in direct conflict and confrontation with the security agencies, especially the police, who are the most vulnerable and direct enemy on the streets. Traditional rulers often got the rough end of their tongues for alleged collaboration with

---

[14] N.A Hassan, "An Analysis of the Gardawa Uprising in Kano," MA Thesis, Bayero University (1986).

[15] Anwar Auwalu, _From Maitatsine Revolts_, 19

[16] Some of these methods include _Wa'azin Turmi_ (preaching on a stool), _Wa'azin fitilar ruwa_ (preaching with a bush lamp), and _Wa'azin Kasuwa_ (Market preaching, _Wa'azin kan hanya_ (Preaching on the road side), among some others forms.

the state and the perceived abandonment of their role as leaders of the faith.

The appeal of these preachers is often wide. The leaders often choose strategic mosques and encourage their followers to open up branches. This is the kind of environment that produced Mallam Yusuf. There may not be any necessary connection between Yusuf's movement known as Jama'atu Ahlil Lidda'awati Wal Jihad and the Boko haram we have today. There are conflicting reports about his place of birth in 1970. He is said to have been enrolled into the local primary school but withdrew in 1979.[17] He is then said to have been an itinerant scholar and supposedly, in a period of twenty years, he was taught by eleven teachers with perhaps different theological and ideological convictions.[18] It is therefore possible to understand how convoluted his mind must have been, drawing from different and sometimes discordant traditions.

When Yusuf founded his organization in 1999, it coincided with Nigeria's return to democracy. It is important to note that by the time the country returned to democracy, it had gone through another phase of almost twenty years of sustained military rule. Additional states had been created in northern Nigeria and, sadly, military dictatorship had closed platforms for protest. Civil society has really not been a part of northern Nigerian Islam and so, there has always been the problem of the lack of outlets for emotions and other forms of protest against the state.

By 1999, millions more Muslims had been to Mecca, and hundreds of millions of dollars, drawn from sources and environments with competing and conflicting ideologies within the Islamic world, had been poured into the various parts of northern Nigeria in support of the Dawah movement. By the late 1990s, some of those the New Nigerian had referred to as *miniature ayatollahs* in 1980 had come of age, with the Muslim Students' Society serving as the platform for radical Islam. The Iranian revolution created the illusion that, somehow, the Nigerian state could be transformed along the lines of what had happened in Iran.

---

[17] Anwar says he was born in in Gidgid, Jankusko Local Government Area, while Ahmad Murtada says he was born in Na'iyya in the Gashua area of Yobe state (Ahmad, *Boko Haram in Nigeria*, 5). Thus, what we see here is the usual development of myths around a controversial individual.

[18] Anwar Auwalu, *From Maitatsine Revolts*, 27.

Some of this fed into the debates over the role and status of Sharia law in the Nigerian Constitution. Again, this is neither the place nor the time to go back to the issues around those series of debates. What is worthy of note however is the fact that this issue has never really been seriously addressed, a factor that continues to heat up the polity today.

International contacts, the annual hajj, globalization, and the rise in the funding of the Dawah, would later turn northern Nigeria into a boiling pot of various shades of movements within Islam which had great appeal and impact on the impressionable minds of many poor and illiterate Muslims. Between the 1980s and 1990s, there were such movements like *Fityanul Islam, Hamas, Hezbollah,* the Ikwan or the Muslim *Brotherhood, The Taliban, Al Qaeda in the Maghreb, AQIM,* the *Salafiyya* and *Wahhabi movements, the Shi'ites, Izalatu Bidia wa Ikamatu Sunna,* and *Al Qaeda* etc. All of these were competing for attention and support against the backdrop of a state whose apparatus of governance had become very weak, while the Muslim ulama was also losing its credibility and moral authority. This created the kind of free-for-all environment that various ideas thrived in while charlatans cashed in and took advantage of the opportunities that were available to offer as an alternative platform for the contestation for power. We also need to truly understand the nature of support that flows into our country from Saudi Arabia, Iran, and elsewhere, and the ideologies behind them.

It is to this world that Yusuf entered in 1999 and successfully negotiated his way to prominence. Apparently, he was a charismatic preacher and there is little to suggest at the early stage that he harboured any ideas of killing people or overthrowing the Nigerian state by violence beyond the rhetorical condemnation of the suffocating injustice of the state. He condemned Muslims for encouraging this corrupt system by active participation, very much like the debates of the rump of the Caliphate one hundred years earlier. The attack on the Nigerian state seemed to be based on the assumption that the state could only be better managed in the hands of not just any kind of Muslim, but the Muslims that believed in his ideas. This is why he preached withdrawal as a tactic, a kind of *Hijra.*

Yusuf travelled around the North extensively, preaching his message. He covered Gombe, Borno, Yobe, Kano, Jigawa, Katsina, and Sokoto states seeking converts. His message was popular, but there were no earth-shaking followers as such. But even then, how is it that no one took serious notice of his antics? How is it that no one thought his sermons and movements should be monitored? Perhaps because at this time, the things he was talking about made a lot of sense to many people against the backdrop of the frustration with the persistence of corruption in our democracy. He also may not have threatened violence to anyone. Yusuf had outlined his beliefs and called on his followers to:

- Oppose and fight the dominance of Western culture as transmitted through Western-type institutions, especially schools.
- Oppose and fight non or anti-Islamic economic and political social systems.
- Strive for the revival and restoration of the Sharia.
- Challenge and eliminate injustice, corruption, and inhumanity in society.
- Inculcate a sense of pride, confidence, honesty, and total reliance on Allah.
- Make good and godly use of science and technology as part of general knowledge and divine heritage entrusted to humanity by God almighty.[19]

This was also summarized in the statement made by Boko Haram, which stated: "We want to reiterate that we are warriors who are carrying out Jihad (religious war) in Nigeria and our struggle is based on the traditions of the holy prophet. We will never accept any system of government apart from the one stipulated by Islam because that is the only way that the Muslims can be liberated. We do not believe in any system of government, be it traditional or orthodox, except the Islamic system and that is why we will keep on fighting against democracy, capitalism, socialism and whatever. We will not allow the Nigerian Constitution to replace the laws that have been enshrined in the Holy Qur'an, we will not allow adulterated conventional education (Boko) to replace Islamic teachings. We will not respect the Nigerian government because it is illegal. We will continue to fight its military and the police because they are not protecting Islam. We do not believe in the Nigerian

---

[19] Anwar Auwalu, *From Maitatsine Revolts.*

judicial system and we will fight anyone who assists the government in perpetrating illegalities".[20]

It would seem that Yusuf himself might have been averse to the adoption of violence as a means of achieving their end. An earlier group which called itself The Taliban, led by Muhammad Alli, had existed around the same Yobe state. They had retreated into the bush where they apparently were living a rather austere lifestyle. They had decided to withdraw to the bush to keep away from contamination by the evil world. They were preparing for what they called the Kannama jihad. Yusuf met up with them, but it seems he found their philosophy incompatible with his. Their leader had preached that he and Yusuf's movement should reject democracy, the civil service, and Western education.[21]

Yusuf seemed to have had some objection to the strategy adopted by the Taliban even though he agreed with their objective of wanting to achieve the dominance of Islam. He was quoted as stating that: "These youths (The Nigerian Talibans) studied the Koran with me and with others. Afterwards they wanted to leave the town, which they thought impure, and head for the bush, believing that Muslims who do not share their ideology are infidels.....I think that an Islamic system of government should be established in Nigeria, and if possible all over the world, but through dialogue".[22]

Unfortunately, we are unable to fathom or verify this strand of thought because Yusuf did not live out his plans and objectives. However, we have enough evidence gleaned from an Open Letter to the President by some prominent citizens of Borno, and we believe that had the government acted quickly, perhaps things would have been different, especially seeing that Yusuf himself may not have been violent nor had he openly preached violence. In said letter, they made the following observations:

- That in the course of his sermons, at no time did Yusuf breach the peace.

---

[20] Statement issued April, 2011.
[21] Ahmad Murtada, _Boko Haram in Nigeria_, 5/6
[22] "Nigeria's Taliban' plot comeback from city hide-outs," AFP, January 11, 2006.

- The followers were able bodied and had Western education, but were frustrated.
- His sermons contained elements of liberation theology, commenting on injustice, social ills, and inequities.
- The killing of 19 of their members over the issue of not wearing helmets by the police led them to seek revenge by attacking the police.
- That the extra judicial execution of Yusuf and Buji Foi, the former Commissioner for Religious Affairs in Borno State, along with some supporters who were invalids, and how the videos were posted on YouTube and broadcast on Al Jazeera television, exacerbated the situation.[23]

6. Addressing the lessons we can learn

The trauma of Boko Haram has taken its toll. However, what I think is most important is for us to address the nature of the lessons that we can learn as a country. Of course, Nigerians continue to look up to the President and they see the persistence of this war as a failure on the part of the President and by extension the security agencies. Whatever might be the merits or demerits of this argument, I am not prepared to wade into it. However, the President himself was quoted widely as having noted that Boko Haram had penetrated his government. In his own words: "Some of them are in the executive arm of government, some of them are in the parliamentary/legislative arm of government, while some of them are even in the judiciary. Some are also in the armed forces, the police and other security agencies. Some continue to dip their hands and eat with you and you won't even know the person who will point a gun at you or plant a bomb behind your house".[24]

How did it get to this point, and how is it that no one was ever charged to court, none of those in the President's cabinet lost his or her job nor was any action taken? But we need to take a rear mirror view of this entire saga to appreciate the fact that too many misjudgements,

---

[23] Mamman Kashim, Kalli Gazali, Dr. Usman Ladan, Abba Kyari, "Letter to the President: Boko Haram: The Real Issues," June 28th, 2011.
[24] Reuters, January 9, 2012.

miscalculations, wrong policy decisions and choices, and inertia at the highest levels, inexorably sucked this movement into violence.

For example, it is worth noting that even after the killing of their leader, the rump leadership of Boko Haram decided to seek redress. They first demanded an apology from the authorities over the treatment they had received and then went to court to demand compensation from the government. They sued the government over the killing of their leaders and members, destruction of their families and so on. The court actually granted their prayers and ordered the government to pay them compensation to the tune of one hundred million Naira (N100,000,000). For over two years, the Federal Government ignored the ruling.[25] By the time the money was paid, harm had already been done, battle lines were drawn and Boko Haram now felt that the stakes were much higher.

To be sure, expenditures on Boko Haram have skyrocketed in a way and manner that is mind boggling. Perhaps this was evidence of the President's commitment to ending the insurgency. However, in my view, this was perhaps the first major mistake. For, I believe this was the product of a wrong diagnosis, namely, the belief that Boko Haram was essentially a problem of law and order and subsequently, a war. By raising the bar and making this a military engagement with humongous budget lines, the government created a situation that would naturally warrant a military solution and almost eliminate the human aspect of this crisis. For, as the military pushed on with greater firepower, we saw more death and destruction. As both sides escalated their war strategies, ordinary citizens became the victims of the excesses. As I said at the beginning, there may be no clear way of knowing how or when this war will end, but we can learn a few lessons from those who have had similar experiences. To address this, I will use just three examples of dynamics whereby nations have managed to integrate belligerent elements in the society and build platforms for national unity.

---

[25] Tukur Mamu, a journalist in Abuja, claims that he had interviewed and raised alarm as far back as 2008 over the nature of the preaching and activities of the movement. See his interview in the Desert Herald, April 4th, 2012.

7. Tales from Elsewhere: Some lessons in Ending Terror

It seems that the timing of terror is often tied to transitions or changes from the old to a new order. And, as we know, transitions, especially from dictatorships to democracy, come with their own challenges. They throw open floodgates of emotions and expectations. The first problem tends to be the issue of power sharing; who wins and who loses, who is in and who is out. For many developing countries, and depending on whether the transition was the result of a hard-fought war (as in Afghanistan, Sudan, or Zimbabwe), or the result of negotiation (as with Nigeria, Ghana, or even South Africa), devising an inclusive power sharing mechanism is the real test.

Algeria: Using undemocratic means to save Democracy

Like other dictatorships around the world, Algeria responded to the winds of change that ushered the collapse of the Berlin Wall. This response was marked by the return to ruling dictatorship opening up the political space. A movement known as al-Jabhah al Islamiya lil-Inqah, the Front Islamique du Salut (FIS), registered itself as a political platform. The movement was founded by a preacher known as Abassi Madani. He and his supporters did not believe in democracy. Yet, they were ready to adopt democracy as a route to achieving their plans for establishing an Islamic state.

The popularity of the movement was not in doubt, as was demonstrated when they contested and won about 54% of the Parliamentary election seats in 1992. The military panicked, especially given that they had planned to close the doors of democracy if they came to power. As such, the military stepped in and banned FIS after the elections.

The FIS responded by embarking on a sustained campaign of violent warfare. The guerrilla war was waged over an eight-year period, leading to the loss of over 150,000 lives. San Egidio, a movement of Lay Catholics based in Italy, brokered a peace agreement in 1996, but it did not hold. However, in 1999, Bouteflika was elected president and he moved quickly to resolve the impasse. FIS declared a unilateral cease-fire while the President presented what was known as the National Harmony Law before the National Assembly. The Law, which was overwhelmingly voted for in the Upper and Lower Houses, granted amnesty to over 2000 members of the group. The political space was opened to them, but the 1996 Constitution has specifically banned political parties founded on the basis of religion. With more integrative policies, some of their members were gradually incorporated into government. From 1999 till his eventual resignation in 2019, Bouteflika remained the president of Algeria despite his ailing health.

Northern Ireland: When Blood was thinner than Water

What came to be known as The Troubles in the history of Northern Ireland had its roots way back in 1919, when the Irish Republican Army (IRA) used force to compel Britain to the negotiating table for a free and united Ireland. A civil war broke out in 1922 leaving very sad memories, and by 1939, the IRA adopted violence as a strategy for dealing with the issues of whether Northern Ireland would remain part of the United Kingdom or join the Republic of Ireland. For over 40 years, from the 1960s, right up to the 1990s, one of the deadliest and most protracted histories of violence was enacted as bombings, hunger strikes, marches, and violent protests came to dominate the landscape. After years of negotiation and ceasefires, the Good Friday Agreement came to force on April 10, 1998, and provided the framework for securing peace. What is most important is the fact that the violence came to an end by way of negotiation.

Uganda: Alice Lakwena and the Holy Spirit Movement

The story of Alice Lakwena and what came to be known as the Holy Spirit Movement is also a demonstration of the ability of the equivalent of the Gardawa in Islam to take advantage of a moral vacuum when people feel a sense of injustice and their universe is threatened.

Ms. Lakwena was variously said to have been a prostitute and a petty trader selling fish and flour. She claimed that the spirit of a dead Italian soldier, Lakwena, had taken possession of her. She became a Catholic and spent 40 years fasting. In the course of her stay, she got a vision that she was to mobilize and take up the challenge of liberating her people. She was a psychic, possessed, and also a healer. Later, she claimed that the spirit had ordered her to stop healing people and to raise an army of liberation. Her followers were ordered to renounce sin, witchcraft, avoid smoking, drinking, and to observe chastity. These were the conditions for the liberation of her Acholi people. She assured her supporters that she had powers to stop the bullets from killing them, and to convince them they were offered holy water and oil. She used voodoo, some say sorcery, and the Bible. The Lord's Resistance Army (LRA) as the soldiers were called, came to a bitter end when they discovered that their oils and water did not really stop the bullets from killing them. Joseph Kony took over from Alice Lakwena after she fled and finally died in exile. He proved to be more diabolical than Ms. Lakwena. However, both held the delusionary view that they were out to liberate the Acholi from being wiped out by the Museveni government.

The important point here is the fact that again, a poor illiterate woman and an equally illiterate young man were able to lead thousands of young men and women, taking advantage of existing ethnic prejudices and hatred. They managed to convince a huge percentage of Acholis that they were indeed under threat of liquidation. The government of Museveni somehow used the threats of the LRA army to also negotiate his way into the attention of a Europe and America that were anxious about the exploits of terrorist groups, a reason that more or less prolonged the tragedy. The lesson again to be learnt is that transitions pose both crises and opportunities, but it is important that new governments bring closure to old wounds and create more inclusive governments.

8. Going Forward in Nigeria: Reconciliation and Construction of a New Order

There is need to try to understand why things have not worked out for us in Nigeria, why the project for national integration and development has been stalled, and why the cumulative impact of all these has created such a fractious, angry, and seemingly frustrated society. We must seek to explore how we ended up with so many years of retarded development, how we became such a severely fractured country, and what can be done to rebuild it again. Boko Haram has tested our wills, but we also have many lessons to learn especially regarding the real history of our country, the levels of injury, grievances, and wounds that our communities carry. We also need to learn the importance of proper and correct diagnosis.

First, we must appreciate the fact that this crisis dragged on because of wrong diagnosis borne out of ignorance, stereotyping, and blind prejudice. When this crisis broke out, we did not allow ourselves to be led by the evidence. Rather, people first from the South-South personalized the crisis and saw it as an affront at their son. The North was accused and demonized, with the belief that Boko Haram had been sponsored by frustrated politicians who had proved unable to live down their defeat at the polls. The conclusion may have been hasty, but it was not totally without some merit.

Of course, targeting churches did not help matters, nor did the popular notion ring hollow that General Buhari had been cheated and his followers were seeking revenge. Clearly, it may not really be true to say that the General necessarily had a hand in the crisis, but matters were not helped by the fact that he did not immediately condemn the activities of this evil group. As it is with our country, time passed, and more and more people dug themselves into these fault lines. We lost time and allowed the group to take advantage of the climate of fractiousness and bickering among the elite.

Second, for whatever reasons, by holding on to power for over a thirty-year period, the region may have created the impression to a younger generation of northern Muslims that somehow, power belonged to the North and in this case, the Muslim North. Unfortunately, and for whatever reasons, beyond grand standing and the manipulation of the sensibilities of their people, this power has hardly brought anything to the ordinary people of the region. Beyond the superficialities of building mosques and sponsoring thousands of people to Mecca, the region has remained trapped in the twilight zone of poverty and destitution. The outward show of religiosity has not really measured up to the expectations of our people. However, for its symbolic benefit, losing this power may have created a traumatic sense of alienation and even humiliation, two concepts that the former *Super Terrorism* Expert and

Harvard Professor, and my teacher, Jessica Stern, identified as driving forces for terrorism.[26]

Third, we need to appreciate the fact that insurgency involves a sophisticated, complex, and multi-layered matrix of actors, networks, financiers, and often non-hierarchical networks. The first thing to do therefore is to try to understand how it works. Their success often feeds on finding and exploiting a weak state architecture, safe havens (forests

---

[26] For a penetrating study, see, Jessica Stern, *Why Religious Militants Kill: Terror in the Name of God* (New York: Harper Collins, 2013). See especially, Chs. 1, 2 on "Alienation and Humiliation," 9-62.

as in our case here), internal or external funding, recruits, supporters, informers within the larger society, enhancing and exploiting existing grievances, real or imagined, a political message and a charismatic leadership, manipulating tribal or religious or regional grievances (read marginalization), and so on.

The challenge here lies in how a country plans for the future of its youth. Youth dreams and idealism need to be properly managed. It is the duty of the government to ensure that it creates the environment to trap the energy of the youth and to channel it towards national development. When a government or a parent fails in this regards, other platforms will become available; drug barons, gang leaders, criminal rings and so on, will recruit our children and offer them a future. So, rather than glibly talk about jobs, there needs to be concerted effort to win the minds of the youth. Like everything else, the nobility of the National Youth Service Corps (NYSC) has come under question because not only are the children of the mighty getting postings of their choices, some of them never stay in their duty posts, but pay others to simply sign a register in their names and they only come home from New York, London, Paris, or Dubai to line up and collect their certificates. Adult recklessness will produce a reckless generation of young people.

Fourth, the Federal Government could have moved quickly to create the office for a counter terrorism unit. This unit should have been manned by experts drawn from different countries with expertise, working closely with Nigerian academicians and officers towards a proper understanding of the problems of insurgency. This is something that would have to be done with discretion given the emotions and conspiracy theories among many northern Muslims regarding the West. This should be an area for the battle of ideas by serious scholars fired by patriotism, seeking to horn their skills and bring in their wealth of knowledge and expertise to serve the common good of the country. We will not resolve these issues by focusing on rehabilitating members of the armed forces. Terrorism is a tactic and it requires science, not sorcery; moral exhortations and pilgrimages resolve the issues.

For a successful counter insurgency program, we need to address the following questions. What respect do the insurgents have in the community? In other words, to what extent do the local people feel that the insurgents represent them or their grievances? Are parents in the community aware of their children's involvement or where they stand with the insurgency? How do parents and relations react to a sudden show of wealth by young people who were hitherto unemployed? Remember the father whose son came back with a huge amount of money boasting that he had made the money from being a member of Boko Haram. He handed him over to the Joint Task Force which summarily shot him, to his father's approval. Elsewhere, this young man would be celebrated as an achiever and sent forward to represent his community at the next election as a favourite son!

There would need to be concerted efforts towards addressing the issues of where the insurgents get their funding. When leaders of religious groups suddenly become like ATM machines, disbursing resources and meeting the needs of the local community, it is helpful to keep an eye on the flow of cash and its influence. Here, there is need to monitor networks, pilgrimages, associations and so on. Without compromising the freedom of citizens to associate freely, Nigerians need to be more circumspect in determining the kinds of preachers who come into our country, their beliefs, and what they think of other religions and the country itself. Here the Ministries for Foreign and Internal Affairs need to work in concert together. Corruption in the Ministry for Internal Affairs through the Immigration Services ensures that dubious businessmen come into our country or cross our borders with no strict examination and monitoring of activities. It has been shown that very often, criminals and terrorists use weak environments to set up dubious businesses such as bakeries or small factories only as a cover for other destabilizing activities. When public officers with powers to monitor put their pockets before the nation, the consequences can be costly.

Fifth, Nigeria has to come to terms with how it will resolve the problems of poverty in the country, especially in the northern states. The northern states on the other hand must not behave as if the rest of Nigeria owes them anything special. The conditions of Northerners and how to resolve the issues should not be the subject of politics and political posturing.

Although there is often the talk about jobs and more jobs, participating and benefitting from jobs requires some levels of education. To prepare for the future requires more than mere tokenism and symbolic gestures. The Federal Government's decision to create separate schools for Almajiri as a step towards rebuilding the North after the insurgency is likely to have the opposite effect. I say so for two reasons, though there could be more.

These children, the Almajiris, will already be stigmatized by virtue of the fact that they will be perceived as being from the streets. The northern elites are not likely to send their children to these schools. But even more dangerous to the program is the likelihood that no non-Muslim child will be allowed into the schools, thus denying the children opportunities to interact with others. Equally dangerous is the fact that their syllabi will be set up and run by Muslim teachers. So, what all this means is that teachers, non-teaching staff, and students are most likely to be Muslims. This is definitely not good enough for children of one country. Behind closed doors, the teachers whose ideology or brand of Islam may not be immediately known could turn these schools into little incubators of hate, thus merely preparing the next generation of Boko Haram.

The Islamiyya school is a seminary of sorts and it is incomprehensible why and how the Federal Government will sink funds into this initiative without appreciating the risk that other religious bodies will start asking to be supported too. Where will we be if various religious bodies should request for the same support? The beauty of Catholic education has been its openness, which can allow a Lamido Sanusi to come out with the best result in Christian Religious Studies in a Catholic school and still be a most devout and dedicated Muslim. I was taken aback when Lamido Sanusi literally challenged me on the origins of the Nicene Creed, various Councils in the history of the Catholic Church, and doctrines such as the Holy Trinity and Transubstantiation. Given the complex religious traditions in our country, especially Islam and Christianity, what we should be looking for are platforms to enable our young people to learn not only about rivers and climatic conditions, but about culture and religious traditions too. In this way, they will grow to respect one another's beliefs.

Sixth, we need to also appreciate the three key strategies that insurgents adopt to pursue their political goals. First is persuasion through the promotion of their ideology by way of propaganda. They also do this through alliances with political leaders and people in high office. This gives them cover and protection, and the stories are not too different. Even Usman dan Fodio first warmed his way to the powers that be during his time. The second strategy is subversion, which they pursue by destruction of public and government installations.

The final strategy insurgents use is coercion. Here, they use violence by way of assassination of opponents and traitors, seeking deliberately to provoke government action against them and often by extension the population. All this is often used to help turn the people against their government and its security agencies who, sooner or later, are accused of indiscriminate destruction of human lives and livelihoods.[27] Terrorists love the publicity that their evil deeds elicit, and often times they want their sponsors to take notice. What this means is that the media has to become more critical and patriotic in how it reports the activities of these evil people. At the height of their wicked bombings of the United Kingdom, the late Mrs. Margaret Thatcher managed to get Parliament to enact a law that criminalized allowing the members of the IRA access to the British media. They could be quoted, but their voices could not be heard. She insisted that the IRA must be denied what she called, the oxygen of publicity. There is a lesson here.

Seventh, it is important to restate what we have said in this paper, namely that Boko Haram has taken advantage and exploited a leadership vacuum that has existed among the ulama in the north. The north has survived by drawing its oxygen of legitimacy from claims of the legacy of the leaders of the caliphate. However, they have not paid much attention to some of the iconic and inspiring words of advice that their forefathers offered them. For example, Othman dan Fodio, the founder of the caliphate, warned his people that, *a nation can live with unbelief, but it cannot live with injustice*[28]. Secondly, his son, Muhammad Bello similarly warned: *Know also that most of the evil that befalls the state comes from the appointment of officers who are anxious to have the appointment because none would be keen on such but a thief in the garb of a hermit and a fox in the guise of a pious worshipper…Whenever I was faced with a problem in my realm, I found out that the cause was the injustice of the governors*[29].

We cannot deny that in many respects, we are reaping what we sowed all these years. Successive Nigerian leaders set the bar of leadership so low that gradually, corruption literally eroded most of the legacy of British colonialism. Public life has lost its glory and in a very strange way, even ordinary citizens have come to expect so little from the public servant. Yet, Abdullahi, the brother of dan Fodio himself, stated as follows: 'Whoever has wealth above what he earns from his

---

[27] See, for some details, "US Government Counterinsurgency Guide," January 13th, 2009.

[28] Hamid Bobboyi (Ed.), "Principles of Leadership According to the Founding Fathers of the Sokoto Caliphate," CRID Leadership Series, 2011.

[29] Hamid Bobboyi, *Principles of Leadership*, 16.

work, the leader shall confiscate and restore it to the treasury".[30] Those we refer to as extremists and fanatics, often draw inspiration from the moral flavour of such words as these, which their elite uncles have not read or are not prepared to abide by.

When ordinary Muslims measure the deeds of their leaders and find them to be at variance with the words of the founding fathers of the Caliphate, they are wont to rebel against the injustice. The rest of Nigeria merely suffers the collateral damage, but the real source of frustrations among ordinary Muslims has largely always been their own elite, who are happy that Christians and the Nigerian state suffer collateral damage. It is fear of the rage of their own people that keeps them quiet and makes them reluctant to condemn the excesses of these fanatics in the face of these crises.

Eight, for any nation, history matters. Without a proper understanding of the past, the future is in jeopardy. In his influential book, *In Defense of History*, Richard Evans has argued that: "Historians should not judge the past in moral terms. Their purpose is rather to understand how the past contributed to human progress".[31] Nigerians like to think of their country and its past in such negative terms as if somehow, nothing has happened to us and no leader has done anything positive or worth celebrating or remembering. There is hardly a former head of state that commands the required respect of Nigerians across the board. Our views about our former public officers are shaped by self-serving assessments, tainted by selfish, clannish, ethnic, regional, or religious considerations. Thus, there can hardly be a common view about any single former head of state or president that commands cross cutting respect and integrity.

The recent reaction to the inclusion of the late General Abacha to the list of those who were honoured in the celebration of Nigeria's centenary speaks to this issue. I have no intention of getting bogged down by the debate except to say that, for whatever reason, had there been no Abacha, there perhaps would have been no President Goodluck Jonathan, no Governor Tinubu, or no Kayode Fayemi, today. This is because there would have been no Ekiti, Nasarawa, or Zamfara States.

---

[30] Hamid Bobboyi, *Principles of Leadership*, 91.
[31] Richard Evans, *In Defense of History* (New York: WW Norton & Company, 1999), 42.

We can judge General Abacha over his theft of state resources, but try telling that to the people of Sierra Leone, where he is revered. History is a highly contested terrain, but we must develop the capacity of managing the good, the bad, and the damn ugly. We can subject them to any interpretation, but we cannot wipe them out of history.

A new generation of Nigerian historians must fill the vacuum left by such giants as the late Professor Dike, R. A. Adeleye, Tekena Tamuno, J. Ade Ajayi, Obaro Ikime, and Toyin Falola, to name just a few. No matter how contested the issues are, we must provide a clear narrative of what our past has been, warts and all, so we can courageously build the future. Our accounts of ourselves have become too incestuous to enable us to create a nation we can be proud of. It is this lack of a collective narrative that has created the room for the endless talk about marginalization. A national discussion among Nigerians is often crowded by primordial sentiments which we invoke to justify why we must hate one another. Thus, Muslims blame Christians, Igbos blame Yorubas, Northerners blame Southerners and vice versa. The result is that we have no more energy left to defend our country, which is why it is in the hands of elements like Boko Haram, among others. It is also the reason why we die as either Christians or Muslims, but never as Nigerians.

Ninth, there is need for a serious review of the role of the military in our democracy. It seems that our politicians are still very much afraid of the ordinary people and their anger. In a genuine democracy, it is the citizens that should occupy center stage, and not proxies such as the military, traditional, and religious leaders, and other non-state actors who have gained prominence in our democracy. The political class continues to court these institutions by co-opting them and making them allies. The increasing politicization of both the military and traditional as well as religious leaders erodes the confidence of the people and the neutrality of these institutions.

As long as the military continues to occupy so much space in our national life, so long will the police remain in retreat. The successes of the so called Civilian Joint Task Force is evidence that the argument about local policing must go beyond the partisan interests of those who feel threatened by the call for policing to become more communal and local. How this plays out is a matter of detail, but we cannot run away from the lessons we have to learn from Boko Haram. Science is key to intelligence, but it has to be fed by or drawn from human intelligence.

Part of the reason for the failure of earlier initiatives is in the fact that local communities felt that the security agencies had become worse than Boko Haram. This was a serious public relations disaster, but it was also a fallout of the military mind that what is ahead of us is war and demolishing the targets. We must change the idea of policing as we know it today in Nigeria, and the matter is well beyond funding or training matters. In Venezuela, it was the police, not the military, that helped to end the violence of Sendero Luminoso, Shining Path.[32]

Tenth, there is the challenge of leadership and the recruitment to public life in Nigeria. This is an area that has occupied much attention, but most of the discussions have been too superficial. We continue to confuse leadership with holding public office. In a country where public office is largely the subject of patronage, what we see is a system that reinforces and feeds on narrow cleavages. For a country like Nigeria where one would expect that public officers should possess a certain level of exposure, what we see is god-fatherism and politics being the defining factors for access to public life. Ethnic jingoists are often concerned with the nature of the portfolios held by their favorite sons and daughters. This is because within the DNA of public life in Nigeria is the tragic belief that you are in office to help yourself, your family, your clan, your tribesmen and women, and indeed, create a government of sorts for your people's welfare.

At the highest levels of government, this is taken for granted. The party in power takes no prisoners and thus, public offices are dispensed. That is why it is natural to expect that every public officer must necessarily be a member of the party in power. The idea of theft of public funds as part of the DNA of being in public life is amply demonstrated by the fact that as elections draw near, ministers are expected to resign to go and run for the office of governor without anyone asking how and where they have found such huge resources.

Too many people from top to bottom are coming into public life with no preparation and no pedigree or evidence of exposure and success in any other form of endeavor beyond the patronage of politics. Too many people are therefore in office but not in power. With too

---

[32] Professor Louis Goodman, (American University, Washington), personal communication with author. *Email communication to the author, dated March 12th 2014.*

many key actors with limited capacity, ability, and exposure, we see that our public officers are soon weighed down by raw power, leading to manufacturing of election results, tinkering with the processes, and wanting to stay in power far too long. As I have said, what we call Boko Haram today is just a handing over the baton in a long relay race of injustice and incompetence in government. Yesterday it was Odua Peoples' Congress who burnt and killed and ended up getting a President Obasanjo. Today, the Niger Delta thinks President Jonathan is a reward for their struggles. Why will Boko Haram not think that it is only violence that will give them a president or an Islamic State? We cannot go on this way and in our situation, perception is reality, tragic as it may be. What we sow is what we shall reap.

9. Conclusion

As we look back at what has happened, it is important that we remind ourselves that almost every protest movement that has arisen anywhere in the world has been based on perceptions of exclusion, injustice, and oppression of one group by another. From the struggle against apartheid and the American civil war, to the Civil Rights Movement and other movements today, the stories are the same. To be sure, human expectations will never ever be met while we are on earth. However, notions of justice are not tied to education or modernity. A sense of justice is a human need. I believe that had the government not made some of the mistakes it made, and not shown such high handedness in dealing with Boko Haram, our story might have been different.

Had Yusuf's murder not been so horrific and perhaps not received such dramatic international coverage, especially by Al Jazeera,[33] followed by his father-in-law's own murder; had the state government paid up the compensation granted by the court to the members of Boko Haram and their families; had the security agencies been less indiscriminate in killing ordinary people; had too many young people not been randomly arrested and detained without trials; had security agencies been more

---

[33] This gory account of these tragic events by Mike Hanna of Al Jazeera is really blood chilling and may have set the tone for the viciousness of the post-Yusuf Boko Haram. http://www.youtube.com/watch?

sensitive in seeking support from local communities and integrating local informants earlier before tensions mounted; had the security agencies adopted and intensified the strategy of cell mating,[34] and other strategies for counter insurgency; perhaps, just perhaps, the outcomes might have been different. But we are at the realm of speculation and what is more, we may never know or appreciate the amount of effort that our men and women have made.

The important thing now is not to blame anyone, but for the Federal Government to think through what kind of security architecture it needs to design now to stabilize our country against internal and external threats. We must also develop a robust intellectual content to get a proper grasp of the history and culture of our people. Too many Nigerians at the top are totally ignorant about the complex nature of the history of the society over which they preside. Once in office, public officers expend energy over the politics of survival in office. Winning the next election and clinging on to power become the reasons why they were elected.

It is a measure of the poor quality of our intelligence gathering tactics and perhaps poor funding that bureaucratic bottle necks, inter-agency competition for resources or influence, government obsession with other non-scientific methods of gathering (listening to medicine men, wearing charms, burying live animals to ward off misfortunes), un-coordinated reporting mechanisms, and infighting at the top are among the difficulties that must be dealt with. Security is in science, not voodoo, as the stories of Maitatsine or Alice Lakwena and others have shown us.

The future? Well, it is in the hands of God, but let me state: Where do we go from here? Our future lies before us. The Federal Government must think seriously about how it will manage an educational blueprint for the country. The other day, Mrs. Oby Ezekwesili spoke about the plans that the Education Ministry had to embark on a comprehensive program of training to be funded by various private sector agencies. The idea was to turn out some 300,000

---

[34] In intelligence, cell mating is adopted to enable security officers to blend in so as to gather relevant information. This means intelligence officers can become cattle herdsmen (for example to get into the cattle rustling problems) or fishermen, say during the militancy in the Niger Delta and so on.

young men and women with different levels of skills. This is the way to go, not for us to boast of building new universities that are turning out job seekers who are dying to get jobs years after graduation (no pun intended).

There is need for us to bring back nobility into the university system. It is men and women of ideas, not politicians, who will change our country. We are where we are today because the academia has surrendered the moral high ground to a political class that clearly lacks both the capacity and disposition to create wealth and a good society based on the knowledge industry.

Nigerian politicians have made life nasty and short in Nigeria. We saw the signals of Boko Haram many years ago, but we were too preoccupied with politics to take note. The endless burning of churches in northern Nigeria by irate Muslim youths, with no governor in the North ever visiting to commiserate with the people. One person who showed how this could be done in the North all these years was Senator Mohammed Makarfi when he was Governor of Kaduna State. He managed to bring peace back to Kaduna, at least during his tenure. He showed leadership and non-discriminatory courage beyond the political posturing of Muslim leaders fearing to be seen openly associated with Christians!

There is now a conference to fashion out a new Nigeria. We have had all this before and been on this road before. Will anything be different? Will the conference really and truly be insulated from the ambitions of those who have set it up? But even assuming for the sake of argument that we really and truly manage to have even a perfect document, what will that mean? We have not been faithful over little things and indeed, we have governed our country more by unconstitutional than constitutional means. We all know that there is no reverence for the document. All the stealing that is going on, all the high costs of governance, all the executive recklessness and individuals in public life treating public funds as if they are private, are any of these in the Constitution?

When we concluded the Oputa Panel, Nigerians were full of appreciation and high hopes. Former President Shehu Shagari said it was the best thing that ever happened in Nigeria, while the Guardian made the panel "the Man of the Year". Today, the work is no better than any average piece of paper. Who will generate the energy that we need to kick start this giant that continues to lie in a state of stupor? Who will provide the road map we need to embark on this long and tortuous journey? Who will provide us with the navigational equipment, and who will the map-readers be?

For any meaningful change to take place in our country, our national character must change. The late John Wooden (1910-2010), the basketball star and coach, once said: *Be concerned with your character than your reputation. Reputation is what people think of you but character is what you are.* Pope John Paul 11 (now St. John Paul) once said that: *Even stupidity is a gift of God, but one must not misuse it.* Nigeria has clearly overdrawn on its store of stupidity with the many avoidable mistakes we have made. Or else, how did we end up as a nation which aggressively exports every valuable thing it has - its professionals, its resources, even its stolen loot - and continues to nurture, conserve, and preserve destitution, poverty and squalor? It is from this bank that we have drawn the Boko Haram cheque.

Everything considered, the words of the late President John F. Kennedy should be the point on which we end this long reflection. He said to the Americans what I want to say to all Nigerians: "Never before has man had such capacity to control his own environment and to end thirst and hunger, to conquer poverty and disease, to banish illiteracy and massive human misery. We have the power to make this the best generation of mankind in the history of the world ".

Thinking about the future requires imagination, and imagination is a function of dreams and visions. The Rev. Martin Luther King had a dream that even though he did not live to see it, created a vision that many thought was impossible. But, it is exactly that vision and that dream that have given birth to a black president in America. Karl Marx visualized a classless society and developed the *Communist Manifesto* in

1948. It created the Soviet Union, which lasted over 50 years and whose message is still alive today. Mao Zedong dreamt of the Great Leap Forward in 1958, and today, we can see the fruits. China, which was despised only a few years ago, is now the world's reference point for growth and wealth. President Nelson Mandela visualized a non-racial society that was baptized as the Rainbow Nation. He fought apartheid with moral force and brought that bastion of evil to its knees. Today, his people are free. President Franklin D. Roosevelt (FDR) responded to the tragedy of the Great Depression in 1933 by offering the New Deal. The United States of America has risen from there to dominate the world. The world has been built and rebuilt by men and women with vision and the power to dream. In 1941, FDR gave the world four freedoms: freedom of speech, freedom of worship, freedom from want, and freedom from fear. Nigeria needs to dream again and the place to dream is here.

Today, our nation has no dreams, and that is why we are threatened by nightmares such as Boko Haram. We have found it fashionable to talk about how the evil British conquered us and created a country without asking us for permission or bringing us to the table. I hear otherwise serious people ranting that Lugard brought together people of conflicting interests and cultures and that somehow, we should sit down and talk about our future. This hypocrisy is as irritating as it is disgusting.

First, neither ideological, cultural, geographical, racial, gender, class, or any other form of homogeneity by itself can guarantee harmony and unity to a people. After all, we cannot conceive of greater harmony than Heaven, but is it not from there that the devil rebelled against God and has become our tormentor on earth (Rev 12: 7-13)? The real challenge we refuse to face is how we have made governance a criminal enterprise in Nigeria, rather than a vocation for service. How did we end up with a country in which almost as a national policy, corruption is the only thing that works and is efficient? How did we lose a sense of shame?

Lord Lugard came to Nigeria one hundred years after the likes of Mungo Park, Hugh Clapperton, or the Lander Brothers. British colonialism was the subject of over one hundred years of adventure by anthropologists, historians, ethnographers and so on, who took interest in Africa and the opportunities it offered for empire building. Rather than excoriating them, we should be asking, how is it that these white men travelled for months and years amidst the wildest of environments, suffered death and desolation, all to fulfill a dream? Compare that with Nigerians and Nigerian academicians who do not want to travel outside their immediate environment out of fear. To Europe, of course, yes, but to Sokoto, Katsina, Kebbi, or Makurdi? No way. This incestuous existence is what has created room for the amount of self-deprecation, stereotyping, and prejudice that characterize debates about ourselves in Nigeria.

Today, our universities, which should be the center of ideas and intellectual curiosity, have become in many respects incubators of ethnic jingoism where professors are competing not for excellence in research in their areas of endeavor, but to get the attention of politicians and secure political appointments. If we lose the nobility of the intellect and its capacity to create ideas and visions, our future will remain in the firm grip of terrorist groups such as Boko Haram. So, if there is any lesson to learn, it is that we must seize the initiative and reclaim the ideals that led us into academia rather than other pursuits.

We are trying to create a new order by way of a new Constitution. Rather than gathering men and women of ideas who know about law making, we have assembled interest groups based on primordial considerations at a time when everyone is angry with everyone and everything else in Nigeria. And, at N12m per month, per participant, as it is alleged, delegates to the Conference must think they are writing a Constitution for the Sultan of Brunei. But this is the beginning of the problem before us.

Looking back, when President Obasanjo set up the Political Reform Conference, I was happy to serve and I was deeply convinced that we could make a difference. Sadly, in my innocence, I did not know that they wanted the Conference as a mere Trojan horse. The President has said openly that the Conference is not about him. I want to believe him. The controversy already raging is a sign of things to come. But, we must remember that the reason why Algeria was led into a war for almost eight years was the fact that the FIS wanted to use democracy to kill democracy. We must note that the reason why Egypt has come to a dead end now is because the Brotherhood wanted to use democracy to kill democracy. If the politicians want to use democracy only as a veneer to cover the nakedness of their ambitions, then our country is set on a slippery slope. It is our job as intellectuals to reflect and point these out as a prophetic responsibility. This country and its survival is larger than any individual or group interests.

Our debates are preoccupied with talk about what Nigerians dubiously call true federalism, and for us, it is about managing the corruption in our rentier economy. The governors are the chief apostles of this creed and all we hear is that the center is too strong (yet it cannot fight to bring Boko Haram to a halt?), by which they mean we must share the proceeds of this theft from the people of Nigeria equally. Take a look at the Federalist Papers, dealing with debates about what would later become the American Constitution. Note how the debates were conducted by passionate patriots who were grounded in political theory, deep-seated passion, keen intellect, love, and knowledge of their country. Think about the likes of George Washington, John Jay, Alexander Hamilton, John Hancock, or the ferociously brilliant James Madison. Their debates were characterized by knowledge and ideas, not narrow partisan political and clannish interests of the moment. The debates were a dream about a world that was not within their reach yet, but a world that would outlast them, a world that would possess the elasticity to accommodate all shades of later generations.

Compare all that with our debates which are supposed to lead us to a new dawn and ask, are we thinking of a generation of Nigerians that are not here now? Are we thinking about a generation of Nigerians who will not be bound by the chains of ethnicity and regionalism or religious bigotry? So far, this Conference is not looking beyond 2015.

Nigerians like to dwell on the word 'experience' as a guide to participation in public life. They focus on experience as a noun, not a *verb*. I prefer to see it as a verb for the purpose of my analysis. If we see it as a noun, then of course, it presupposes knowledge. And for our purpose, having too many old men and women in circulation on grounds of experience means we need to look back at what this experience has been. Is it experience with corruption, experience with stealing elections, experience with the inefficiency that has continued to deepen inequalities, destitution, and poverty in our land? Is it the experience which has given us no electricity, no railways, and nothing but despondency and death?

Experience as a verb suggests that it is I who is the subject of experience. I drive on a road with potholes; I experience discomfort; I am a student risking going blind because I am reading with candles every night; I am a woman, and I know I am not safe because I can be raped or forced into marriage and disposed of; I am a student and I know that just going out to look for a job, I could get killed. It is this that should galvanize us into seeking change in our society. It was the life experience of students in the university that determined when they would be on the streets. It was when university students translated their experiences of frustration, whether it is over increase in fees, food, or other hardships such as fuel crises, that their protests sharpened their political consciousness and prepared them for public life. But now, students are too busy with seeking which politician to sponsor their own ambitions and which one to serve. If we can channel our pains and sufferings, our frustrations and grievances, then, experience as a verb is what can displace the dubious claim of experience as an adverb by which gerontocracy has gradually been made to displace democracy.

Presently, I have set up what I call The Kukah Centre as a nursery bed for generating new ideas. I am frustrated by the seeming death of the rigor of debate, controversy, and the constant confrontation with the demons of injustice. I am nostalgic about the day of the Professor Nzimiros, the Claude Akes, the Bala Usmans, and so on. That was when scholarship was alluring and enduring. If scholars do not wrestle the demons that threaten our collective present and future, we will remain hostages to nightmares, convulsing in swivel chairs, turning and turning but going nowhere. By the Kukah Centre, we are trying our best to see if now, and in the future, we can light more candles rather than cursing the darkness. I thank you for your patience. The Lord bless Nigeria.

43rd Convocation Lecture, University of Nigeria, Nsukka, March 27th, 2014.

CHAPTER THREE

To Heal A Fractured Nation: Education And Leadership For A New Nigeria

A house divided against itself cannot stand. I believe this government cannot endure, permanently half slave and half free. I do not expect the Union to be dissolved -- I do not expect the house to fall -- but I do expect it will cease to be divided...It will become all one thing or all the other.

The above quotation comes from Abraham Lincoln's famous speech, known now as the *House Divided Speech*, which was delivered in Springfield, Illinois on June 16th, 1858. It was one of his greatest, moment defining speeches, delivered at a very critical period of the nation's life. In a slightly different, less dramatic, context, I believe it speaks to our moment because it draws attention to the moral choices a society has to make. We may be physically free from slavery in Nigeria today, but we are in a form of bondage that requires that we respond with the same candour that drove Abraham Lincoln in the United States, because I believe that our nation requires a balm of healing well beyond the silence of the guns.

Today, we are told that the Boko Haram insurgency is only a foretaste of what is still to come. We are told that Nigeria is likely to split into tiny pieces sooner than later. We have the words of a scapegoat or a prophet to prove this. Professors, politicians, traditional rulers, bishops, priests, and market women are all talking about it in fear and trepidation. The red flag has been raised by the moral policeman of the world; the United States of America has predicted that Nigeria will collapse in 2015. We are only to prepare to take our place in the funeral parlour as we prepare to bury Nigeria. Moving **home** and returning **home** have become routine scarecrows that prey on our fears. This lecture is about exploring some of the fractures that have produced these fears, anxieties, and hopes.

In this lecture, I wish to address what I call the state of fracture of the Nigerian state and explore what steps we need to take to work towards some form of healing. We have developed different longstanding vocabularies for expressing the manifestation of these fractures in our daily lives: *marginalization, Nigerian factor, ethnicity, national character, federal character, North* and *South, Christians* and *Muslims, Minorities* and *Majorities.* These catch phrases continue to haunt almost every sphere of our national life.

This will be divided lecture in four sections. **Firstly,** I will try to identify the fractures in our nation and briefly look at the causes and their impact. **Secondly,** I will identify what I call the three 'vehicles' for healing the fractures of our nation. Here, I will choose politics, education and the bureaucracy only to illustrate the point. **Thirdly**, I will specifically address the issues around the so-called impending collapse of Nigeria in 2015 as being predicted. **Fourthly**, and by way of conclusion, I will argue that our situation requires a particular typology of leadership to mend our fractures.

1. Nigeria's Fracture: Colonialism and the Wheels of Human History

On a visit to Jordan in 1998, I was told of a place called Churchill's hiccup. According to the anecdote, Churchill, who was Colonial Secretary for Colonies, boasted that he created Jordan *by the stroke of a pen*! Apparently, on the said day in 1921, Churchill had taken one drink too many at lunch and then went on to create what accounts for the sharp zig-zag that constitutes the strip of land on the eastern border between Jordan and Saudi Arabia. Some people would say that Nigeria has just celebrated 100 years of its own Churchill's hiccup! This therefore is the first fracture of what is today modern Nigeria.

It is largely a waste of time for us to continue to argue today about the pros and cons of colonialism and about whether colonial fractures were right or wrong. After all, had the British not come, we are not sure what our collective fates would have been in the face of the conquering and slave raiding armies of the Sokoto Caliphate, the empire builders of Benin, Kwararafa, or Oyo and Zamfara, among many others.

A lot of those who agonise about colonialism focus on its conquest and subjugation but pay little attention to the fact that this was in fact part of the turning of the wheel of human history. The disciplines of both history and anthropology have shown that colonialism is the universal process of movement of human civilization, it is part of the human experience with domination, control, and oppression, and it is part and parcel of the struggle and negotiation for power among peoples. The story of colonialism is a vital part of the tapestry of the history of all nations of the world. The colonial state laid the foundation for the emergence of the modern state as we know it today in developing nations. The structure and forms of colonial governments were inherently unequal, and inequalities lay at the roots of the system. Some nations seem to have been able to mend their colonial fractures with some success. Why has Nigeria been unable to make the transition? How have succeeding elites exacerbated the fractures and wounded the nation further? It is to these that I now wish to turn my attention.

2. Nigeria's Fracture: Its Causes and Consequences

At independence, Nigeria adopted the Westminster Parliamentary system of government. The historical development of those processes is the subject for another platform. However, the nation's greatest achievement was sealed when the British flag was lowered, and the Nigerian flag of green-white-green was hoisted. The Parliament was a galleon of colours filled with a paroxysm of voices.

To honour Nigeria and to show its promise, the very influential international TIME Magazine (December 5th, 1960 edition) took the historic decision of making Sir Abubakar Tafawa Balewa its cover person. It followed with a subheading: "The Other Africa:Independence Without Chaos". This pointed at the optimism about the prospects of Nigeria developing along the path of honour, non-violence, and progress. In the lead story, the magazine noted: "Along with its echoes of Britain's Westminster, the legislature over which Sir Abubakar presided last week had some flavour of Pan African Congress. On its benches, tall, haughty Hausas, splendidly robed in green and scarlet, sat among volatile Ibos draped in white azure gowns. Across the aisle were Yoruba tribesmen wrapped in gold, yellow and orange with little porkpie beanies on their heads. Between them, they constituted the world's noisiest Parliament. Each Speaker was greeted with cries of 'Hear, heath' from his friends and derisory shots of 'Sit down, you wretched fool' from his foes. From the rostrum came the perennial plea for 'Oda, Odah'". But somehow, through the din, the nation's problems got discussed and decided.

The reporter was far more generous than these early lines suggested because he went on to raise a banner of hope for Nigeria. He continued:

"In the hurly burly of the 1960s African avalanche of freedom, Nigeria's impressive demonstration of democracy's workability in Africa is too often overlooked…Nigeria entered the world community without noisy birth pangs or ominous warnings of its determination to avenge ancient wrongs. Since moderation and common sense are not the stuff that headlines are made of, the world's eyes slid past Nigeria to focus worriedly on the imperialistic elbowings of Ghana's Nkrumah….In the long run, the most important and enduring face of Africa might well prove to be that (face) presented by Nigeria. Where so many of its neigbhbours have shaken off colonialism only to sink into strong man rule, Nigeria not only preaches but practices the dignity of the individual".

So how did Nigeria take its eyes off this ball which was heading straight into the goalpost of opportunity, dignity, and freedom? How did Nigeria end up delaying its journey to greatness? There are bound to be many and contradictory explanations. There is enough blame to go around all the regions, religions, communities, individuals, the political class, the military, and weavers of national and international conspiracy theories. However, our intention here is merely to highlight just three phases in our national life that account for the major fractures that we are referring to.

First Fracture Caused by the First Military Coup: Northern Dominance

The first fracture in post-colonial and post-independent Nigeria was caused by the blow of the first military coup. By this singular act, the military shattered the glass of optimism elevated by the writers in TIME Magazine and chose bullets rather than the organized noise that represents the very essence of the democracy that Nigeria had inherited. Many attempts have been made to justify and explain how gallant the intentions of the coup plotters were and how they would have resolved some of our lingering national issues and created a truly just polity. This truly begs the question because, the truth is that in principle, to the extent that military intervention is not the will of the people, its rape on democracy can never be justified, no matter the nobility of the cause. For, as we shall show, that coup opened up a can of worms that would afflict the entire nation and throw up challenges that would delay the healing of our nation. For some inexplicable reason, the period of military rule after the coup that overthrew General Gowon in 1975, witnessed the prolonged dominance of the levers of power by northern Muslims. This phase of our national life witnessed major policy shifts such as the ill-advised misadventure of the Babangida administration with the Organisation of Islamic Conference (OIC), the lingering anxieties over the status of Islamic law in the Constitution, and the rise in the curve of religiously induced violence across the northern states. These left severe fractures, some of which still haunt our nation.

Second fracture caused by the Civil War: Eastern Grievances

The second major fracture in the Nigerian polity was caused by the civil war. General Gowon's policy of three R's, Rehabilitation, Reconstruction and Reconciliation, did not go far because many of those who worked with him did not share his enthusiasm in the philosophy of 'no winner, no vanquished'. Thus, today, the Igbos still nurse grievances that they have not been fully integrated in national life across the nation. Whether one agrees with these claims or not, time has not healed the fracture and we cannot ignore its feature in our national life. However, right till date, this feeling of injury permeates every facet of our national life, from politics, the bureaucracy, the military, and the economy to almost everything else.

Third fracture caused by the Creation of states: Loss of sense of national unity

The third fracture was the creation of states which replaced the regions left behind by the colonial administration. Unlike post-colonial states such as Ghana, Kenya, India, South Africa, and other African countries, it seems that only Nigeria enthusiastically and, to my mind, wrongly opted for state creation as a means of resolving the crisis that followed independence. Other countries soldiered on, coping with military interventions, corruption, and violence, and still saw wisdom in leaving the internal colonial boundaries such as regions or provinces largely intact with very minor adjustments. The painstaking care and thought that went into the creation of provinces and regions by the colonial administration contrasts very sharply with the arbitrariness that followed the creation of states and Local Government Areas in Nigeria.

Whereas the local bureaucrats greeted the creation of states with enthusiasm, facts have shown that the balkanization of the political space has only deepened the frustrations, bitterness, and hatred among Nigerians. The creation of these states, and later Local Government Areas, merely offered local elites new fiefdoms with yesterday's majorities becoming minorities or vice versa. The first noble intention was to avert the civil war. It did not work. The second was to allay the fears of minorities. That too has not worked, as we can see from the embarrassing demands today for over 100 new states and a thousand Local Government Councils. The effects of these fractures still haunt our nation today as more bitterness, angst, suspicion, and fear continue to stalk the land. At local levels, the ubiquity of Emirates and traditional institutions have all further opened up new fractures as communities, clans, and families have all turned on one another.

Tragically, whereas the colonial state left us a workable state with some infrastructure relative to the resources of the time, a sound educational base, and a bureaucracy, subsequent military regimes merely superintended over the destruction, collapse, and decay of these institutions one after the other. Rather than diagnosing and seeking cure to these ailments, successive regimes only deepened the wounds of the nation by institutionalising violence. The execution of alleged coup plotters and armed robbers only added to the sense of injury and the glorification of violence. The children who saw this waste of lives would later grow into adults and glorify violence.

How then do we address the problem of national healing? Some of us, including myself, have an injury in some part of our body that is the result of a fight or a sport, an accident of one form or the other. These injuries have since been cured. However, healing has not taken place. What I mean here is that although we may not feel the injury, each time we look at the scar we remember what caused it. I argue that healing of our national injuries will be the result of a combination of factors. If we gloss over injuries as we have tended to do, we will surely pay the price, as we can see in the volatility that has become part and parcel of our national life. The resort to violence by many communities today arises from that feeling of unhealed injury, leading to frustration. What strategies, then, should we adopt to effect deep and lasting national healing?

3. Vehicles for Healing the Fractures of our Nation

What is the best strategy for effecting healing in post-conflict societies or societies in transition? What policy measures should a society in transition take to ameliorate the trauma of the past? How should the accounts of the past be read and written? These and many other questions need to be asked.

There are many strategies but the most common for many nations in the last twenty years was the resort to Truth Commissions. These initiatives have their own logic and often they may have opened the wounds of society, but they tended to leave the society even more divided than healed. Nigeria has already experimented with the Truth Commission model. The Federal Government under President Obasanjo attempted to commence a process for healing our fracture through the setting up of the Human Rights Violation Investigation Commission. Sadly, that initiative got caught up in the web of politics and intrigues and became a victim of the politics of the day. It was illustrative of the fact that our nation was still not ready to lance the boil so as to commence a process towards healing.

The report of the Oputa Panel, released or not, should have been the stuff of research in the political science faculties in our universities so that we can work towards writing a better history of our nation for the next generation. Sadly, from my experience, there is more interest among foreign researchers abroad in the work of the Commission than in Nigerian universities. My book, *Witness to Justice*, gives an account of my personal experience, the trials, and also the hopes and opportunities I saw in the work.

It is not my intention to explore this theme here or to ask why this did not work for us. What I think I need to do is to focus more on what is before us, namely, the fact that we are faced with a broken country in need of healing, to see what other options there might be. To do this, I have decided to look at what I call vehicles for service delivery, vehicles which I believe, if properly deployed, can help our country heal from the some of the fractures that I have listed above.

3: 1. Education as a Vehicle for Healing

The history of Nigeria's educational system has been well told and needs no repetition. However, our concern here is not with the history. I am concerned with whether or not education has been a vehicle for exacerbating the fracture, or if it has effected some level of healing. The reality and the facts before us do not inspire any kind of inspiration.

It is difficult to find any other country in the world that has done as much disservice to its educational system as Nigeria has done. This destruction is really another word for describing almost every facet of our national life. Looking at all public institutions of yesterday, from hospitals, roads, railways, bureaucracy etc., one would be forgiven for believing that those who governed us all these years came to deliberately preside over the destruction of everything they laid their hands on. Their inefficiency and corruption merely deepened the sense of fracture and frustration.

Many Nigerians are wont to argue that the takeover of schools by the Gowon administration was the first strike that dealt the most severe fracture on the nation's educational system. Looking back, whatever good intentions the Gowon government may have had, these intentions were later turned into a license for vengeance, victimization, and high expressions of envy.

Since Nigeria's return to democracy in 1999, we have witnessed a new turn, marked by a combination of passion for our people and a sense of remorse and repentance. In all the southern states, we have seen governors genuinely becoming aware of the fact that the takeover of schools was a mistake and that to restore quality in education, the state needs to collaborate with the faith communities. We today witness a return to what ought to have been, namely, federal and state governments seeing the faith and ethnic community associations as partners. These commendable efforts are now bearing fruit in almost all the southern states. But not so in the North, ironically, the worst hit in calculating every index of development.

In the northern states, those in power are still looking backwards, weighed down by fear, prejudice, and pure ignorance. Sadly, Northerners have come to see the takeover of schools as an arrest of the growth of Christianity. Many northern Muslims seem to be blinded to the opportunities that secular education holds out for the future. They continue to tinker with education, refusing to create a more integrative system that can harmonize the rich cultures and diversity of our nation. They continue to hoist the word religion as an excuse for not opening up the society. The result is that the region continues to produce generations of young men and women who cannot compete with the larger society. Driven by this insecurity, they fear change and are quick to reject the unknown. They are more comfortable in the womb of religion. This is what has produced the toxic, nihilist, and murderous doctrines that drive the madness called Boko Haram.

What is important for our reflection here is to answer the question: how can education become a tool for healing and integrating a fractured nation? Indeed, there can be no healing without education. Education must be a tool for nation building because it is the source of knowledge. Therefore, the kinds of people and the environment around which that knowledge is transmitted must not be left to chance. We have witnessed the systematic decline of the status of the teacher, the pivot of education.

In the murky waters of corruption in Nigeria, teachers have fallen victim and are involved in nearly all the petty crimes of survival that the rest of us are involved in, except of course, such lucrative ones as fuel subsidy or pension fund scams, kidnapping or oil bunkering, which are the preoccupation of their ex and current students! Other nations have not been as irresponsible and criminal as Nigeria has been despite having the same colonial roots and experiences. Asian and Latin American countries have used education to uplift their people, restore their dignity, and create viable nations. The problems have not gone away, but clearly, from these, we have a few lessons to learn.

Costa Rica

Take Costa Rica, a small country which in many respects is the model for the value of education. I came into contact with the news of their system purely by accident. In 1998, I was invited to speak at a conference in the United States on the military and the struggle for democracy. After my presentation, we went on a tea break. A man walked up to me and introduced himself. "I am Oscar," he said to me, "Oscar Arias". The name rang a bell, but I did not wish to speculate. He moved me gently in the direction where coffee was being served. Our conversation went something like this: "Father," he said to me, "I enjoyed your presentation and your enthusiasm. But I must tell you, the military is not what you think it is. It is not as powerful as you think. It can be overthrown peacefully. You do not need the military. My country has the experience and I can show you how this can be done". I wondered who this man was. His humility was striking, and his eloquence suggested a man who had a lot of experience in what he was talking about. He continued: "Education is the key to ridding any country of the virus of the military. In my country, we invested a lot in education, and we have reaped the fruits. Now, we do not have a military and, rather than feel threatened, we actually feel stronger as a people and as a nation."

He went on to explain how the founders of modern Costa Rica had battled to lay the foundation for a sound educational system as the basis for security. They believed that an educated populace would be able to defend themselves against the greatest enemy, ignorance and poverty. Suddenly, the co-ordinator of the Conference walked to us and I heard him say, "This way, Mr. Arias, the next session is about to start, and you are the Chairman". He walked away, and it was when he was introduced at the session that I realized that I had been with Mr. Oscar Arias, the former President of Costa Rica and winner of the Nobel Peace Prize!

Arias was also the epitome of those leaders who left their countries, got a good education, and came back home with a clear idea of how to fix their societies. He received his education in Costa Rica, but then went on to Boston University in Massachusetts, and the London School of Economics and the University of Essex in the United Kingdom. These roundly educated persons often are great reformers who effect change arising from the quality of education they received and the time they may have had to plan a future for themselves and their countries. Dr. Arias was president from 1986-1990 and received a Nobel Peace Prize in 1987 for the great and courageous work he did to bring about peace in the Americas.

Yes, Costa Rica still has no military. They also have no oil or any known resources. Education is their oil and it is the anchor for almost every facet of life. Teaching is the most prestigious and precious calling-card for every citizen. If you want to win elections in Costa Rica, it is not money that you need to have. No, if you are lucky to have parents or even better still grandparents who were teachers, you have nothing to fear. Teaching is the most prestigious engagement and that is why they can afford to be a country without an army and still be one of the most peaceful countries. Dr. Arias received the Peace Prize at a period of the greatest display of US power in the region. It is a measure of the triumph of moral authority over weapons that he won the Prize with no standing army!

As an aside, let me divert our attention a bit. In our own situation,

Nigerians have also demonstrated that if they are truly allowed to make their choices, they value the teacher, his/her probity and contribution. Teachers have also received their reward here on earth in ways that Nigerians would seem to have forgotten or do not appreciate. Let me give you some examples: President Shagari was a teacher before politics. He was neither rich nor ambitious for politics. This is why his biography is titled, *Beckoned to Serve*! Governor Ibrahim Shekarau was a teacher before politics. He won his elections as Governor of Kano State even though he was unemployed and had no house of his own at the time he joined politics. Dr. Goodluck Jonathan, who is President of Nigeria, was a teacher. Today, Jonathan and Shekarau are President and Minister of Education, respectively. We expect to see qualitative and measurable changes.

Singapore

The world continues to bow to Singapore and South Korea, among other Asian countries. Since Nigeria's return to democracy, Lee Kwan Yew's autobiography, *From Third World to First,* has sold more copies in Nigeria than anywhere else in the whole world. President Obasanjo and his successors apparently ensured that all Ministers had copies of the book. While it is doubtful if these Ministers ever went beyond the first few pages, it is even more doubtful that those who may have managed to read the book had any real intention of borrowing the sense of discipline and patriotism that Mr. Lee so eloquently spoke of. It is a measure of our dilemma that, apart from Alhaji Shehu Shagari, none of our former heads of state has had the courage to publish an autobiography.

Like others who have been to Singapore, the beauty, order, serenity, and the sense of patriotism, efficiency, dedication, and commitment of the Singaporeans struck me. Most of what the country is today has been attributed to the vision of Lee Kwan Yew. But vision is not enough if you do not build a sound educational system to inspire sharers of your vision to see through your window. Lee himself speaks about the deliberate efforts he made to reserve and recruit some of the most brilliant minds into public life and politics. Neither patriotism nor anything else in life can be left to chance.

For example, there is a fascinating educational grid in Singapore that ensures that all Singaporean children acquire certain values and traits as they go through the system. It is organized in such a way that all children are literally indoctrinated to achieve an already defined outcome. The result is that in the end, there is a set of shared values that all children imbibe from primary to secondary school and junior college. That means that by the time one finishes junior college and is ready for university, between the ages of 16-18, these values have been deeply ingrained. This ensures that after 18, when one has become an adult and is released into the larger society, one is fully equipped with what it is to be a Singaporean citizen, and prepared to take one's place in society.

The table below speaks to the story[1]:

After Primary School	After Secondary School	After Junior College
Children should distinguish between right and wrong	Children must have imbibed moral Integrity	Youth must be resilient and resolute
Learnt the art of sharing and putting others first	Have care and concern for others	Have a sense of social responsibility
Must know how to build friendships with others	Be able to work in teams and value contribution	Understand how to inspire others
Developed intellectual curiosity	Be enterprising and innovative	Have an entrepreneurial and creative spirit
Must know how to think and self-expression	Possession of the foundation for further education	Able to think independently and creatively
Take pride in work	Believe in their personal ability	Strive for excellence
Cultivate healthy habits	Have an appreciation of aesthetics	Have a zest for Life
Love SINGAPORE	Believe in SINGAPORE	Know what it takes to lead SINGAPORE

Moving Forward in Nigeria through Education

We do not need to look far to know why our nation has seemingly lost its soul. Education, which constitutes the backbone, the central nervous system of any nation, has collapsed in our country. It is not as if the system has been taken over by bad men and women. No, it is just that

---

[1] Claudio Castro & Aimee Verdisco (eds.), *Making Education Work: Latin American Ideas and Asian Results* (Inter-American Development Bank, 2002) 22.

we have had a complete system collapse, triggered by years of military rule which had total disregard for systems and processes. It is not that bad or unpatriotic soldiers governed us. On the contrary, with all the derision and criticisms, we have had some of the most patriotic leaders who actually were convinced that they were doing their best for this nation. Sadly, they were like men driving expensive cars; driving really hard, but in the wrong direction. This has resulted in a fractured society with no shared values and no clear navigational aids.

Today, from top to bottom, the rut is noticeable. The noble ideas behind the engagement of the Federal Government's involvement in education have been compromised by a combination of wrong policy options and poor vigilance. The noble ideas for national unity behind the establishment and funding of institutions like the Federal Government Unity Colleges, Federal Special Science Colleges, Federal Colleges of Education, Federal Universities, Polytechnics, and so on, have been reduced to mere fiefdoms at the mercy of local cabals.

Appointments, promotions, and so on have been hijacked by local tribal, regional, and religious war lords who see these institutions as federal government patronage to their territory, while a morally weakened Federal Government sees these institutions as extensions of domains of patronage to the local elites. The bureaucrats, politicians and public officers have filled up these federal schools with their children not because they measure up but because of nepotism. The result is that the sense of common citizenship and nationhood that guided these visions has been severely compromised. How can these institutions possibly breed graduates that can, as they say in Singapore, *know, believe and dream of what it takes to lead Nigeria?*

In fairness to ex-President Obasanjo, he did a lot in his second term to reverse the rut in education. He set up universal platforms and initiatives to bridge the gaps and deficits in the educational systems from primary to the university. The problems here relate to the fact that the State Governments have turned these boards into platforms for patronage of their political cronies. There is more emphasis on procurements, construction, renovation, and other avenues for slush funds.

Given the complexity of our nation, can we find a Professor of Fulfulde in the University of Ibadan, a Professor of Tiv in Benin, a Professor of Hausa in Uyo, or a Professor of Efik in Usman Dan Fodio? Are there specialists in Nok or Ife civilizations in the University of

Maiduguri or specialists in the Sokoto Caliphate in the University of Lagos? Are our universities prepared to confront the demons of our past historical experiences? Can a Fulani Professor teach history of the civil war, or an Igbo Professor specialize in the history of the Caliphate? What will the results of their research look like? These are the demons that the academia must confront if we are to dredge up and confront our common histories and narratives. This incestuous territoriality and domestication of the academia has stunted national politics and discourse, and the result is that even the best of our academicians is vulnerable to be bait of their regional, religious, and ethnic hegemons. Can we carry on like this and hope to build a nation?

Undoubtedly, and not withstanding all our difficulties, we can still make progress. There needs to be some very vigorous competition for excellence and professional achievement among our universities. At a local level, we should be asking how many National Merit Awardees our university has produced, which university has produced more renowned scientists in the various fields, and so on. Is the hope for a Nobel Prize in Science being nurtured in some laboratory somewhere in this country? There is need for universities to address the issues of self-sufficiency. The way to do this has to be by research, endowments, and consultancies with academicians interested not in their own self-serving projects, but in the development of their department, faculty or university.

Universities must seek to position themselves so that their research results can change their environments. Since the Federal Government decided to pool resources by setting up a body like TETFUND, many universities seem to have gone to sleep, merely waiting for funds to come from that body. The universities must do more to ensure that they achieve some level of independence so that they can become insulated from politics and politicians who wish to use them as extensions of their political fiefdoms. There is need to energize the alumni offices so as to reposition our universities to become more competitive.

Going forward, Nigeria must address the need to deliberately plan how to raise up a huge army of professionals covering all fields, especially in the sciences, developing expertise to address our domestic and international needs. This means that the government must turn to the universities, immediately free them from the stranglehold of politicians, and deliberately seek how best to return the academic community to its days of glory as an incubator of new ideas to drive progress.

Can the universities recover from the choking hold of ethno-centricism to which they have been consigned today and become mere expressions of ethnic, religious, or regional hegemonies? In the hey days, we had Professor E. A. Ayandele, Gilbert Onuaguluchi and Professor G. Tasie as Vice Chancellors for the University of Jos, from its inception in 1971-1994. The University of Ibadan had the phenomenal historian Onwuka Dike, Horatio Thomas, and Tekena Tamuno, the first alumnus, as Vice Chancellors. The first Vice Chancellor of the University of Lagos was not a Yoruba man, but Professor Eni Njoku. Ahmadu Bello University and the University of Benin had Professor Akingubge and Adamu Bakie as Vice Chancellors. Our universities are now severely constrained and can hardly serve as vehicles for national integration.

3: 2: The Bureaucracy as a Vehicle for Healing

This is not the place to discuss either the notion of bureaucracy or its origins in Nigeria's national life. Max Weber has addressed these issues in his theories of the bureaucracy. Weber's *Seven Rules of the Bureaucracy* remains a timeless take-off point: *fixed division of labour* (to avoid whimsical caprice of moving people from one point of labour to the other), *hierarchy of offices* (the guarantee of authority and each knowing his or her place), *rational-legal authority* (by which everyone knows where they legally derive their powers from), *governance performance rules* (by which everyone knows their place and ensures stability), *separation of private from official properties* (to avoid conflict of interest), *selection based on qualification* (to avoid nepotism and arbitrariness), and finally, *clarity of career path* (through a steady ladder of promotion). Imperfect as these have been, they have continued to guide the bureaucracy as a viable vehicle for service delivery.

Rd. Tunji Oloapa has undertaken some extensive, and perhaps the most up to date analysis, of the evolution and the challenges of the Nigerian bureaucracy today.[2] But, this is outside the purview of this presentation.

---

[2] Tunji Oloapa, *Public Administration and Civil Service Reforms in Nigeria* (Bookcraft, 2012).

Successive governments have made serious attempts at improving the quality and capacity of the bureaucracy to deliver efficient results and services to Nigerians. From the 1963 Morgan Commission, through Simeon Adebo, Jerome Udoji, right up to the Stephen Orosanya Panels, the Bureaucracy has been drowned in the ocean of its own papers. However, despite a deluge of paper, Commissions, Committees and Panels over the years, not much has been achieved due to the volatility of the bureaucracy itself and the arrival of too many heads of government with little preparation and knowledge of the system. The military compounded all this by their actions, and so an institution which elsewhere has always operated under a strict code of discipline, process, and procedure, was soon reduced to the whims and caprices of the military authorities.

The rules guiding the civil service, such as threats, sanctions, promotion exams and so on, are well known to civil servants, but most of this energy remains lost in the system. The civil service has continued to reinvent the rules to accommodate and domesticate public service into personal fiefdoms. As the years have rolled by, we have witnessed the gradual erosion of the values and culture of public service. In between these bouts of frustration, we hear the nostalgic wails of an Alison Ayida, Philip Asiodu, Ahmed Joda, or Adamu Fika, about what might have been in the years past.

A scholar, M. Sani Abdallah, in a reflection on the Service, noted that: "Whereas the civil service rule prevents officials from engaging in any economic endeavour except Agriculture, official duty has become the side business for the well-connected officials while their various private businesses are their real concern. Civil servants are now engaged in any and every business".[3] He identified areas within the system which continue to provide avenues for civil servants to subvert the system, and noted as one of the most lucrative platforms the area of public procurement.

Despite there being an Act along with rules and regulations, he argues that: "Officials make proposals not because they believe the item

---

[3] M. Sani Abdallah, "The Nigerian Civil Service and the Burden of Development."*African Development Magazine* 1, No. 12: 31.

to be procured is of any value or in the public interest. Often times, these procurements are never installed. There is the popular belief that there is hardly any procurement concluded, especially in Abuja, without top officials reaping a handsome gratification or houses, cash and sponsored exotic holidays". He cited the multi-billion naira CCTV camera project in Abuja as a good example of the many failed public procurement initiatives that merely re-enforce this culture of theft.[4] The stories of ghost workers, scams in the pension sections of the various government agencies, abandoned projects, payments for unexecuted jobs, and employment rackets are some of the areas of immense graft in the civil service.

It would be wrong to look at this issue in isolation as if the civil service is merely a forest of crime and criminals. On the contrary, there are many honest, patriotic, and dedicated Nigerians who are helplessly held captive by a corrupt political elite that has continued to hold the entire system to ransom. We cannot confront the rut in the civil service today without addressing the way and manner that successive military and civilian administrations have continued to tamper with its rules and culture. Greedy politicians and their political appointees insist on making the bureaucracy serve their interests.

The failure or the weakness in the civil service today is a combination of factors. How long we shall be on this road and whether we shall climb out sooner rather than later remains to be seen. Our future lies in what we need to do to truncate the gargantuan appetite of public officers in our country. Resolving this is the duty and responsibility of whistle blowers within civil society and the arms of government, law enforcement agencies, and the courts. If we do not reverse this ugly trend, the civil service will merely continue to increase the depth of the fracture of the Nigerian state, thus making healing impossible. If the civil service can be made to serve our people, it will indeed be a great vehicle for healing the wounds inflicted by our massive oceans of poverty.

---

[4] M. Sani Abdallah, *The Nigerian Civil Service and the Burden of Development*, 36.

3: 3: Politics as a Vehicle for Healing

It is difficult to imagine where to start assessing African politics. Both Aristotle and Plato dwelt on the nobility of politics and its inevitability in our human genes. Politics remains so far the most noble of all tools for organising society.

Politics is about the management and allocation of resources for the benefit of the greatest number of people in any given society. Democracy has been adopted as the most popular form of expressing political choices, especially in diverse societies. Political parties are the platforms on which people with common visions congregate to seek power. They seek the mandate of the people to govern by articulating their visions through manifestoes. Political parties are managed by their own guidelines, but also according to the provisions of the nation's laws. The electoral management bodies provide the rules of engagement and they also serve as referees. Once these platforms have come into being, politics takes on a life of its own, and competition among parties ought to become routine. In settled democracies, politics has become part and parcel of life, and it has been adopted as a vehicle for development and integration.

Sadly, for us in Africa, politics has deteriorated into an instrument of war and death. As a vehicle for ascent to power, it has caused far more destruction than perhaps any other institution in Africa. Nigeria's failure presents us with one of the most ignoble manifestations of this dance of death called politics, whose corrosive effect is shattering our communities. Today, Nigeria's politics is choking from the stranglehold of godfathers who have turned the parties into fiefdoms.

Why has politics failed to heal our people in Nigeria? Why have we been unable to raise a political class worthy of the name of politics? Is democracy alien to us, or is our culture unable to develop a democratic reflex? Will democracy further divide us or heal us as a people? Will the high cost of getting into public office continue to gnaw at our body politic, further deepening the ostracisation of the weak and the vulnerable from the table of opportunity in a nation so richly endowed? How long can we contain the lava of frustration and anger, some of which has been spewed and is being spewed by Boko Haram? For a nation used to seeing politics and government as a means of self-gratification, are the likely losers of the next elections already preparing their armies to ensure that the country remains ungovernable if their candidate does not win?

Despite the much-touted flaws in the 2007 elections, Professor Maurice Iwu, the then INEC Chairman, remained quite upbeat about its perceived success. In a television interview recently, he argued that when he was given the job, the then President Obasanjo said all they wanted was a successful election that would guarantee three years of back-to-back, uninterrupted elections. In his view, this was where the success of the elections lay. This is not an insignificant point, and its hidden meaning should not be lost on Nigerians. The fact that imperfect elections were greeted with judicial processes and not a call for the military is quite important for the deepening of our democracy. It means that while rejecting flaws in the processes, we must seek to resolve them through the legal and democratic processes.

Whatever may be the strength of that argument, we can now boast that we have gone ahead and doubled the back-to-back achievement. That being the case, one would expect that by now, going into our fifth elections, Nigerian politicians and the electorate should be supremely confident. We would by now be proud of the fact that we have clear ideas about what to do and what outcomes to expect, that the political class would have learnt the rules and predisposed themselves to accepting the rules of engagement and the outcomes. Sadly, if what we see is anything to go by, the politicians have learnt nothing and forgotten nothing. They seem to have perfected their rules of perfidy; they seem determined to enact their own rules and have come to the conclusion that violence must be in the DNA of Nigerian politics. With allegations of imposition across the parties, and both governors and senators at loggerheads over access to Senate slots, it remains to be seen how this will impact on the process. The future lies with whether the politicians themselves decide to play the game in the most mature and patriotic manner.

How else do we explain the tremor, the palpitation of our collective hearts and the splitting headache that characterized the 2015 elections? In my encounter with journalists in the last year, no interview is complete without reference to what is often presented as the looming clouds around the 2015 elections. Yet, rather than worrying about the quality of those who will participate in the process and ensuring a transparent process of elections, the parties are showing signs that they have merely improved on the quality of their desperation for power. The dictatorship inherent in the imposition of party candidates, and the stupendous display of ill-gotten wealth that has turned our experiment into a plutocracy, are all causes for anxiety. The stranglehold of the governors over the entire party apparatus of power has led one commentator to refer to what we have as a *governorcracy*, rather than a democracy. The governors have become mini gods, presiding over fiefdoms with literal powers over life and death. Their tight grip and control of the electoral rigging machines in their states is total.

Two weeks ago, I chaired an event organized by civil society groups to enable them to get an update on the state of INEC's preparedness for the next elections. I was quite impressed with Professor Jega's eloquent demonstration of the fact that INEC had learnt quite a lot of lessons and had deployed some technological innovation to ensure that the elections are free, fair, and transparent. INEC's preparations can be thrown into the garbage if the political class persists in its wayward and criminal ways. The entire political class must concede that politics must become a vehicle for healing. Going forward, we must ask, what options do we have? I will list and address three of these options.

To learn from the history of northern domination: Develop the skills for managing diversity and creating a sense of national identity

First, is the issue of how we responded to the post-colonial state that was handed over to us by the British. In my book, *Religion, Politics and Power*, I have clearly demonstrated the fact that the British distrusted the southern educated elite, whom they considered too troublesome (in asking for independence), and feared they would create too many problems for them. Their wish to hand over power to the North was not in doubt and was clearly illustrated in even the geographical decisions that were taken in the allocation of regions and populations. The dominant role assigned to Islam then as now enabled the northern elite to consolidate their stranglehold on power in a way and manner that further deepened the anxieties of both their non-Muslim constituencies and the larger society outside its boundaries. There was little or no sensitivity in addressing the lingering feelings of alienation that had been captured in the Report of the Minorities Commission in 1958. Tribunals, conferences, commissions and committees have done very little to ameliorate the grievances and trauma of the minorities.

Discussions about Northern domination have been clouded by

churlish and fragmented arguments over distributions of industries or allocation of offices and so on between the North and South, Christians and Muslims. Little attention was paid to developing strategies for the co-operation and collaboration of the various communities even in the North itself. Allegations of open and blatant discrimination against non-Muslims in most northern states in areas such as federal representation, the takeover of mission schools with no compensation, and the lack of a clear policy of integration, all deepened angst and frustration and distrust. Barely five years after independence, these frustrations were already bubbling over in the form of political violence.

The Tiv riots in the Middle Belt in 1964, and the violence in the Midwest, popularly known as *Operation Wetie,* in 1965, became the preludes to the coup and then civil war which followed. When the civil war broke out, it inflicted the deepest fracture and shattered the optimism captured by TIME Magazine just five years earlier. The point here is that if we are to heal the fractures in our nation, our leaders and people must effectively think through very clearly how to develop the skills for managing diversity, sharing power, and creating a sense of national identity and belonging.

To learn from the history of state creations and on-going oppressions: Understand the social structure of society and the distinctiveness of its groups

Second, the military responded to these crises by adopting state fracture as a solution. The creation of states out of the old regional arrangement generated a lot of excitement and cries of **independence** across the land. Each time a new state was created, the minority elites who had felt oppressed by the dominant group, whether by virtue of religion, ethnicity, or class, felt the new space was an opportunity to breathe fresh air. They went on to celebrate their independence by reproducing the same dynamics of perceived oppression that they had experienced. The oppression is usually related to the skewed distribution of state offices, especially what Nigerians call *juicy offices* by the local elites. Sooner or later, the logic flows all the way through, and yesterday's victims become today's oppressors. The oppressed then begin to demand their own space within which to also oppress others. This is what explains the upsurge in the demands for states, new Local Government Areas, Emirates, chiefdoms and kingdoms. The cumulative impact of all this is what we see in the rise of ethnic, religious, or regional loyalties and the diminishing interest in national unity. This must be revised if we are to heal nationally.

Resolving these distortions requires deep critical and analytical knowledge, and a high degree of imagination and courage, which no single Nigerian leader has been able to bring to the table. All through, we have had office holders whose obsession with clinging to raw power has blinded them to these processes. Without a clear understanding of the social structure of a society and the distinctiveness of its groups, it is impossible to design a satisfactory system that can unite them. There are too many people who are governing over their people but know next to nothing about them, even the ethnic composition of these communities. One of the key demands for a place in public life must be that Nigerians must show that they are familiar with the history, culture, and structure of the Nigerian society. There are too many ill-informed people in public life.

To learn from the illusion of a binary North-South, Christian-Muslim universe: see an end to the manipulation of religion, ethnicity, and region in election processes

Third, is the very irritating fallacy of representation in power. Carrying on with what the British left behind, the political elite has deepened our differences by focusing on North and South, Christians and Muslims, as categories of power-sharing mechanisms. The British operated in this binary universe because it suited them; it kept us divided and we could therefore never rally around to deal with our issues as citizens. Tragically, but not surprisingly, the military and the political elite have sustained this illusion of our division, and they have carried it as a vehicle of mending the fracture of our pain.

Recently, General Obasanjo, our former president who we believe should know better, has persisted with this dubious construct by warning the political parties against fielding presidential and vice-presidential candidates from one faith. This observation is a measure of how little we have progressed in understanding the heart of democracy. President Obasanjo is speaking as a military man who benefited from this duplicitous *army arrangement* that has been carried into what is at best a mockery of democracy. Let us subject this piece of illogic to reason and the realities of the Nigerian experience.

First, if this dubious arrangement were the solution to our problems, why did President Obasanjo and Atiku fight all the way through their presidency? Secondly, why did huge majorities of Igbos and Yorubas, or call them Christians, vote massively for the late General Yar'adua in an election that was cancelled by a Northerner, General Babangida? Thirdly, how and why did huge majorities of Christians across this country massively vote for Chief Abiola and Kingibe in 1993? And before then, why are we still a bit nostalgic about the Buhari-Idiagbon regime, with all its skewed regional and religious preferences? As an aside, we might only pose the question: would the Muslim elite, especially in northern Nigeria, even have contemplated supporting a ticket of two Christians, then as now? Muslims in Nigeria must reflect on their sincerity in this regard.

This thesis is, at best, a shibboleth, no more than a heuristic device which hides the fear of the consequences of our people's choices if they were to be exercised freely. The primary kernel of democracy is choice, and its essence is the efficacious management of diverse groups and interests. For example, in all honesty, General Buhari knows that his greatest opposition is not Christians but the Muslim elite in the North. Therefore, to continue to hoist this mannequin on the window of our democracy is to take us back and to dig us deeper into the cesspool of atavism, stoking our worst fears and keeping us permanently on the boil. If we remain on this path, we will never defeat violence, we will never have free and fair elections, we will never see an end to the manipulation of religion, ethnicity, and region.

To push this further, we should appreciate that religious identity is just one out of many identities that make up our social structure as a society. Why do we suggest that a religious identity is more important than gender or class? If we push this logic, then why are we assuming that justice has been done when two men run and no provision is being made for women? Or, put another way, why not field, *old* and *young*, or *rich* and *poor*, or *tall* and *short*, candidates in our elections? The challenge is whether our politicians are prepared to subject themselves to the scrutiny and discipline that the rules and dictates of democracy demand. The only qualification anyone has for contesting office in our country is and should be the fact that they are citizens of Nigeria. How they organize to achieve this must only be decided by its legality and compliance with the rules of engagement, not sentiments and emotions. Let experience expose the foolishness or otherwise of these decisions.

4. The so called, impending collapse of Nigeria in 2015?

Before I conclude, I would like to say a few words about the thorny issue of the future of our nation. As I said earlier, everywhere one turns, we hear the tales of gloom about Nigeria's impending collapse. The Boko Haram insurgency is being touted as the final evidence. It would seem that in this popular narrative, the 2015 elections will mark the final phase of this scenario.

I feel quite sad about this development, because although this story has been making the rounds for some five or so years now, it has increasingly taken on a life of its own, climbing all the way from the *ise ewu joints* and meetings of tribal associations to some serious academic institutions and, finally, even into the heart of government. This prediction accounts for the reason why Nigerians are now blaming the United States for not working hard enough to help us end the Boko Haram insurgency. Others have created even a bizarre scenario linking the United States with Boko Haram. This tragedy would have been a subject of debate and could be taken as part of our conspiracy theories if ever it were founded on some reason and common sense. Now, Nigerians are already moving or planning to move in different directions for fear that the 2015 elections will be the fulfilment of the American prophesy of doom.

However, the thesis that Nigeria would collapse as a nation initially evolved from a report released in January 2005 as the proceedings of a one-day conference of US experts on Africa. The consultation was sponsored by the National Intelligence Council under the auspices of the Office for Africa. The thrust was to discuss trends in Sub Saharan Africa over the next fifteen years, with the United States' concern being primarily to ensure its security and interests. This is in keeping with America's concern over its power and dominance in world affairs. The United States takes very seriously its role and place in the world and is focused on how to secure and continue its dominance and to ensure that no one threatens these interests. The US is not unaware of the fact that its power and dominance are under threat by other forces, and it has refused to leave anything to chance. The report has some staggering conclusions which have proved its experts right. Let me take just five key issues highlighted in the report to illustrate this point. Among other issues, the report calls attention to the following:

- The level of violence in Africa is unlikely to change appreciably in the next 15 years. Most conflicts will be internal. Many African security forces will undergo further atrophy due to low economic growth, shrinking foreign military aid, and the impact of AIDS.

- Africa is unlikely to become a major supplier of international terrorists due to the profound differences between Islam practiced in Africa and in the Middle East. Foreign terrorists, however, may seek sanctuary in Africa or attempt to hide weapons and assets there. The overwhelming majority of terrorist activity in Africa will involve or be caused by indigenous groups waging war against local governments and populations.

- The most important terrorist-related trend in Africa affecting the United States is the further development of pockets of radical Islam that actively provide support and sanctuary to international terrorists. Most African countries will continue to proclaim a public adherence to democracy and no other form of government will significantly challenge the nominal allegiance to regular elections; however, commitment to democracy in Africa will remain a "mile wide and inch thick".

- While Nigeria's leaders are locked in a bad marriage that all dislike, but dare not leave, there are possibilities that could disrupt the precarious equilibrium in Abuja.

- An overwhelming majority of terrorism in Africa will be caused by indigenous groups waging war against their own or neighbouring governments or against other population groups, defined by religion or ethnicity.

The report went on to single out northern Nigeria, pointing out how radical Islam, supported by some northern Muslim politicians, will continue to be funded largely by Saudi Arabia, and the threat that this will continue to pose. Looking back, it is hard to find a more embarrassing reflection of the lack of seriousness on the part of the Nigerian government in terms of how it defines or conceives of its security. Intelligence is not mere acquisition of weapons. In a serious country, the business of intelligence is a robust intellectual exercise. Governments all over the world do this by securing the support of think tanks and universities, commissioning, sponsoring, and supporting serious research in areas and countries that might negatively or positively impact on our country's interests. Rather than face these realities, senior foreign and intelligence government officials in Nigeria resort to intimidating the messenger and calling them enemies of Nigeria. A simple example of this is how we have dealt with the matter of Dr. John Campbell, the former US Ambassador to Nigeria, whose penetrating insights and prognostications about Islam in Nigeria continue to prove true to our collective embarrassment.

It is not the fault of other countries that the Nigerian leadership has not been able to consider strategic thinking as a vital tool for strategic development. It is not enough that Nigeria is producing oil and has a huge population. It is important that the leadership in Nigeria defines its interests very clearly. We hear much talk about this but there is no policy clarity and vision. The Office of the National Security Adviser is the brain box of the nation and should therefore not be seen only in purely military terms. This is borne out of our military past. Evidence of a tough intellectual understanding of world politics and strategic thinking should be the preoccupation of that office, and not merely the acquisition of military hardware.

Why is Nigeria not thinking beyond its borders? Why is Nigeria not concerned about the threat to its interests from Alaska to Zimbabwe? Why are we only focusing on those who hate us, or those who are conspiring against us? In a serious country, the university communities and think tanks should have been buzzing with analysis of these claims. But, does it not worry us that while the United States of America has designed tools and is thinking and projecting about our future in the next fifteen years, we are merely panicking about the next few months? Leadership is about prophecy, and prophecy is not foretelling the future, but a mere projection of the future based on present realities as we see them. Acquiring these tools and these platforms for forecasting or mapping our future is an inevitable part of our democracy that requires substantial investment. It is a challenge that our universities must take up as an annual ritual. We should therefore not blame America. We should be courageous enough to learn from them and plan our future.

5. Summary and Conclusion: Leadership and the Courage to Heal

I have argued in this paper that Nigeria is riddled with fractures. The first was the fracture of the colonial state. Subsequent scars have been inflicted by the succeeding military and political elites, leaving the country scar-faced. In my view, the effects of those fractures are responsible for the endless cycles of violent protestations that afflict our dear nation. I have argued that there are many vehicles that can be designed to help heal our fractures. I chose to look at three and I know that there are many more. By skipping the judiciary, I may be accused of leaving out a very important institution and I do perfectly agree. However, the lecture cannot address everything and indeed, I believe that this conversation is not conclusive. To return to where we started, how do we heal our fractured nation? How did we throw away the opportunities for greatness which TIME Magazine predicted? Where did we take the wrong turn? Let me make my point by relating a little personal story that might hold a few lessons for the point that I am making.

I spent some of my early years with my grandmother and she was, then as now, my favourite person of all time. I was of course pampered, but I still have one or two painful memories of my life with her that have impacted my life. I will share one with you.

One day, I picked up an injury while playing with my cousins. I got a cut behind my shin. I hid it from my grandmother because I feared that she would stop me from playing and I did not want her to feel vindicated since she had often warned me. Then it became painful and I began to limp. She noticed it and waited for a perfect time to confront me. I came back from school and after I had eaten, she deliberately sent me on an errand. I walked out and after a few steps, she called me back. "You are limping, what is wrong with your leg," she said. "Nothing," I muttered, "it is only a small injury". "Where is it?" she asked. I showed her, even though I suspected she had already seen it. It was right behind my shin and clearly the wound had gotten far worse than I knew.

She waited patiently until a Saturday when we did not have to go school. I did not know that she had arranged for an ordeal for me. It seemed that a plot had been hatched to get hold of me. My uncle called me and I thought he wanted to send me on an errand, so I innocently went to him. He grabbed me, and two of my other cousins who seemed to have been part of the plot emerged from nowhere. They all held me and turned me face down and went to work. I have no idea of the details of what followed but the pain of that ordeal never left me. While they held me down, my grandmother used sliced lime to clean the wound which had begun to fester. Even now, I do not recall any other ordeal half as painful as what I went through that day. But that was the beginning of the end of my wound whose scar I still carry till date.

I am telling this story because the reasons for Nigeria's festering wound have been the subject of subterfuge; but deceit and machination must be lanced and cleansed. The military and the political elites have tried to solve Nigeria's problems by presenting the symptoms as a disease. State and local government creation only deepened our wounds, and those wounds are still festering. We now believe that we can resolve our problems by creating new fractures even when the old fractures have not healed.

The colonial state did an excellent job of trying to hold our diverse communities together. We often get carried away with colonialism and fail to learn some great lessons from the way the colonial project was executed. An understanding of this will help us understand the longevity of the project, its relative peace, and its ability to first impose its will and dominance and finally to acquire control through co-option and integration. Getting the defeated Caliphate on its side required some incredible diplomacy. But this came about as a result of an amalgam of forces that were chiselled together by the skill and knowledge that the British brought to the project. Prior to the conquest and afterwards, the British recruited and co-opted anthropologists, bureaucrats, explorers, historians, and military officers. Colonialism was sustained by a combination of the knowledge of these experts to develop policies of the colonial state.

So, what has happened that the succeeding Nigerian elites have proved totally incapable of managing the inheritance? The reasons are many, but they are not unrelated to the accidental processes by which all our former heads of state and presidents have come to power. The average newcomer to the presidency of Nigeria comes totally unprepared, with no knowledge of the environment itself, no experience in public life, no knowledge of the bureaucracy or those who run the system, no knowledge of politics, and power derived from some years of loyal pupillage.

Countries in transition, whether from colonialism, or military or civilian dictatorships, require a certain set of skills. These include a clarity of vision, an understanding of the country, the people, the resources, and its challenges. A leader has to develop the ability to read the mood of his people and their expectations, communicate the challenges, create synergy, and develop a most effective strategy for holding his diverse people and their ambitions, fears and hopes together. Most importantly, is the courage needed to lance a few boils despite the inherent pain. We have a few examples to draw from.

Transitional leaders like President Abraham Lincoln, Fredrick D. Roosevelt or Churchill of yester years, or those of our modern times like Mikhail Gorbachev, Margaret Thatcher, Lee Kwan Yew, P.W. de Klerk and Nelson Mandela, have left us some of the lessons I am speaking about. Sometimes, two leaders arrive on the scene at the same time, face the same challenges, and their decisions change history. A few examples are President Roosevelt, Churchill, and Stalin, who confronted Nazism in Germany. Pope John Paul II, who with President Reagan and Margaret Thatcher teamed up with Gorbachev and helped to end Communism and bring about a new world order. Another example is the courageous William de Klerk, who paired up with Nelson Mandela and presided over the funeral rites of apartheid.

President Lincoln's resolute commitment to ending slavery in the United States was at the heart of his private engagement as a lawyer even before he got into politics. Lincoln believed that fighting to end slavery was a battle he was prepared to live and die for. Over two hundred years later, Mandela would state the same sentiments during the Rivonia trial, when he said freedom was something he was prepared to die for. Indeed, on the day he signed the Emancipation Proclamation, on December 31st, 1863, Lincoln stated: "If my name ever goes into history, it will be for this act, and my whole soul is in it".

A leader must have a vision that is larger than his personal ambition. He must therefore know where the good of the nation starts and where his personal ambition ends. All the great leaders of the world always knew when to bow out after they believed their vision had been accomplished. The tragic contrast is illustrated in the African situation, where our leaders have buried the future of their nations in the wombs of their personal ambitions, as we see in the gerontocratic tragedies that still afflict the continent and have stunted the growth of our democracies and freedoms.

Franklin Delano Roosevelt, the only American president to have served four terms, and the 32nd President of the United States (March 1933 to April 1945), stands shoulder to shoulder with Abraham Lincoln in many respects. His legacy and memory in the history of the United States is tied to his vision called the *New Deal*, a reconstruction and rehabilitation programme that enabled him to team up with his political opponents at home and abroad to achieve a most spectacular record of four terms of office as president.

Under the New deal coalition, he mobilized Republicans and others around his themes and programme beyond the shores of the United States; he mobilized Churchill and Stalin to confront Nazism. His spectacular initiatives would later lay the foundation for the emergence of such historic institutions like the United Nations, the World Bank and the International Monetary Fund. Little wonder, after a war, he still campaigned on the theme song, *Happy Days are Here Again*. His policies gave the Democrats an unprecedented control of government in the United States over a long period of time.

In conclusion, all transitional societies carry fractures, but identifying them is a challenge that requires certain leadership skills. As I have illustrated, our beloved country remains severely fractured because too many citizens are, in the words of Abraham Lincoln, *half slave, half free,* despite over fifty years of independence and huge resources. Boko Haram is merely a metaphor for understanding the depth and extent of our fractured nation.

Boko Haram is the fruit of a country whose leadership has not had the courage to break the eggs of different identities to make the omelette of a united country. The undefined role of the feudal institutions continues to get in the way of our building a united nation, not because there is anything wrong with ethnic identity, but because increasingly, our sense of nationhood and loyalty to a common flag and Constitution remain subordinated to other loyalties. This has left a huge vacuum that Boko Haram has exploited.

Confronting what seemed like a rag tag army of misguided fanatics has turned into a nightmare and has further exposed the underbelly of our nation. We have watched helplessly as the competence and commitment of members of the Nigerian military has been tested. Wrong diagnosis has led to a total misreading of the context and our inability to identify the best strategy for fighting the war. Now, before our own eyes, it is an unconventional gathering of illiterate hunters who are scoring victories where the Nigerian military has failed. There could not be a further metaphorical expression of our predicament. The people of Nigeria must note that there are lessons for us. The collapse of the army is usually the prelude to state collapse. The stories of the collapse of the armies in the Democratic Republic of Congo, Liberia and Sierra Leone are all before us. We know what followed.

Our fractures have been the result of bad politics. However, it would be suicidal for us to think that the process of healing should be left to the politicians. Healing our nation is too serious a business to be left to our politicians. Those who aspire to lead us must know who we are and what our fears, anxieties, and hopes are. When they win our votes, they ought to know what to do because they have asked to lead us and our votes have given them the job. Creating a team of rivals should then be the real challenge. Therefore vigilance on our part remains a key part of politics. The time to start is now and the place to start is here. Thank you very much. God bless Nigeria.

Convocation Lecture, University of Uyo, Uyo, Akwa Ibom State, Nigeria
November 20, 2014

CHAPTER FOUR

Transition to Democracy: Can Nigeria Ride The Wave?

"Whether Democracy succeeds or fails continues to depend significantly on choices, behaviours, and decisions of political leaders and groups"
(Seymour Martin Lipset, 1994)

Now that the euphoria over the elections has reasonably subsided, perhaps this is the time for more sober reflection. We have enjoyed the huge outpour of self-praise, conviviality, and gregarious ululations over what we might refer to as the great crossing by our country. Public reactions have called the elections one of Nigeria's greatest moments. Commentators have offered a wide array of explanations for the success. There is definitely no taking away the significance of this event. I have no intention of disrupting our much-deserved celebrations. However, my concern is that we will focus so much on the celebration that we will not give sufficient thought to the challenges that lie ahead. This would be a fatal mistake.

This lecture seeks to bring to sharp focus something I have often spoken about, particularly since the beginning of what is now referred to as the Fourth Republic. That is, the transition to democracy. After an analysis of transitions to democracy globally, I once concluded that Nigeria would require a minimum of sixteen years to be able to assess the quality of our democracy. I did not imagine that my analysis would be so precise. My argument went like this: given our kind of transition, I thought that the party in power would win the first and second sets of elections because the departing regime literally handed victory over to them. The opposition might try, with some hard work, but it could come so close and not really win the third elections. I concluded that by the fourth elections, if the opposition did not surrender, it could build on its failures and aim to win, but the elections might go to a run-off. Consequently, even if the opposition lost, it would be so energized that it would win the fifth elections, thus marking the beginning of a new experience for the people and the parties. Looking back, it seems I did not win the argument but was also not disappointed with the way things have turned out.

In this lecture, I will argue that we must not underestimate the sheer amount of work that remains to be done, because I believe that our country is still in a transition. The mass exodus from the rump of the Peoples' Democratic Party (PDP) to the victorious All Progressive Congress (APC) suggests that we still have carpetbaggers and contractors rather than politicians with principles.

I will divide this lecture into four parts. The first part will attempt to locate our reflection within the context of the debate about transitions to democracy. In the second part I will look at a few lessons from other transitions that will enable us better appreciate our own situation. Thirdly, I will look at the last elections and see what lessons we must learn from them. By way of conclusion, I will identify some specific themes that should occupy our attention.

1. Transitions to Democracy: Can Nigeria Ride the 4th Wave?

In our nation, not given to serious scholarship and diagnosis, very little has been done to address and explain the causative factors of our debilitating journey to democracy. In my many essays and lectures, I have labored to make the point that our nation's intelligentsia and academia have not done enough to consolidate our democracy. Perhaps this is not unconnected with the debilitating impact of the military on the psyche of the ivory tower. Years of military rule and assault have left in its wake a traumatized series of ivory towers, riddled with infighting, politics, intrigues, cultism, bigotry, and all the ills that afflict the larger society. This has taken a toll on the student body and robbed them of the energy and vitality of youth, hunger for mentorship, quest for idealism, and love of learning. Student unionism, the school for leadership, has been filled with young men and women merely rehearsing how to replace their superiors in crookedness and greed. No one, including the students, now wants to take the long road.

The late Professor Samuel Huntington was the one who introduced the notion of what he called "the waves of democracy".[1] He identified

---

[1] Samuel Huntington, *Democracy's Third Wave* (University of Oklahoma, 1991).

three waves of democracy since the beginning of modernization. According to him, the first wave occurred between 1828 and 1926. Even a mere passing knowledge of some little history would lead us to an understanding of where in the worldview Africa was at this period. What passed for democracy at this time did not include our continent in any serious sense. Africans and women everywhere, even those who lived in the United States and Europe, were not considered as capable of participating in the process. At this time, democracy was adopted as a means of consolidating the gains of empire building and industrialization across Europe.

The second wave of democracy, according to Huntington, occurred between 1926 and 1942. Here, the First World War had already been fought and brought to an end. The struggle for industrial and territorial power had taken its toll and human greed had driven the world to a severe war. This time, it was Europe fighting itself with no external provocation. Within the four or five years of the war, most of Europe lay in ruins. Europeans surveyed the total cost and loss of war: 16 million lives were lost, and some 20 million people injured. Waking from this gross folly, Europe quickly set up the League of Nations to serve as an umbrella of protection. Set up in 1920, the League sought to build on earlier initiatives which had found little success in keeping Europe together.

According to Huntington, the third wave of democracy occurred between 1960 and 1970. After over one hundred years of slavery, rape, banditry, and exploitation of the African continent, African and Asian countries were variously granted flag independence and were on the path of democracy. This was more an attempt at ending the white man's burden than demonstrating any altruistic love. Independence was hinged on the adoption of Constitutional forms of government along with bureaucracies and standing armies. A wiser world now decided to rethink the notion and philosophy of the League of Nations.

Now, the world realized that there was need to focus on our common humanity. Democracy seemed a veritable platform on which to hinge this notion. Thus, the United Nations came up with a Universal Declaration of Human Rights in 1948, focusing on the belief that all of us were created equal in the image and likeness of the creator. Its preamble read in parts as follows:

> Whereas recognition of the inherent dignity and of the equal and inalienable rights of all members of the human family is the foundation of freedom, justice, and peace in the world. Whereas disregard and contempt for human rights have resulted in barbarous acts which have outraged the conscience of mankind, and the advent of a world in which human beings shall enjoy freedom of speech and belief and freedom from fear and want has been proclaimed as the highest aspiration of the common people. Whereas it is essential, if man is not to be compelled to have recourse, as a last resort, to rebellion against tyranny and oppression, that human rights should be protected by the rule of law…Now the UN General Assembly proclaims the Universal Declaration of Human Rights as a common standard of achievement for all peoples and nations.[2]

These noble words have served as a compass for guiding the world out of its barbaric inclinations leading to wars.

For the better part of the so-called third wave of democracy, it seems doubtful to suggest that Africans and Asians really experienced the benefits and fruits of true independence and democratic governance. Under the heat of the Cold War, a form of colonialism continued as proxy wars, military coups, and authoritarian regimes became instruments of control. For the better part of almost 50 years, authoritarian, one-man dictatorial regimes were the norm of most of Africa. From the late 1970s through the 80s and 90s, the Afrikaners stood rock solid, convinced that their theft of African lands and their scorched earth brutality and modern-day slavery against Africans would last forever. While the world looked away, Africans rallied and struggled for freedom for their kith and kin in Angola, Mozambique, and South Africa. Those countries that had managed to secure flag independence were firmly in leashes and their masters ensured that they, their resources and citizens, remained tied to their former colonial powers.

---

[2] *UN Declaration of Human Rights* (New York, 1948), Preamble.

Chapter Four | Matthew Hassan Kukah

We can argue that in reality, most of Africa did not really ride on the third wave of democracy. I will rather argue that it was at the fourth wave of democracy that Africa seems to have come of age. This period for me would be from the late 1980s through the 1990s till date. This is the period which Professor Francis Fukuyama controversially referred to as the end of history. His argument was that the end of communism had marked the terminal point of communism and ideology, and now opened the world to the frontiers of Western liberal democracy. Despite the elegance of his argument, the future would prove this prediction to be both true and false. Professor Fukuyama did not foretell the confusion, blood bath, and terror that would mark what Professor Huntington himself controversially argued as the clash of civilisations in the wake of this quest.

This fourth wave, marked by the collapse of the Berlin Wall, is what has opened up new vistas for us. It is on this crest that Nigeria has had a most bumpy ride. Like a man on a horse ride, we should feel proud that despite the bumps, the rider is still firmly on the saddle, determined to continue this journey. It is against this backdrop, that we might say, with the great Chinua Achebe, that although the democratic wave started in the nineteenth century, the train never really arrived at our station until 1999. Before then, we seemed like Sisyphus, the one cursed by the Greek gods, who after painfully rolling the stone up the hill, watched it roll back to the bottom of the hill, and he had to start all over again.

Now since it seems that we have crossed to the other side, can we look back at the land of Egypt and remember that it was a land of pain and suffering? Can we look back at the years devoured by the locusts and think about how to plan for the green years ahead? What is there to suggest that the politicians have learnt any lessons? Given the fact that there is so little to choose from between the PDP and the APC, what are we to expect? We are being warned about the ugly challenges that lie ahead against the backdrop of the dwindling oil prices. Will the subsidy racketeers merely change their jerseys? What about the threats of Boko Haram? In other words, has Nigeria turned the corner? Have we finally placed the stone firmly on top of the mountain? Is it so well protected that it can withstand the hostile elements, or will something trigger its roll back to the bottom of the mountain? We shall return to this at the end.

2. Transitions and the Land Mines Ahead

In my reflections on transitions, I have always drawn attention to the need for countries to understand that transitions are not linear in progression, and that their outcomes are never predetermined or conclusive. Successful transitions cannot be measured by the quality of the ink and the signatures on the agreements or Constitutions. Expectations often vary; suspicion, fear, and anger are often part and parcel of the process. This is why we must note that all transitions from authoritarian regimes do not necessarily lead to democracy, unity, and progress. More often, they lead to destruction of the foundation on which a country was built. There will always be those who would look back and prefer the chains of slavery; they will prefer those days when "they sat beside the flesh pots of meat, when they ate bread to the full" *(Ex. 16:3)*. The difficulties of transitions may rob them of their privileges, and they will seek to disrupt the process by various means. However, different transitions lead to different outcomes.

First, you could have a transition that is the result of the end of war in which one side triumphs and another surrenders or decides that they want an end to the war. Some examples are Algeria, Angola, Mozambique, Uganda, Rwanda, and Zimbabwe. When countries transition, it is not uncommon for them to lapse into civil war, even if temporarily. Expectations vary, and a good example is what happened in South Africa when some of the Afrikaners stage-managed a rash of black-on-black violence so as to stall the process of transition.

In the transitions in Zimbabwe, Uganda, Rwanda, and now the Democratic Republic of Congo, for example, Presidents Robert Mugabe, Yoweri Museveni, Paul Kagame, and Joseph Kabila seem determined to create only a nominal form of democracy while consolidating the hegemony of the ruling elite under one party dictatorships. The claims often are that the diversities do not permit multi-partyism in the real sense, or that no one can be trusted to rule the country. In each situation, those in power so demonize the past that they create the impression that a vote against them is a vote for a return to the past.

Somehow, the countries continue to stagnate or grow at their own pace, with muted opposition. In each of these cases, the countries are still holding together, and stability remains a veneer for sustaining dictatorship. In the case of Rwanda, the pouring of foreign aid and the development of infrastructure seems to be the excuse that the government has for ensuring that it remains in power. How long these developments will last, no one knows. They present us with possibilities and lessons in Nigeria.

The extreme case of transitions leading to great anarchy is to be found in the developments after the end of the Cold War, especially in the former Soviet Union. We witnessed an upsurge of old antagonisms, leading to the use of identity (religion and ethnicity) as the means of seeking separation and independence. Today, many of these countries are better off than they were. They are prospering and enjoying the fruits and benefits of democracy. The wars of Bosnia, Yugoslavia and so on are an example. Rwanda's case is also an example.

We must of course ask, why do some transitions succeed, and others fail? There are many reasons but essentially, we can collapse them into two. First, is the quality of internal leadership in the country. New leaders often seek to replace the old ones by merely inheriting their privileges and the tools of violence which they willingly deploy on the new opposition. Mandela's ability to use his moral authority to rein in his own people and manage the emergence of a rainbow coalition, which was a government of national unity, is an example of a different kind of new leader. The second reason, which builds on the first, is the question of the reaction of the international community and donor agencies. The reaction of the Western world towards Mandela, largely an exercise in conscience cleansing, saw foreign aid pour into South Africa and Mandela being elevated to the status of a secular saint. After ignoring Rwanda and allowing the genocide to happen, again, the international community has rallied around Kagame and offered his country aid. South Sudan for example, has not had the same response from the international community. Little wonder it is caught up in war.

3. Has Nigeria Crossed the Rubicon: Lessons to be learnt

The elections have come and gone. Except for some extremists within the ruling party, who were looking forward to purchasing new yachts, private jets, new homes in Dubai and so on, we all seem to have felt reasonably happy with the outcome of the elections. How do we move ahead?

It is true that these elections could have swung either way. Many would argue that President Jonathan and his Peoples' Democratic Party (PDP) could have won the elections had they not succumbed to the hubris that has become the hallmark of the PDP. We all know the story of the peculiar circumstances that brought the party into being. We also know that despite that, the Party became an association of takers and buccaneers more than anything else. The Party could not deal quickly with the issues of greed and the arrogance of some of its men and women in power. The Party could not control the excesses of some of its ministers and henchmen/women. It simply saw itself as presiding over a distribution agency. Many would argue that it became insensitive to the needs of its supporters. It had no mechanism for internal cohesion, and simply believed that it was the elephant that could never be slayed.

I have raised these issues when the opportunities provided themselves. In almost all the opportunities I had to speak at the Party's retreats, I called attention to the fact that the PDP needed to change its ways, move beyond prebendalism, greed, and primitive accumulation so as to institutionalize democracy in our country.[3]

The important thing now is that the All Progressive Congress (APC) has won the elections. The APC does not have a track record. It is a gathering of takers and there is no reason why it could not end up like the PDP, from where it has drawn most of its leaders today. President Buhari has won after contesting for the elections three times under three different political platforms. Most people agree that the APC is a conglomerate of factions and fractions of disparate groups which were welded together by a common belief that things must change. There are no angels anywhere in sight. There are many lessons for us to draw from, but I will only take five.

---

[3] I must thank God for the opportunities I had to make my points. What surprised me was that they kept inviting me to these events. For example, in 1999, I was invited to speak at the first PDP Retreat ahead of President Obasanjo's inauguration on the theme of "Ethics in Government". In 2007, just ahead of Yar'adua's inauguration, I spoke at the PDP retreat on the topic "Another Nigeria is Possible". In 2011, I spoke at another Retreat for the PDP, and I presented a paper titled, "How did We Get Here?" Since 2014, I have been a Guest at the annual post-election Governors' Forum Retreat for all newly elected Governors across Party lines.

3.1 How to interpret the victory

The first is how to interpret the victory itself. There is no need for us to go over the issue of President Jonathan's magnanimous and graceful concession. What is most troubling is the nature of the victory of General Buhari in the northern parts of the country, and the reactions to his victory in the northern states. Ordinary young men literally killed themselves in celebration of an election victory! For the youth of northern Nigeria, this victory was not just any victory. The amount of psychological and physical terror that had been visited on non-supporters of the APC was frightening. Openly, there have been stories of young Northern Muslims telling Christians that they are lucky because had the election gone the other way, they would all be dead. Those of us living in the North also heaved a sigh of relief to the end of what had been a long night of uncertainty and trauma. What are the implications of this for the new government?

3.2 Restoring public confidence in government and politics

This brings us to the second point, namely, what should General Buhari do? Or, to put it another way, what can he do? To be sure, restoring public confidence in government and politics will have to be General Buhari's immediate challenge. This will come about by the nature of the choices he makes in assembling a team. Here, he must move away from seeing assembling a team as the sharing of a carcass, a typical characteristic of governments in Nigeria. Nigerians have shown that they trust his judgment and his integrity. The detractors of the APC say that Buhari is APC and APC is Buhari. Well, in a way, this may not be such a bad idea. After all, Lew Kwan Yew was Singapore and Singapore was Lee Kwan Yew. Mandela was South Africa and South Africa was Mandela. A tree may not make a forest but counting the trees in a forest starts from one tree. Buhari can therefore shape both the APC as a party and Nigeria as a country. He may have integrity, but integrity by itself does not win elections. The challenge before him would be to have the sagacity to manage his patrons and their choices. The Hausas say in a proverb: "Whoever takes a leper's money must give a leper a haircut". So, you cannot take his money and then suddenly realize that he is leprous.

Fighting corruption sounds fantastic and is a great calling card. But, where in this country is corruption not written all over? What would be the consequences of fighting the corrupt men and women? Will the victory amount to merely replacing one band of robbers with another? My take is that the idea of a fight against corruption is a no brainer. The greatest and most successful weapon against development is development. The late Professor Claude Ake captured it well when he said something to the effect that the democratization of development is the best development of democracy. So, rather than chasing the thieves, the President should work hard at addressing the issues of the misery and squalor that have come to define Nigeria. Development will raise the best army to fight corruption.

3.3 Reconstruction, reconciliation, and rehabilitation

Thirdly, how should the President embark on the policy of reconstruction, reconciliation, and rehabilitation? This country has had three attempts at dealing with the issues of reconciliation, but none has achieved the required outcome. From the "three Rs" of the Gowon regime after the civil war, the Oputa Panel by President Obasanjo, and the Yar'adua Amnesty Programme, we have not come anywhere near resolving the issues of long buried animosities, real or perceived injuries and so on. This is not the place to review these developments, but clearly there is a great need for some form of healing across the country. President Jonathan tried his best to stay the course. However, there are many Northerners who believe that now is their turn to get their own amnesty deal. Unpacking the racketeering that reduced the insurgency into a highly lucrative venture would require a programme of its own. The President's challenge will lie in how he responds to the perceived interpretations of his victory, especially within the various institutions, networks, and interest groups in the North. He has to contain with traditional rulers, the various ideological strands within Islam, for example, Kadiriya, Tijaniya, Izala, Ansar, Boko Haram and the whole. Most of the interests of these groups under the banner of Islam are in direct opposition to one another. They conflict, intersect, counter-penetrate and are territorially divergent from one another. All of them are fighting for different things for Islam and for themselves. These groups believe that a Buhari victory is a victory for Islam. Managing these will require uncommon skill.

He is lucky that he has the unassailable credentials that his base requires: honesty, asceticism, a sense of justice, integrity, and lack of visible show of greed. The belief that he will not be an enemy of Islam will help to make his judgment trustworthy. He can, with courage, pull the nation away from the combustibility that has come to define northern Islam today. He has to identify those areas of state intervention that the northern Muslim elite have continued to use to line up their pockets under the pretext of defending Islam.

The President has to move the state away from the stranglehold of all religions so as to free both religion and the state to fulfill their role in the attainment of social welfare and justice. Will the state, at the Federal, State and Local Government levels continue to spend money on pilgrimages, the building of places of worship and so on? How will the Northern governors deal with the issues of return of schools and the funding of education as a means of bridging the yawning gap in the northern states? A secular, just, and democratic Nigeria should be our vision.

3.4 Be careful of the intention and the ambition of those in the wings

Fourth, from the reactions to the elections, it is clear that we have a lot of work to do. Across the northern states, APC Youth supporters openly derided Christians, telling them that they were lucky that they voted rightly, and that had Buhari lost the elections, there would have been war. What this comes down to is the need to appreciate that free, fair, credible elections are not a guarantee that we will get the right outcomes. The references I made above illustrate this point.

We must therefore not get carried away by the euphoria of having achieved credible and peaceful elections in Nigeria. A lot can still go wrong if we do not watch out for the demagogue who has other intentions for democracy. For example, Hitler came to power not through a coup but through a democratic process of free and fair elections. The Brotherhood in Egypt came to power barely three years ago by riding on the crest of the Arab spring, which opened them up for democracy. Some years back, the FIS in Algeria were almost about to take power by a democratic process, not a military coup. They wanted to use democracy to kill a democratic ethos and culture. The challenge therefore is not the process, but the intention and the ambition of those in the wings. We must therefore keep vigil of the precious prize we have won.

3.5 Rebuild our common humanity

Fifth and finally, the President has to manage the egos of those who believe that now it is their turn to eat.[4] Professor Ake has noted that ego is indeed a great challenge to Democracy in Africa. He spoke of the men and women with large egos who have tended to manipulate democracy for other non-democratic means.[5] Today, in my view, Nigeria's challenge is not so much the popular idea of fighting corruption. It is rather the need to see that corruption is the symptom of the cancerous ailment of a society that has lost its soul. How to rebuild our common humanity is one of the greatest challenges that lies before us. Let me now conclude.

4. Summary and Conclusion: Moving Forward

In this lecture, I have tried to address the issues of transition to democracy. I have noted that Nigeria has come very late to the table, but we believe that the last elections have placed us on a positive platform to enable us deepen our democracy and hopefully take our place with other respectable nations in the world. We must now renew our commitment to democracy and seek to place our country on an irreversible path of democracy. It is, as Professor Amartya Sen has argued, the guarantee of freedom and development. It is also the antidote to war and hunger.[6] The plausibility of democracy and its correlation with qualitative human development is verifiable.

In a study undertaken by the World Bank in 1989, it was discovered that out of the 24 richest countries in the world, only three of them were not democratic. The same study showed that out of 42 of the poorest countries in the world, only two of them had ever experienced democracy. The visible correlation between democracy, wealth creation,

---

[4] Michela Wrong, *It is our Turn to Eat* (London: Harper, 2009). This is an excellent book that deals with the fruitlessness of issues of fighting corruption in Kenya. The story is one that can be sadly replicated across the continent of Africa.

[5] Claude Ake, *The Feasibility of Democracy in Africa* (Senegal: Codesria, 2000), 25.

[6] Amartya Sen, *Democracy and Freedom* (Oxford University Press, 1999).

and security has made democracy attractive to the world. For example, in 1973, only 32% of the world's population lived in free, democratic societies. Between 1990 and 1994, the number went up to between 38 and 58%. Today, the number hovers between 60 and 70%, and this is because of the population of China!

It was Professor Robert Dahl who argued that the essence of democracy is competition, inclusiveness, and civil liberties. Democracy will die if it does not serve as a platform for creating opportunities, managing diversity, and encouraging the attainment of the common good. For too long, we have defined ourselves as Christians, Muslims, Northerners, Southerners, Minorities and so on. General Buhari's elections have shown us the need for coalition and consensus building, and that no group can go it alone.

It was great to see General Buhari in his various regalia. One must commend those who rebranded him. However, the challenge is for the new president to see beyond voting patterns, to concretize the plurality of colours that marked his elections. I asked my friend Dr. Kayode Fayemi, the former Governor of Ekiti, how the APC intends to deal with the many desperados flocking to the APC. He gave me a simple but deep response: "You are a Bishop. You cannot stop all people from coming to Church, rich, poor, rascals, sinners, and saints. However, you can at least determine who can become a priest among them". As we surge forward to build our country, let us pray that by the end of four years, this country would be better, stronger, and much improved.

I cannot end without repeating what has become a bit boring now, namely, the graciousness of President Goodluck Jonathan. When I had a chance to speak to the President, I told him that I was convinced he was not yet aware of the significance of what he had done. He has made politics honorable. We know from what we have now heard that what he did was the result of his very strong, deep, and patriotic convictions as a statesman. May God bless him and bless our country.

Let me leave you with the immortal words of Wendell Phillips, who, in an address to the Anti-Slavery Movement in Massachusetts on January 28th, 1852, stated that:

> Eternal vigilance is the price of liberty; power is ever stealing from the many to the few. The manna of popular liberty must be gathered each day or it is rotten. The living sap of today outgrows the dead rind of yesterday. The hand entrusted with power becomes, either from human depravity or esprit de corps, the necessary enemy of the people. Only

by continued oversight can the democrat in office be prevented from hardening into a despot; only by agitation can a people be sufficiently awake to the principle not to let liberty be smothered in material prosperity.

Convocation Lecture, Ebonyi State University, Abakaliki, April 25th, 2015

CHAPTER FIVE

Education & Leadership Recruitment for a Plural Society: A Case for Nigeria

1. Preamble

L et me make a public confession: I am not an educationist. Therefore, my concern is not to attempt to bore you with any analysis of the state of education in our country today. We are all in agreement that like almost every facet of our national life, education is also lying prostrate. We are nowhere on the radar of the top ten universities in Africa, not to talk of the rest of the world. The irony however, is that somehow, without Nigerians, the state of education in the rest of the world would be totally different. Despite not being an educationist, I believe that, as we say of politics and other areas of human survival, education is too serious a business to be left to educationists.

This is the right environment for us to explore the theme of leadership, because of the prospects that lie ahead and also because of the urgent need to find answers to the huge treasure that is our teeming and highly sophisticated youth. As I will show, it is in our interest as parents and as a nation to fall in line with the hopes, fears, and aspirations of the youth today. They are far better skilled than we could ever have dreamt of, and increasingly, they no long rely on the conventional ladders of opportunity that worked for the old generation. They are becoming leaders in their own ways and on their own terms.

The story of ISIS and Boko Haram today are evidence of the capacity of the youth to exploit the possibilities that are open to them, albeit negatively. The emergence of ISIS and their creation of a cyber state, using the sophisticated technology that the earlier generation of extremist groups like Al-Qaeda could never have dreamt of, is a warning to us. For ISIS and its murderous agenda marks a major generational shift in strategy and focus. Therefore, for the sake of self-preservation, we need a generational conversation, and quickly too.

Many things conspired against us and led to the leadership conundrum in Nigeria. First, we inherited a convoluted colonial legacy that left behind a country hurriedly put together by the British colonialists as they opted to cut their losses when they realized that running empires was no longer a profitable and sustainable enterprise. Second, a hurriedly assembled and inexperienced bureaucracy and political class that were ill prepared for the challenges of managing a plural society were put in place. Despite their relative inexperience, this first generation of men and women were devout, dedicated, patriotic, honest, and loved their jobs. Third, the military interrupted this journey, destroyed the foundation of our politics, poisoned our dreams, and stained the banner of our national pride. A rapacious and predatory military elite, propelled into power by greed and lust for power, engaged in an endless orgy of fratricidal coups and counter coups. A coup culture destroyed both the military ethos of esprit de corps, took us to a civil war, and left us as a nation severely wounded by the trauma of violence. Therefore, those who praise the Asian Tigers and denigrate us must understand that had their democracy been encumbered by military coups as we had in Nigeria, their fate would have been similar to ours. And, had the military left us alone, I am convinced we would have been standing shoulder to shoulder with the Asian Tigers in almost every sense.

I argue that it is a combination of the cumulative effect of these distorted experiences with leadership that accounts for Nigeria's state of anomie. By the time the military left, a culture of coups had turned access to power into a violent preoccupation, based on the laws of the good, the bad, and the ugly. Survival depended on who pulled the gun first. The military would over time diminish due process and integrity as a basis for access to power, and assign to themselves the right to decide who would govern and who would not. Thus, as General Babangida eloquently stated, the military could set up an election still and say: "We do not know who will succeed us, but we know who will not". By narrowing this entrance of access to power, the military saw politics as a long, intricate, tiresome, and negotiated exercise in co-optation and exclusion. It was somehow uncanny that in the same transition where General Babangida had said he knew those who would not succeed them, he was wrong footed by the decision of the people of Nigeria.

The abortion of that process did not derogate its significance or lessons. The rest is history, but ordinary Nigerians had, by their action in those elections, issued a yellow card to the military.

I believe that we must have a society where the race for any office or position has clear finishing lines. Just pause for a moment and imagine: If today, I were President Buhari, Senate President Saracen, Speaker Degaru, or any Governor, and a young man said to me: "I would like to occupy your position one day, what should I do?", what answers would I or any of us here give to such a young person? Would we tell them what courses to study, what friends to make, what war chests to build, what godfathers to seek for, or would we just say, "It is the Lords' doing"?

The most dangerous thing in our politics is not so much the issue of our electoral body and its competence or lack of it. Thankfully and happily, my friend and my brother, Professor Attahiru Jega, the patron saint of card readers, is Chairman of this event. The qualities of electoral bodies are necessary but they are never sufficient conditions for ensuring the right electoral outcomes. However, the real issues remain the questions around who qualifies to contest elections, what machinery or qualifications should they have, how much money should they have, and so on. The political class remains the culprits because it is their actions or inactions that determine the outcomes.

Among the worldwide commendations that the National Peace Committee (NPC) for the 2015 Elections received, that of the Office of the Secretary General of the United Nations was quite salutary. In one of our many interactions, the Special Representative of the Secretary General, Dr. Ibn. Chambas, stated how impressed the UN had been with the contributions of the Peace Committee. In a meeting with the Committee, he suggested the idea of a replication of this initiative around West Africa at least. As he said: "Conducting elections in Africa should not be left to the major contenders in the contest. Our people require a mediating institution such as the NPC".

The point I am making here is that yes, we are turning the corner and we are all proud of what Professor Jega and his team achieved. However, the challenge now is how to ensure that there is really a level playing field that does not exclude anyone on any grounds whatsoever. We need to pose more questions. For example, in a plural and highly divided society like ours, how do we prepare the youth for a role in public life? It is not enough that a group of men simply sit around in the middle of the night and appoint a few women and elderly people to serve as Women or Youth Leaders. Why don't we have Adult Leaders too? In most cases, all that these groups are expected to do is to merely serve as members of a supporter's club with no sense or hope of direct participation. Our challenge is to knock and insist that the doors of opportunity are opened to everyone in the most free and fair manner possible.

2. Managing Diversity: Education as a Foundation

This is not the place for me to attempt a review of the educational policies of our dear country, Nigeria. Suffice it to state what is already well known, namely, that we owe what we are today in the area of education in most parts of southern and mid-northern Nigeria largely to the work of Christian missionaries.

In northern Nigeria, the missionary presence was fraught with tensions due to the colonial policy of non-interference with Islam. This found expression in the segregatory decision to create Sabon gari[1] among other divisive policies. The colonial state may have gained some measure of peace to enable it continue its exploitation of a colony and its people. However, in the long run, Nigeria has had to pay the price as the notion of a united and strong nation has remained a dream deferred. Sadly, we have not found a leader with enough vision to rouse our nation from slumber and to find a way of gently breaking the eggs of miniature nationalisms so as to make a national omelet of unity.

For example, when the colonial state stepped in to take on the challenges of providing Western education in northern Nigeria, they targeted the ruling classes and saw education as a means of consolidating the hold of the feudal classes. In his book, "An Imperil Twilight", Sir Gawain Bell, the last colonial Governor of Northern Nigeria, noted, among other things, that although education came late to the North and was open to all children with character, there was always a bias in favor of: "a boy whose father was an Emir or District Head, and who was likely to succeed to the responsibility of his father's office"[2].

---

[1] Literally translated as, *new town*, the idea behind these settlements was to keep the southerners who were settling in northern towns from mixing with their Muslim counterparts. Despite some levels of modernisation, these settlements still exist.

[2] Gawain Bell, *An Imperial Twilight* (London: Lester Crook Academic Publishing, 1989), 75.

The substance and thrust of the colonial narrative focused on the fact that we were a "dark continent" infested with paganism and sorcery. Their mission, they said, was one of civilizing and taming the African mind. To acquire this education or civilization required that our hearts and minds be emptied of the demons that had held us down. The asymmetrical nature of the relationship was never in doubt. The perception or assumption of the superiority of the white man was also taken for granted.

Rudyard Kipling's epic poem, "The White Man's Burden", remains one of the most cited pieces of writing that sought to legitimate imperialism. Although written for a different context, the essence was the same. Kipling wrote his poem in 1899 as a paean to imperialism, and although the United States had itself been a victim of British colonialism, he nonetheless recommended this bitter pill to them. The United States had already signed a treaty which brought Cuba, Puerto Rico, the Philippines, and Guam under American control. The words of the poem had power and resonance, and even President Roosevelt confessed that although it was not a great poem, still, it was a historic piece of writing. Some lines of the poem went as follows:

> Take up the White Man's burden—
> Send forth the best ye breed—
> Go send your sons to exile
> To serve your captives' need
> To wait in heavy harness
> On fluttered folk and wild—
> Your new-caught, sullen peoples,
> Half devil and half child
> Take up the White Man's burden
> In patience to abide
> To veil the threat of terror
> And check the show of pride.

This is not the time or the place for us to review the history of colonialism and the literature that accompanied it. The challenge now is not so much the need to dwell on how we were wronged by colonialism. It is not even to pose the sterile question of whether it was good or bad for us. The real challenge is, what lessons have we learnt? How have others risen from the rubbles of colonialism to build great nations, while Nigeria still remains at the bottom of the hill? Will we manage diversity in an age of globalisation, or shall we remain weighed down by the yoke of our own internal slavery, driven by constant self-flagellation and self-doubt? Globalisation is now before us like a broken dam, and we either learn how to swim, fish, or risk being drowned by it.

Clearly, Nigerians generally decided to make peace with the colonial state and accept it as a necessary evil. Indeed, even when the first generation of Nigerians rose up to clamor for independence, it was based on the new tools that Western education had given to them either through the missionaries or the state. The struggle for freedom was also tied to the privilege to move to the European quarters or the Government Reservation Areas (GRAs), taking over the offices and the paraphernalia of power. Not much has changed. Check out the location of the big boys, those who live in Asokoro and those who live in Nyanya, and ask why the Nyanya of this world have become the fault lines of death.

Understandably, the focus on education was largely to ensure the quality of personnel required to run an efficient civil service. Some scholars have argued rather controversially that the prestige of the civil service attracted some of the best brains, while those who could not compete went into the army or politics. This may not be the case in reality, but it definitely has a place in part of the popular narrative. If we reject all of this, then we must find an explanation for why it took us almost fifty years to have a university graduate as a president, and why we actually did not have any as a military head of state!

It is difficult to identify any clear evidence that we had leaders who thought through very clearly the challenges of managing a plural society. At a gathering of African bishops in Rome some two years ago, we had to discuss the issues of religion and violence in Africa. Understandably, since it is an area in which we have achieved optimal notoriety, most of the attention turned to me and our endless crises with Boko Haram. As it is with these issues, you try to put up a brave face. However, two bishops from Tanzania and Zambia intervened giving account of their experience with managing diversity. They both concluded that although they were materially poor, ethnic violence had not been much on their menu. They all explained the fact that both President Nyerere and Kaunda had developed policies that deliberately sought to create a united and peaceful country. Therefore, they ensured that senior civil servants were sent far away from their areas of birth. In this way, they argued, most of their educated elite and their children spoke at least three languages, namely, those of their ethnic origin, those of their adopted homes, along with Swahili and English. Here, we did not seem to have had a language or cultural policy, and this is why language and culture have become weapons of war among our people today. Sadly, we have been left neither rich nor peaceful, but victims of self-immolation, violence and death.

The founding fathers did not do enough to address the issues of education as a tool for national integration. The idea of a sound education as a basis for entering public life was not given much attention. The North, which was, then as now, still far behind on the ladder, had come to rely on civil servants from the South to fill such jobs in the civil service, especially in the areas of education, healthcare and the Judiciary. With time, the presence of Southerners would later be seen by politicians as a threat to the North.

The pursuit of the Northernization policy of the Sardauna would later set the Northern political elite against their Southern colleagues, and prepare the ground for the events that led to the civil war. Still, not much has changed today because there is hardly any single state or federal university or hospital in the North that has enough local manpower to sustain itself. There are therefore still rumbling complaints about professionalism and sons or daughters of the soil taking over the tables of power because they have arrived. The result is that we cannot meet international standards because the only qualifications people often have are that they have arrived to take over their commonwealth. For a diverse nation, this is dangerous to growth and diminishes national cohesion. What could we have done differently? To answer this question, let us see what others have done differently.

3. Some tales from Elsewhere: Education for Managing Diversity

Nigerians like to argue that, somehow, our problems lie in the pluralism of our ethnic and cultural differences. We focus so much on these differences that we do not see their possibilities and prospects for uniting our peoples and countries. Managing pluralism requires some clarity of vision, purposeful commitment, discipline, and sacrifice on the part of the leadership. How these leaders are recruited, the platform from which they emerge, the development of an internal culture and succession plans are the key drivers. It is the vision of a leader or leaders that shape the goals to be achieved and the individuals or groups required to drive and achieve these visions.

All of this, or most of this, is tied to the nature of the choices a nation makes in its educational policy choices. If a man has five children, four males and one female or vice versa, something is likely to give. The girl with four brothers is likely to end up as a tomboy. She will likely play games like football and so on. Conversely, four girls and one boy will probably give you a spoilt brat who believes that he has five women looking after him, or, he could end up loving netball! A family with a disabled child will have to help the siblings understand how to deal with their brother or sister. Nothing is precise, but these examples are just to say that managing differences requires diplomacy, skills, and honesty. Mere good will is not enough. There have to be policies to integrate and support the weak or the vulnerable so as to ensure that everyone can make their contribution.

For a nation, the challenge is not too different, only bigger. It requires that leaders possess deep knowledge of their environment and then set about mobilizing the people to a collective vision. Our question here is, how have other countries managed diversity, and developed and achieved national cohesion? The issues here fall under what our historians and social scientists have often referred to as the "national question". The national question is an aggregate summary of the visions, the dreams, fears, hopes, and the imagination of a world that is possible but not necessarily in sight. Such visions are often captured in speeches made by leaders. Let us take two examples.

The timeless Gettysburg speech of Abraham Lincoln, delivered literally against the backdrop of the debris of the destruction caused by the civil war over one hundred and fifty years ago, captured a vision that has continued to drive the very philosophy and being of the United States of America. In the speech, he announced the birth of:
a new nation, conceived in liberty and dedicated to the proposition that all men are born equal. The world will little note, nor long remember, what we say here, but it can never forget what they did here. It is for us the living, rather, to be dedicated here to the unfinished work which they who fought here .....It is rather for us to be here dedicated to the great

task remaining before us….that from these honored dead we take increased devotion to that cause for which they gave the last full measure of devotion -- that we here highly resolve that these dead shall not have died in vain….that this nation, under God, shall have a new birth of freedom -- and that government of the people, by the people, for the people, shall not perish from the earth.

Taken together with the nation's Constitution, along with the notion of a people under God (the Bible), successive American leaders have emerged to build the greatest country on earth with the adoption of the principles of democracy captured in the last line of the speech. The vision of the founding fathers of "a city on a hill" has been kept alive and has continued to guide the leadership of that great country. For over two hundred years of its history, it was an unwritten dictum that aspirants to the White House had to be White, Anglo Saxon Protestant (WASP), and of course male!

Today, to aspire to the Presidency of the United States of America has to be firmly anchored on the assurance that one will uphold the Constitution, that one holds the founding fathers in reverence and awe, that one has a military background or some record of public service, and that one has a record of having attended an Ivy League institution. So, clearly, no matter how rich one may be, it is almost impossible to gate crash into the White House without possessing any of the above indicators in your backpack. Those aspiring for public office know where to start making the connections.

After his swearing in as President of the United States on January 20th, 1997, the world was shocked by the release of a photograph showing a teenager, Bill Clinton, shaking hands with President John Kennedy on July 24th, 1963. The world took notice and everyone wondered, how had this kid nursed this ambition? Other teenagers who had been with him on that fateful day recalled that the young Bill had told his friends that one day he would like to take up President Kennedy's job. How could anyone dream that 34 years later, Bill Clinton would raise his hand on January 20th, 1997, and be sworn in as the President of the United States? This is no ordinary story, but its importance lay in the stability of a ship of state which could allow a young boy to dream well beyond the limits of his little vision.

When Barrack Obama went to Harvard Law School and pushed on until he had become Editor of the prestigious Harvard Law Review, he knew he was adding something special to the backpack of his future life.

When he worked tirelessly with homeless people in Chicago and collaborated with churches to push the boundaries of opportunity for the poor, he knew where he was putting his investment. When he chose a disciplined lifestyle and lived a life of deferred gratification, quickly turning away from drugs, alcohol and irresponsible youthful exuberance, he knew what he was investing in. These young men merely trusted their brains and knew they lived in a country where there was no limit to one's imagination, and that raw brainpower and determination were the issues, not social status. So, for the youth in Nigeria, night vigils and hope for miracles are not substitute for hard work and determination.

Next, let us look at Singapore and Costa Rica, two countries that have outstanding records in having used education to advance their countries. The mythical story of Lee Kwan Yew, Singapore's founding Prime Minister, looms larger than life and does not require repetition here. Nigerians have been hopelessly carried away by Lee Kwan Yew's epic achievements, with so many of our public officers making endless references to him and his country. That is the easy part. The difficult part is whether any of these public officers are ever ready to subject themselves to the kind of mental discipline and sacrifice that he subjected himself to.

Dr. Lee Kwan Yew first visited Harvard in 1967, shortly after he became Prime Minister. He would return to that institution, send his son there, and continue to use it as a touchstone for sharpening the required leadership skills and knowledge needed to sustain his vision. Little wonder, his son, the current Prime Minister of Singapore, is an alumnus of the Mid-Career program at the Kennedy School of Government. Lee surrounded himself with intellectuals, focused on developing human beings, and used education to lift up his people above the shallow and murky waters of ethnic, racial, and religious conflicts. He avoided sterile and empty ideological rhetoric. Indeed, he went on to set up a Lee Kwan Yew School of Government modeled after the Kennedy School of Government!

When he died, his friend of almost fifty years, Henry Kissinger, stated in his tribute to him that Lee was so respected that his visit to Washington was a national event. According to Kissinger, Lee never lobbied in Washington; rather, people flocked to him to learn because he taught American officials how Asians think, their values, and how they saw development. What was more, a conversation with him was always a vote of confidence, Kissinger said. Compare this with what

African leaders spend just to see senators and undersecretaries in the United States today.

Singapore developed an educational system that focused on how to recruit an educated elite and turn them into an army for national development. From the day a child enters primary school till he or she completes what is known as junior college, there are basic levels of knowledge that all Singaporean children must acquire. From primary school, every child must know how to distinguish between right and wrong, learn the art of sharing and putting others first, build friendships, work as a member of a team, develop a sense of creativity, and master self-expression. A child must strive for excellence, develop a sense of aesthetics, love Singapore, believe in Singapore, and by the time they complete the equivalent of secondary school, they would have learnt what it takes to govern Singapore! You can see clearly that gradually, education helps to suck a child away from the clutches of ethnicity, class, and religion, and transfers their loyalty to the nation. For them, it is the nation first, and every other form of identity is merely a building block to the higher goals of nationhood.

So, those of you who wonder why Singapore is so clean or why it is that you can lose your telephone in a taxi and be told where to pick it up in the city must understand that they did not get there by organizing endless night vigils, shouting, "holy ghost fire, back to sender", or going to pilgrimages! The products of this system will not consider collecting estacode as the most important and primary goal of the civil service. Compare this with our own civil service where, as a senior permanent secretary said to me, "estacode is the civil servant's energizer"!

Take another look at my favorite country in regards to education, that is, Costa Rica, a little country of less than five million people. They have no standing army in Costa Rica. Their former President, Oscar Arias, told me that they had since come to the conclusion that their nation's security did not depend on the military but in education. Education was the best form of security, he argued. In a sense, in a country with a well-educated people, everyone is a soldier by way of being educated.

To be a president or to seek high office in Singapore, money, class, or status are not so important determinants. The most important of all requirements is a legacy of public service, especially in the area of coming from a family of teachers. To have grandparents or parents who were teachers means more to them than to have an oil well or to be a political godfather! Clearly, a country has to choose what values it places a premium on. As we have seen, service to others and country seems to take first place before service to self. What lessons can we learn from all this?

4. Leadership Recruitment: Leaders, Institutions and Strategy

For any institution or nation, longevity and stability are very important attributes. To stay successful and avoid crisis or collapse, a country or an institution has to anchor its future on a vision. Today, businesses have continued to rebrand to stay on top, but also to keep other competitors at bay. Developing even the best brand is not good enough. Staying power is almost everything. Today, Coca Cola, Dangote, Apple, Microsoft, HP, various Airlines, Hotels are in constant competition. You do not develop a brand just to sell your products. You also need to attract the right men and women to sustain the brand. This is where recruitment and head hunting come in.

It is not enough, for example, that Steve Jobs and Steve Wozniak wowed us all with Apple. There have to be successors to them. It is not enough that Barcelona is Messi and ten other players; there has to be a plan for both his successor and someone to pair with him. It is not enough that Arsenal walloped Manchester United; they have to plan to also beat Chelsea as well. On a serious note, the challenge therefore is not so much that a country has a leader with a vision, what is most important is how it plans for others to share this vision. Without a national policy, all the efforts made by individuals in the area of education are likely to be too insignificant to make a major impact on society.

The nation has been aglow with President Buhari, and we are all poised to see an end to corruption and the enthronement of a new dawn. However, despite being misunderstood, I will continue to insist that we need to pose more questions than answers. What is the vision that we are pursuing? How has it been crafted and what is the narrative or the plot? Who are the key actors or drivers? What is the post-Buhari succession plan beyond his term? Beyond the rather undefined rhetoric about fighting corruption, what assurance will young Nigerians have about opportunities to realize their dreams?

The absence of a clear pathway or road map for the development of a culture of leadership recruitment has meant that the purveyors of violence, the rich, those famously known as godfathers, and the criminal have continued to provide the syllabus for access to power written in the dark recesses of their dark habitats. The real challenge now is not so much the promises that President Buhari has made, his good intentions, or his new team of ministers. From what we can see, there is a long way for us to go. The challenge is how to avoid the predicament of Sisyphus, how to ensure that this rock does not roll back to the bottom of the hill only for us to start all over again.

Chinese President Xi Jinping confessed that one question he is often asked by other world leaders is how difficult it is to manage a huge country like China, which has 9.6 million square kilometers of land, 56 ethnic groups, and 1.3 billion people. He said he often responds by saying: "It is as delicate as managing frying a small fish". He further said that the Chinese believe high level officers must have served as local officials, and generals (in the military) must have risen from the ranks; recruitment to public office in China requires evidence of service at local levels. He said that he himself served the country at the municipal, provincial and central level before getting to the top. He concluded: extensive experience gained from working at local levels can help officials develop a sound attitude towards the people, know what their country is like and what the people really need, and be better versed in various jobs and professions.[3]

Thus, when we hear that China lifted about 400 million people out of poverty, we can understand what this has come from. This did not happen because of theories manufactured in city centers and universities. Rather, the experiences gained by senior officials and their familiarity with the periphery of life are what prepared them and made them sensitive to the conditions of their people.

This means that the first requirement of any leader who is managing a plural society is to understand the length and breadth of their country and its diverse peoples, their cultures, fears, hopes, and dreams. Lee Kwan Yew, Mahatma Gandhi, Martin Luther King, Nelson Mandela, Obafemi Awolowo, Ahmadu Bello, Nnamdi Azikiwe, Julius Nyerere,

---

[3] Xi Jinping, *The Governance of China* (Beijing: Foreign Languages Press, 2014), 457.

Kenneth Kaunda, Sedar Senghor, all had an affinity with their people and knew their immediate needs. It showed in the choices they made and the kind of language and idioms that they used.

Chief Awolowo's clarity of vision remains largely unsurpassed, and by placing education before everything else, he put his people at an unassailable advantage. The Sardauna was saddled with a bigger burden of how to manage the feudal hegemonic hold of the Hausa-Fulani founded on the ideology of Islam, and the motley group of ethnic groups that had conflicting expectations with the Hausa-Fulani. Azikiwe's pan-Nigerian vision saw him develop a view well beyond the confines of his local Igbo nationalism. Looking back, it is a pity that we have not covered much ground in the area of national cohesion.

5. Summary and Conclusion: Who are the Turning Point Generation?

Diversity is a gift of God and managing it requires more than good will. Effective management of diversity requires that we understand its polar opposite and what it can generate. Selfishness causes us to feel threatened by what we cannot control and leads to uncertainty and induces fear. For example, Cain killed his brother Abel because of jealousy. Selfishness is the elder brother of jealousy. To manage diversity properly, we have to overcome fear and insecurity.

Business schools teach the management of diversity as a subject, but their focus is on how to harmonize various skills so as to ensure higher profits for their corporations. In our own case, diversity should similarly be channeled towards achieving the maximum profit for the larger society. The challenge is, how and why is it that Africans have failed to be able to manage diversity? Why has ethnic and religious intolerance proved to be an obstacle to development? Again, a simple answer is to state that we have had leaders who have known very little about their own people, their cultures, fears, hopes, and anxieties.

Mr. Chude Jideonwo is one in the galaxy of brilliant young men and women that published an excellent book with a provocative title: "Are we the Turning Point Generation?" What is most important in my view is that Nigeria is changing so dramatically but we do not have the right attitude to catch the wave. We are confused as to how to tell our own stories ourselves and for ourselves. The country has been almost at a standstill, on a four-month prayer vigil, waiting for the heavens to open so that President Buhari's angel will tumble out. Characteristically, we seem sad, unable and unwilling to even give those on the list a chance.

The release of the List of Ministers has largely elicited wide yawns from across the nation. But, as the brilliant columnist Azu Ishiekwene has argued, we actually should be paying more attention to what he calls the "Other List". The "Other List" is a story of young Nigerians who are doing great things, not as a result of borrowing someone else's laboratory or driving on someone else's thoroughfare in the diaspora. It is about those young Nigerians who are sweating it out here in this great country called Nigeria. It is about brave young Nigerians swimming in shark-infested waters against the tide of a corrupt bureaucracy, armed robbers, crooked politicians, bandit economists, false prophets, and the clouds of suffocating helplessness. In spite of it all, they are dreaming big and doing great things with so little. They are the future.

They are making bricks without straw. They are pulling out chestnuts from the fumes of volcanic lava. They deserve our ovation and celebration. The "Other List" contains such names as Sim Shagaya, founder of Konga; Tunde and Raphael, founders of Jumia; Mosunmola Umoru, founder of Honeysuckles; Bankole Cardoso, co-founder of Easy Taxi Nigeria; Julius Agwu; Ify Aniebo; Bright Okpocha, also known as Basketmouth; Klint da Drunk; Femi and Seun Kuti; Asa; Banky W.; Mark Nwani; One-On-One; Mark Essien, Founder of Hotels.ng; Eseoghene Odiete, founder of Hesey Designs; and the trio of Opeyemi, Olalekan and Ayodeji of Jobberman. And, guess what, they all, like Basketmouth would say, still **WANT MORE**.

The dam of energy that held us back using corrupt, semi feudal, and blue-blooded mafia connections to survive is broken. This generation of young men and women will destroy the foundations of the corrupt empires that were built by the generations of their fathers and uncles. They represent a future of a country that will be based on ideas and knowledge. They will lead the way out of the dark tunnels that have held our nation down.

The other day, on a plane, I saw a very interesting story in the International New York Times. It carried a report from Forbes Magazine, showing how DJs—yes, DJs—were now making as much money as some corporate bodies. It reported, for example, that Calvin Harris, a young Scot, was making $66 million in a year as a DJ, while 19-year-old Martin Garrix, a Dutchman, was earning $17 million. Afrojack, also a Dutchman, was earning $16 million per annum and so on. And here I was thinking that DJs were just a bunch of rascals who took to playing records because they could not pass their examinations! Ditto the football and the tennis stars. So everywhere we turn, we see young people who are not looking for government to give them work, but they are looking for government to sanitize and create an environment for them to use their God-given talents.

The concept of "shared values" is the brainchild of Michael Porter and Mark Kramer. They used the concept to illustrate the fact that businesses and companies can increase profits while doing good for their local communities. In New York, Exxon Mobil decided to commit $125 million to training teachers in science, engineering, and technology, so they will produce a great work force. The percentage of school graduates in engineering in New York went up. SOUTHWIRE, a cable and wire company, hired some of the fresh engineers and made a profit of $1.7 million in its business[4].

This is why, even for the university, the notion of "town and gown" is another word for social corporate responsibility. The idea here is that working together in collaboration, we can create a win-win situation. Increasingly, the vocabulary is expanding as we hear such expressions as: "social capital", "corporate social responsibility", "enlightened self-interests", "good business" and so on.

Like everything else in our country, the notion of a private sector is somehow fraudulent, and the idea needs further interrogation. This country has always been one whole private sector, with its resources held by a tiny few. Today, what is the private sector is simply the left arm of government patronage. There is no business outside government business. So, when we speak of the private sector, we need to be more cautious. Bankers are more interested in cheques from Abuja than the sweat of small people; the media is glued to government advertisements for survival, and so on. However, even in its weakness, the so-called private sector and its father, the government, must appreciate the simple logic that poverty is bad for business. Hunger is bad for business. Illiteracy is bad for business. Violence is bad for business. The universities must appreciate that illiteracy is bad for business.

In conclusion, we must remember that a good leader must be a good manager of diversity, one who focuses on inclusiveness, and is obsessed

---

[4] Eduardo Porter, "Corporate Efforts to Address Social Problems Have Limits," *The New York Times*, Sept. 8, 2015, https://www.nytimes.com/2015/09/09/business/economy/corporate-efforts-to-address-social-problems-have-limits.html

with building a big tent to accommodate everyone. Often, the biggest setback for democracy is when leaders fail to manage pluralism and diversity and focus on limited self-interests. Here, the key word is power sharing.

Our democracy in Africa has been endangered by the greed of elected officials who soon turn power entrusted to them into personal weapons by which they deny their opponents their rights. It is easy for politicians who win elections to behave as if their responsibility is only to those who voted for them, or, to use the Nigerian expression, those who worked for their victory. These politicians soon erect a wall around themselves to which they retreat, and they end up turning their community into a fortified city. The problem with the fortified city is that those inside cannot get out, while those outside cannot get in.

The leader then denies himself the energy and vitality of the larger society and the opposition becomes engrossed in a war for all against all. Narrow-minded and selfish politicians who encourage or pursue policies of exclusion of others based on grounds of opposition or ethnic and religious hatred only build up resentment and endanger democracy. They bury the seeds of frustration and hatred only to see them germinate again after the next election, where revenge becomes a philosophy and violence becomes a culture. They tragically try to use democracy to kill democracy, as the Brotherhood tried to do in Egypt. Democracy opens doors and expands frontiers of tolerance and diversity.

Abraham Lincoln taught all Democrats the benefits of managing diversity. The story has been well told in the book by Doris Kearns Goodwill, titled "A Team of Rivals". It is a great story of how Abraham Lincoln, after winning the elections, assembled to his government those who had bitterly contested against him. He realized that rebuilding a country ravaged by war and making his people great was more important to him than allowing pettiness and jealousy to eat him up. This famous team of rivals was made up of William Henry Seaward, whom he named Secretary of State; Edward Bates, who became Attorney General; Salmon Chase, who became Secretary of the Treasury; and Edward Stanton, who became Secretary of War. Edward Stanton stands out because he was the top-drawer lawyer who thoroughly humiliated Abraham Lincoln in an earlier life at the Bar. Both men were polar opposites with sharply divided dispositions on different issues, including the war. However, Lincoln's sagacity saw him manage diversity so effectively that he was able to look beyond their weaknesses and draw out their inner strengths. This is the measure of a good leader.

Building networks and friendships is perhaps one of the most important and enduring lessons for any aspiring leader. A good example is the relationship between Dick Cheney, the former Vice President under President George Bush, Jr., and Donald Rumsfeld, who served as Secretary of State for Defense. To see both men simply within the frame of the Bush years is to miss the point. They had a rather interesting history and it is worth repeating because in his autobiography, "Known and Unknown", Rumsfeld tells part of the story.

He recalled that in 1968, a young man called Dick Cheney who had won an American Political Science Association Congressional Fellowship, had applied to serve in the Office of Economic Opportunity, then held by a young Senator by the name of Donald Rumsfeld. Dick was interviewed, and the detailed result of the interview has been the subject of controversy between both men. Cheney believed he failed the interview, but Rumsfeld said that he really did not hire Cheney because at that time, he needed a lawyer in the office and not a young budding academic! The relationship did not end there because Rumsfeld was promoted to the position of Chief of Staff to President Ford in 1974. A year later, when Ford appointed him Secretary of Defense, he decided to recommend Cheney for the position of Chief of Staff to replace him. Rumsfeld would make history as the youngest Secretary of State for Defense (1975-76). However, nearly thirty years later, Dick Cheney repaid the favor when he became Vice President by recommending Rumsfeld as the Secretary of State for Defense to President Bush in 2001. Again, in the process, Rumsfeld would go down in history as the oldest Secretary of State.

Those in public life, those holders of public office, must love their people. Addressing the members of the Standing Committee of the Political Bureau of the Chinese Communist Party in 2012, after his election, Mr. Xi Jinping, the new Secretary General and President of China, made an astonishing statement that very few would have associated with the leader of the Communist regime in China. I want to use the words to end my lecture. M

Mr. Jinping said: " The people are the creators of history. They are the real heroes and the source of our strength. We are aware that the capability of the individual is limited, but as long as we unite as one like a fortress, there is no difficulty we cannot overcome. One can only work for a limited period of time, but there is no limit to serving the people with dedication. Our responsibility is weightier than the mountains, our task is arduous and the road ahead long. We must bear in mind what the people think and we must work together with them diligently for the public good and for the expectations of history and the people".

_____

3rd Convocation Ceremony of the Afe Babalola University, Ado Ekiti, October 20, 2015

CHAPTER SIX

The Pursuit of Happiness: Some Thoughts on Human Rights, Freedom and Justice in Nigeria

We hold these truths to be self-evident, that all people are created equal, that they are endowed by their Creator with certain unalienable Rights, that among these are Life, Liberty and the Pursuit of Happiness, Declaration of Independence, July 4, 1776

It is difficult to find a better and clearer summary of the notion of the pursuit of happiness than that found in what used to be called the Penny Catholic Catechism. In it, we find the following questions and answers:

Q: Who made you?
Ans: God made me.
Q: Why did God make you?
Ans: God made me to know him, serve him, and be happy with him in Heaven.

One does not need to be a Catholic to appreciate the weight of these simple words. Cultures, ideologies, philosophies, religions, traditions, and so on, all propose paths to achieve happiness, and while these might all be different, the objectives are all basically the same. The attainment of happiness, in this life or in the future, is what inspires, motivates, and pumps the adrenalin of the hardest worker, the saint, and the sinner. But, we pursue it by different routes. Let me illustrate this by a short story.

A tourist was taking a walk along the Lagos beach at around 11 o'clock in the morning when he chanced by a one Mr. Ade sitting under a canopy. From the radio beside him, Ade was crooning away. On the fire by him, a fish was roasting. Beside him sat a bottle of red wine whose contents were visibly hurrying to the southern end of the bottle. His bowler hat sat precariously towards the end of the bridge of his nose as he seemed lost in a world of his own. Out of curiosity, the tourist stopped, and the following conversation ensued:

Tourist: Good morning, my friend. Nice morning on a nice beach.

Ade: Yeah, that's why I am here to enjoy it.

Tourist: So, what are you up to this morning?

Ade: I am relaxing and enjoying myself as you can see.

Tourist: But don't you think it is a bit too early to be drinking and roasting a fish? You could be out there catching some fish, you know?

Ade: And then what?

Tourist: Well, imagine what money you could have made if you had started early.

Ade: (Lifts up his bowler hat), And then what?

Tourist: With much money from fishing, you could build yourself a good house, buy a really nice car and who knows, take a holiday to any of those fun places like Hawaii.

Ade: Wow, sounds nice, but then what?

Tourist: But you know, with some good money kept away, you could really retire and have a real great life.

Ade: So, what am I doing now? Why do I have to go through all that hassle? Move on my friend. It is a long beach. Keep walking. I am already having a great life.

What exactly constitutes happiness? It is possible for us to equate happiness with exhilarated and expanded laughter, visible expressions of joy, and so on. However, on a philosophical level, does this external manifestation of what we call happiness approximate what is inside of us? Is there a way we can gauge or measure happiness? Is it some episodic experience, or is it a destination, an object, a notion that we can work towards? Is it personal or universal? What drives or inhibits us from attaining it?

This lecture is not about the philosophy of happiness. Nor is it about judging whether one source or content of happiness is morally good or otherwise. It is not about imposing any judgment on any individual, whether he or she derives happiness from a bottle of beer, sex, sports, drugs, reading, or watching a movie. What we are concerned with here is to examine and discuss the extent to which each individual has an inalienable right and opportunity to pursue his or her own goals of what they define as happiness. We will then allow the community or the state to develop the necessary instruments to either enhance the quest, or restrain those who threaten other people's quest for happiness. I am unambiguously convinced that protecting this right must constitute the cornerstone, the raison d'être, for state existence and its legitimacy.

I will divide the lecture into four sections. Section one will briefly examine some theories of happiness and its pursuit. Section two will argue that human rights and justice are essential aspects of this pursuit. Section three will examine how faith (not religion) and the judiciary can enhance the pursuit of happiness. I will do this by drawing some lessons from elsewhere to illustrate my point. Finally, in section four, I will conclude with some insights from the past for our own role today in shaping humanity's pursuit of happiness

1.1: Pursuit of Happiness: Philosophy, Faith, Culture, or Politics?

If we take the pursuit of happiness as a philosophical preoccupation, our concern will be with how to measure happiness, whether happiness can be acquired and lost, and so on. We will go back to the teachings and reflections of the various schools of philosophy. For example, Aristotle saw the pursuit of happiness as being based on the acquisition of such virtues as wisdom, courage, moderation, justice and friendship.

If we see the pursuit of happiness as based on faith, then we must return to the beginning of this lecture, namely, put God and His plan for human beings as a basis. In this case, we will reflect on happiness as being ultimately based on doing the will of God and being in His presence in eternity.

If we see it as culture, we will have to look at what value a particular cultural milieu see as constituting happiness. For example, perhaps, happiness will be based on acquiring and amassing property, marrying and having children (preferably boys?) etc. In some cultures, it might just be the pursuit of a good name and reputation.

If we see it through the prism of politics, then, we will have to examine the manifestoes and the ideologies of the various political parties to see the activities that they think constitute the path to happiness. For the moment, it would seem that the APC-led government and the rest of us in Nigeria see it ultimately as winning the war against corruption.

For the purpose of our discussion and given my background, please permit me to explore just in passing the notion of the pursuit of happiness that has come to form part of the corpus of material that is out there in the reflections on this theme. It has been the subject of great intellectual preoccupation for Christian theology. St. Thomas Aquinas and Augustine stand apart as the greatest teachers who worked very much on this theme. Permit me to therefore turn to them, because they are in the territory with which I am slightly familiar and, of course, being a Catholic Bishop, you can understand where I am coming from.

Thomas Aquinas (1225-1274) believed that perfect or absolute happiness could not be found here on earth, no matter how much we tried. This, in his thinking was tied to the reality of the transitory nature of life here on earth and the fallibility of the human person. For Aquinas, therefore, the ultimate happiness, **beatitudo**, is only attainable in heaven, in God's presence. He argues that here on earth, what is attainable is what he calls **felicitas,** a kind of an imperfect state of being happy. As with Aristotle, he argues that we can attain this temporal happiness by living a life of virtue, here, anchored on the Christian virtues of faith, hope and charity.

In this pursuit, Aquinas distinguishes between happiness and enjoyment. Enjoyment, in his view, satisfied by human good, tends to be of limited value and cannot be an end because it is ephemeral. Not only does it tend to end very quickly, it actually increases the craving either for more or for something different. Enjoyment therefore does not constitute happiness because in the end, it is often abandoned when the real happiness is found. This theme was more eloquently taken up by St. Augustine. His own life had been one of a limitless quest for happiness and actually far away from the idea of God. When he finally found God, he came to the most astonishing conclusion that: *You have made us for yourself O Lord, and our hearts are restless until they rest in thee!* He envisioned a social order, inspired by the divine order here on earth, where the pursuit of happiness could be undertaken. He referred to this as *tranquilitas ordinis.*

Indeed, Aquinas himself was also a good example of this quest. He was born of an aristocratic family but as an adult relinquished this, took a vow of celibacy, joined the Dominican order, studied, and was ordained a priest. This was only the beginning. He turned out to be an extraordinarily brilliant scholar, teaching in various Dominican houses and universities in Europe. After twenty years of extensive research, he completed his magnus opus, the *Summa Theologica*, the Summation of all Theology. The book itself remains a masterful piece of work. However, we are told that one day, while celebrating the Mass, Aquinas experienced what was probably a mystical beatific vision, which is what he had always taught as the summit of happiness. Rather than seeing this as the summit of the validation of what he has taught all his life, he literally shut down totally. He never wrote anything again and referred to his earlier works as mere straw! Aquinas died six months after this experience, thus raising the question: having attained or experienced the perfection of a beatific vision of happiness, what else was left in life?

This therefore forces us to raise another question: is a beatific vision or experience possible? Can it be sought? The answer of course is yes, because whatever our own beliefs may be, in a way, the spiritual life, particularly as lived by the mystics, seeks to achieve this. In Islam, this is at the heart of Sufi mysticism. This is the ultimate pursuit, the Nirvana that is sought in Buddhism and Hinduism, and in a sense the Heaven or divine Communion that is sought in Christianity. Again, this is not the place for us to go into a debate on these claims and beliefs. Whatever their merits or demerits, this pursuit remains an eternal quest that has persisted since the beginning of time. How or whether people find it is a subjective question and only the one who searches can answer that question.

It is significant that the image of the end of life, known as the final judgment, is tied to our state of accountability for our actions here on earth. For Christians, the idea of the Incarnation, that is God taking on human form in Jesus Christ, changes the context of our relationship with God. It becomes the thread that connects our lives here on earth with the afterlife. And so, this is why, in the course of that final judgment, as the parable tells us, we shall enter communion with God in heaven or eternal damnation in hell depending on how we treated all human beings, those Jesus calls the least of my brethren (Mt. 25:40).
But, in more practical terms, while we are here on earth, how should we pursue happiness? In other words, what should we do to make our heaven or hell here on earth in this transitory world, before we get to eternity? It is for this purpose that governments exist, and it is to this that we shall now turn.

2. Human Rights and Justice as the Pursuit of Happiness

We have illustrated above that there is what Thomas Aquinas referred to as a state of imperfect happiness, what St. Paul meant when he said, for now, we see as in a mirror (1 Cor. 13:12). Since governments exist to enable us to pursue this happiness with all its imperfections, what should we do to attain this? Here, I want to argue that enthroning a culture of human rights and justice should be at the heart of the pursuit of happiness, even in its imperfect form.

Irrespective of what way we understand creation or evolution, we can see that the pursuit of happiness has been part of human civilization. The idea of civilization itself has developed as a means of taking human beings further and further away from our animal state with its tendencies towards the survival of the fittest and dog eat dog attitude.

The story of Cain and Abel suggests to us that, somehow, in the pursuit of happiness there would always be conflict of interests. In the film *The Godfather*, the Godfather told Sollozo the Turk: "It does not matter to me what a man does for a living as long as his interests don't conflict with mine". Then as now, the question is, how do we ensure that when there is a conflict of interests, none has to lose his or her right to pursue a life of happiness? In a world where the powerful believe that the laws apply only to those weaker than them, in a society where the powerful believe that the only persons entitled to any legitimate pursuit of happiness are they, their families, friends or associates, how do we ensure a level playing field? To attempt to answer these questions, I will look at the nature of the struggle for the realisation of what today we refer to as human rights and justice.

Colonial exploitation, and its resulting human slavery, emerged as a vehicle to support and sustain the European model of nation states which was based on the philosophical foundation that we can sustain and extend our happiness by appropriating from others. This is not the place for us to engage in an analysis about the ills of slavery and other forms of human exploitation and degradation which are still extant in our world today. Indeed, the fact that today, the quest for domination persists among peoples, merely suggests that this instinct is inherent in us. Therefore, the real challenge is not to believe we can eliminate it totally; the real challenge lies in helping victims seek appropriate redress if their pursuit of happiness is endangered.

Since the emergence of the nation-state, what we now call the international community has, over time, continued to design and improve the best system to help all human beings pursue happiness within the boundaries of local and international laws. These various declarations or covenants and a host of other initiatives have offered a broad template, a moral fence to monitor and ensure that the project of the pursuit of happiness becomes a legitimate right of all nations and peoples. The challenge is how to ensure enforcement and compliance.

Beginning with the Edict of Nantes (1598), which ended the ferocious hostility between the Catholics and the Protestants (Huguenots); the Treaty of Wesphalia (1648), which ended the 30 year war; the Toleration Act in England (1689), which guaranteed religious freedom; the Bill of Rights (1689) which provided for rights of citizens even within the Monarchy; to the Declaration of Independence (1776), by which the founding fathers of America decided they had had enough of the excesses of the British powers; and the French Revolution, which flowed from the Declaration of the Rights of Man and Citizen (1879) whose philosophy was, Liberty, Equality and Fraternity... The struggle for domination and territorial ambitions, and the internal revolutions to overthrow existing orders, continued among the new powers until it all came to a climax with the outbreak of the First World War (WWI) from 1914 to 1918.

The experience of WWI left behind a legacy of almost 40 million dead civilians and military. The same powers woke up to the fact that there was need to create a culture of honour even among thieves. It was clear that territorial greed, as seen through the war, had taken human civilisation back to the dark ages from where they thought they had escaped. The world powers began to find the best means of putting a leash on their ambitions and lust for power. Thus, the adoption of the Covenant of the League of Nations came into being in 1920. The League of Nations had arisen from the Paris Conference, which had helped to end the war. Its objective was to create world peace by working for collective security through disarmament. However, war did not end. It soon became necessary to contemplate a new war to end all wars. Thus, from 1934 to 39, a Second World War (WWII) was again fought, with even more devastating consequences for humanity. After dropping between 3 and 4 million bombs, the war left behind almost 80 million military and civilians dead, with Europe in ruins.

The atrocities of the Second World War exposed the limits of human cruelty, bestiality, and savagery. The ideals of the League of Nations had proved inadequate and it was followed immediately with the establishment of the United Nations in 1948. This was followed in 1965 with the adoption of the International Covenant for Civic and Peoples' Rights, and then the Declaration on the Elimination of All Forms of Intolerance and Religious Discrimination based on Religion or Belief (1981).

The United Nations has proved to be quite successful in nudging the world on the path of peace. We can only wonder what things would have been like had the organisation not come into being. With all its imperfections, it remains a moral force. If at all peace remains a distant echo today, it is not so much that this organisation has not been alive to its duties. Rather, the real challenge has been the inability of the various superpowers to put a leash on their ambitions.

Subsequent years would see the United Nations playing the role of providing a home, a platform for everyone. That body has continued to expand the limits of the opportunities for the pursuit of happiness of nations and their peoples. Through covenants, declarations, and other instruments, the UN has continued to provide more and more opportunities for the children of a lesser god to sit at the same table with the powerful and speak as equals. The poor nations can at least take their pains, tears, and sorrows to what we have come to know as the international community. Despite the subtle apartheid that still exists in the system such as the existence of the exclusive club known as the Security Council, nations feel a sense of belonging through the General Assembly, that annual bazaar where world leaders, accompanied by their spouses and a coterie of civil servants, line up their pockets with estacode. There, every leader takes the podium to tell the world about their struggle over the obstacles to their pursuit of happiness.

The first lines of the preamble in the UN Declaration clearly state the all-encompassing ambition of the leaders of the world for all people to aspire to full equality as citizens of one planet called earth. It states:

> Whereas recognition of the inherent dignity and of the equal and inalienable rights of all members of the human family is the foundation of freedom, Justice and peace in the world.

Article 1, almost borrowing from the Declaration of Independence, repeats the same claims when it states that: "All human beings are born free and equal in dignity and rights. They are endowed with reason and conscience and should act towards one another in the spirit of brotherhood and sisterhood".

Against this backdrop, we might ask, why has the idea of our common humanity, the spirit of brotherhood and sisterhood, and the pursuit of happiness remained a challenge? In fairness though, we can see that in the last twenty or so years, much has changed in the world. More and more doors have opened. Ideology and dictatorships have collapsed. Even in Africa, where some old tyrants are still clinging to the delusion of war heroism or messianic mentality as a means of staying in power (Burundi, DRC Congo, Uganda, Rwanda and The Gambia), things are not easy for them.

The end of dictatorship came at great cost for many countries around the world, including many in Africa. However, since the beginning of this century, we have had cause for celebration. The legendary story of the collapse of Apartheid should serve us as a lesson. However, this was also anchored on the larger stories of heroism across the world. In these struggles, men and women have given up their lives by way of martyrdom, imprisonment, and exile to secure the rights of their people to pursue happiness. Now, the question is, what lessons can we draw from these experiences? To try to answer these questions, we shall look at how some individuals, associations or societies have appealed to faith and the judiciary in their struggles for the pursuit of happiness in their environments.

3. Faith and Judiciary as Platforms for the Pursuit of Happiness

In the struggles for happiness, religion has often been summoned as a platform. Religious leaders often appeal to the moral authority of the holy books, especially during moments of national crisis. Societies, even where it is claimed that religion is not important, have watched as its people turn to God as a means of coping with tragedies or difficulties. During natural or human disasters, we see churches, mosques or shrines often full of worshippers in supplication and consolation.

Today, when we look back at how religion has helped to restore some kind of moral order in society, we can appreciate the point that is being made. There are many stories of the monumental struggles by religious leaders who used their moral authority to change the courses of history. We think immediately of the very significant and visible roles of people like the late Martin Luther King, Pope John Paul II (Poland), Cardinal Sin (Philippines), Helder Cardinal Camara, Archbishop Romero (El Salvador) or Archbishop Tutu (South Africa). Within Islam, the role of Ayatollah Khomeini comes to mind.

All religions hold the view that although God has prepared a good life for us here on earth and a higher and eternal one in the hereafter, getting to our ultimate destination depends on the choices we make on earth.

Very often, our right to the pursuit of happiness is circumscribed by the decisions other individuals or institutions make by way of discriminations through policies of exclusion. For example, in the United States of America, under what came to be known as the Jim Crow Laws, the fate of Americans of African descent as inferior, second-class citizens was institutionalized in some states. In South Africa, after apartheid was formally institutionalized as a form of government in 1948, laws were in place to ensure the perpetual enslavement of black citizens on grounds of their colour.

The Jim Crow Laws were based on the assumed superiority of the white race. They were also a means of protecting white privilege from black encroachment. Although they are all but gone now, at least on paper, it is necessary to know what the struggle has been all about. Let me choose just a few of these laws to illustrate the point:

Marriage: All marriages between a white person and a Negro, or between a white person and a person of Negro descent to the fourth generation inclusive, are hereby forever prohibited.

Barbering: No colored person shall serve as a barber [to] white women or girls.

Toilets: Every employer of white or Negro males shall provide for such white or Negro males reasonably accessible and separate toilet facilities.

Buses: All passenger stations in this state operated by any motor transportation company shall have separate waiting rooms or space and separate ticket windows for the white and colored races.

Restaurants: It shall be unlawful to conduct a restaurant or other place for the serving of food in the city, at which white and colored people are served in the same room, unless such white and colored persons are effectually separated by a solid partition extending from the floor upward to a distance of seven feet or higher, and unless a separate entrance from the street is provided for each compartment.

Teaching: Any instructor who shall teach in any school, college or institution where members of the white and colored races are received and enrolled as pupils for instruction shall be deemed guilty of a misdemeanor, and upon conviction thereof, shall be fined.

In South Africa, a wide range of evil laws sustained the apartheid regime. These laws assumed and sought to institutionalize the racial superiority of the white people and the inferiority of the blacks. A few examples serve to illustrate the point:

Prohibition of Mixed Marriages Act (1948): This law which came into existence barely one year after the coming of the apartheid regime to power in 1948 sought to ensure the purity of the white race.

Immorality Amendment Act (1950): This law sought to prohibit such acts of immorality as adultery or fornication across the race lines.

Population Registration Act (1950): This law ensured the registration of all births again to avoid any contamination of the white race. It also ensured that the whites kept an eye on the growth of the black population.

Group Areas Act (1950): This law ensured the separation of the races along the lines of residences. It also enabled the government to remove black people who were considered to be living in the wrong places.

Bantu Education Act (1953): This law was to ensure that black people did not receive the kind of education that might raise their expectations and lead them to seek higher offices in future. They were to receive the minimum education that would enable them to work among their own people in the homelands.

In all of this, the world has not stood still and surrendered to evil. Over time, men and women have risen to defend freedom and sought to end the heinous crimes of inequality and injustice created by policies which have denied ordinary citizens the rights to seek the pursuit of happiness. Let me illustrate by briefly making reference to three judicial trials that will illustrate my point. I will refer to one of the most important cases in US legal history as far as the issues we are dealing with are concerned to illustrate how and why the judiciary is so important in enforcing the ideals of the pursuit of happiness.

For the United States of America, I think the natural case to look at is the case that came to be known as Brown vs. Board of Education in 1954. This is not the time or the place to review the case, except to refer to its significance and life changing relevance which opened the doors for ordinary people of African descent in the United States of America today. This case was not only a landmark case, but also it turned centuries of history and culture upside down. In the process, it laid the foundation for a new America and extended the opportunity for black people to have access to education as a means of the pursuit of happiness. Indeed, were it not for this spectacular victory in the Supreme Court, it is doubtful that people like President Obama, as well as hundreds of thousands of other Americans of African descent, would have had a seat at the table of public life today.

Education is the ladder and the key to the pursuit of happiness. By denying or out rightly limiting for black people both in the United States and South Africa an opportunity to pursue quality education, the system was basically shutting the door to their future in the pursuit of happiness.

The case of Brown vs. Board of Education was brought by 13 black parents who sought to assert the rights of their 20 children to attend schools that were within their vicinity rather than being bused to black schools that were inferior but also very far away from their neighbourhoods. The lead counsel in the Brown vs. Board of Education case was the legendary Thurgood Marshall. This case had Americans of various persuasions on the edges of their seat. Imagine a group of black lawyers in America in the 1950s, heading to and addressing the Supreme Court of the United States where there was no single black person in that court. The case for the plaintiffs was based on the belief that the inferior education that black children were exposed to had inflicted psychological wounds that scarred them for life. It imposed a culture of inferiority complex in them and in the long run, made it impossible for them to achieve their goals in life (in our case, the attainment of the education necessary for the pursuit of happiness). In his historic ruling, the Chief Justice of the Supreme Court of the United States of America,

Justice Earl Warren, ruled that: To separate black children from others of similar age and qualification solely because of their race generates a feeling of inferiority as to their status in the community that may affect their hearts and minds in a way unlikely ever to be undone.

A combination of these struggles is what informed Martin Luther King's now famous "I have a Dream" speech. In that speech, Rev. King, although a preacher and inspired by the Bible, made no direct appeal to Scripture. Rather, he focused on the claims made by both the Declaration of Independence and the American Constitution. He literally dared, challenged, and taunted the successors of the founding fathers of the Union to live up to the ideals enunciated in these texts. Dramatising the systematic use of policies of exclusion against the people of African descent, Rev. King accused the political leaders of his day of a mortal sin against the black people. He said:

> The Negro is still languishing in the corners of American society and finds himself in exile in his own land. So, we have come here today to dramatize our shameful condition. In a sense we've come to our nation's Capital to cash a check. Instead of honoring this sacred obligation, America has given the Negro people a bad check; a check which has come back marked "insufficient funds." But we refuse to believe that the bank of Justice is bankrupt. We refuse to believe that there are insufficient funds in the great vaults of opportunity of this nation.

Thus, those who seek for freedom do not seek it for themselves. The only evidence of a just society is one in which citizens are free to pursue their goals and ambitions in life. Therefore, whether they are shut out or denied opportunities on the grounds of colour, religion, gender, or status, the issues are the same. As the saying goes, in the end, injury to one is injury to all.

4. Summary and Conclusion:

I have tried to make a case for the pursuit of happiness as a legitimate human endeavour. In doing so, I have made passing reference to some thoughts of Catholic thinkers such as Thomas Aquinas and St. Augustine, as well as to landmark statements such as the American Declaration of Independence, the UN Human Rights Declaration, and other initiatives relating to the struggle for the pursuit of happiness. I have argued that creating space for this struggle for happiness is the sole basis for the legitimacy of governments. There is no doubt that not everyone will achieve happiness. The issue is whether everyone has had a fair chance, uninhibited by humanly created obstacles.

To return to the source of our inspiration for this topic, the signatories to the Declaration of Independence had further stated: "That to secure these rights, Governments are instituted among Men, deriving their just powers from the consent of the governed….That whenever any form of Government becomes destructive of these ends, it is the right of the People to alter or to abolish it, and to institute new Government. But when a long train of abuses and usurpations, pursuing invariably the same object evinces a design to reduce them under absolute Despotism, it is their right, it is their duty, to throw off such Government, and to provide new Guards for their future security."[1]

The age of revolutions seems to have come to an end with the arrival, or should I say, the discovery of democracy. Democracy seems to be a much more useful way of curbing the excesses of the human person. It seems best suited for helping in the pursuit of happiness. The history of this struggle is what Samuel Huntington has called the three waves of democracy. Although there is an old saying that democracies do not go to war, it is clear that democracy has its own imperfections. The democratic quest is not an end in itself. It must be assumed that there is a threshold that a democratic society must achieve in the fulfillment of the human spirit's quest for happiness. The evidence suggests that the quest for democracy is simply another way of speaking about the pursuit of happiness.

In this effort, we must acknowledge and appreciate those gallant men and women who have provided a template for the attainment of the right to the pursuit of happiness. The father of the Declaration of Emancipation (also known as the Emancipation Proclamation), Abraham Lincoln, remains the legendary father of the values and principles of democracy, freedom, and human rights. It is instructive that in the whole of his life, winning the war and being President were not the most important achievements for which Lincoln wanted to be remembered. Rather, for him, signing the Declaration of Emancipation

---

[1] https://www.ushistory.org/declaration/document/

was the most spectacular, life changing achievement for which he wanted to be remembered. Taken together with the Gettysburg Speech, this document represents a timeless piece of writing that focuses on the importance of the human person as a creature of God and centre of human activities.

His biographer, James McPherson, tells us that on New Year's Day, 1863, Lincoln stood for three hours shaking the hands of friends and visitors whom he had invited to the White House for the celebration of that day. When he retired to sign the Declaration, his hand had become sore from shaking hands and was trembling when he tried to sign the document. He changed his mind and decided to wait because he feared that when generations to come examined the document and saw evidence that his hand was shaking as he signed it, they would say he hesitated. When he signed the document, Lincoln said: "If my name ever goes into history, it will be for this act, and my whole soul is in it".[2]

As we acknowledge and appreciate those gallant people who have provided a template for the attainment of the right to the pursuit of happiness. We must first pay homage to God the Father and Creator of Heaven and Earth. We thank God for the gift of faith and for all forms of religious expressions through which, although we see as in a mirror the promises of a future, continue to serve as a means of restraining human beings from destroying one another and creation.

We must acknowledge theologians, philosophers, and scholars like Aristotle, Plato, Thomas Aquinas, St. Augustine, Bentham, John Rawls, Amartya Sen, and a host of scholars whose thinking has shaped the way we think about the pursuit of happiness.

We have to acknowledge great statesmen and women, who, in their personal and public lives, have designed a template for the pursuit of happiness through their roles in office. They are gallant men and women, across faith and politics, who have given humanity a dream, a vision for the pursuit of happiness. Some of them have done this within our lifetime. We must celebrate people like Nelson Mandela, Julius Nyerere, Mother Theresa, Konrad Adenauer, Winston Churchill, Mahatma Gandhi, Ayatollah Khomeini, Pope John Paul II, Pope John XXIII, Fredrick Delano Roosevelt, Doris Day, Martin Luther King,

---

[2] James McPherson, *Abraham Lincoln* (Oxford, 2009), 64.

Desmond Tutu, Lyndon Johnson, John Kennedy, and Peter Benonson. The list is endless, and it is my hope that the reader can add his or her own list of heroes and heroines.

Lawyers and judges have played a very significant role in shaping the outcomes of the struggle for the pursuit of happiness as citizens have confronted the barricades of injustice. In our situation in Nigeria, lust for power and greed for material gain has seen our judges grovel to do the devil's job for governments over the years. In my book, *Witness to Justice*, I devoted a chapter to what I called "Military Decrees and Judicial Impunity", and here I explore the ugly and sad phase of our national life when under the book of the military. Judges angled and struggled to be appointed trial judges in military tribunals often set up to settle scores. In most of these trials, the outcomes were predetermined. The most famous of these tribunals were those that tried the Ogoni 9 and that of General Lekwot and his kinsmen. Richard Akinnola has completed a book on the trial of General Lekwot with the title, *Judicial Terrorism*. It paints an ugly picture that the judiciary in Nigeria should be ashamed of.

The Supreme Court under Earl Warren (1891-1974) turned the tide of judicial activism during his term as the Chief Justice of the Supreme Court of the United States of America. He had served a three-term tenure as the Governor of California before President Dwight Eisenhower nominated him. He is famous for his commitment to issues of human rights and is remembered for his role in the famous case of Brown vs. Board of Education. He also led the investigation commission on the assassination of President John Kennedy.

On the side of lawyers, my prize goes to Thurgood Marshall (1908-1993), the lead counsel for case of Brown vs. Board of Education. Marshall's place in the history of law and human rights will remain very special. He fought 32 cases in the US Supreme Court and won 29 of them. He was the lawyer for the National Association for the Advancement of Coloured Peoples, NAACP, and his sobriquet was Mr. Civil Rights. When President Lyndon Johnson nominated him to the Supreme Court in 1967, President Johnson himself was reported to have said: "The appointment was the right thing to do, the right time to do it, the right man for it and to the right place".

Very often, most of us wonder, what can a poor, invisible person like me do? Can I change the world alone? How can I end corruption? Who am I and with what? I am not rich, no one knows me. People like me can take cover and say, I am a Priest or a Bishop. I should be praying and blessing people. I should be found in my chapel praying for corruption to end in Nigeria. I should be praying for God to give us good leaders. I should wait for the penitents to come to my Church. I could actually rise to become an influential religious leader, blessing or prophesying for politicians, businessmen, infertile women, praying for husbands or wives for young people and so on. There is nothing wrong with all this.

However, many apples fell and so many people saw apples fall. It took Newton's curiosity to know why and what made the apple fall, so that today we have the law of gravity. The airplane, the computer, Facebook, the Internet, all were a response to some kind of curiosity and the belief that I can do something, I can make a change.

When he saw that two young men had lost their freedom just for toasting to freedom, Peter Benonson decided to pray first and then wrote an article in the London Observer titled, "The Forgotten Prisoners", published on May 28th, 1961. That marked the beginning of what today is called Amnesty International. Mother Theresa did not set out the change the world. She just thought that she would do something beautiful for God by helping the poor on the streets of Calcutta to die in dignity. She did this by just washing them and feeding them.

Sensing that the many world leaders were still doing horrible things against their own people despite being signatories to many International Human Rights Laws, the United Nations decided it would step up its game. Countries were required to support the claims of their national Constitutions by setting up National Human Rights Commissions to monitor the guarantee of these rights. Sadly, Nigeria for a long time, and some would say up till now, never really took very seriously the issues of the enforcement of these rights. Today, the United Nations' notion of the Responsibility to Protect (R2P) has come into force as a means of ensuring that the struggle for human rights and dignity is now an international obligation and cannot be left to the whims and caprices of those who lead. This norm argues that: "States could forfeit their sovereignty when they fail to protect their populations from mass atrocities, crimes and human rights violations".[3] The challenge here of course is how to detect these atrocities before they assume larger proportions.

---

[3] https://www.un.org/en/genocideprevention/about-responsibility-to-protect.shtml

Chapters 2 and 4 of our Constitution have copious claims about the rights of citizens to what we might say constitutes the ingredients for the pursuit of happiness. We have all kinds of promises of the good life; promises about what the government owes its citizens. We have a basket of freedoms, from freedom of religion, right to fair hearing, privacy, freedom of association or not to even associate and so on. Yet, right before our eyes, under the claims of religion and culture, these rights are being denied to women as well as to minorities across the country, most often with the collusion of federal and state governments. Right before our eyes, women and Christian or Muslim minorities are constantly living beneath the radar of freedom. And we all look on without concern. The courts do not feel there is much they can do while the lawyers are more inclined to cases that can enhance their economic goals.

We need a generation of lawyers and judges who can bend the arc of justice in favour of the poor. But, over and above all this, what are teachers of law teaching students and how can the law faculties serve as laboratories for monitoring injustice in the universities? Students do not need to wait until they can go to courts to seek justice when daily, young women have their dignity being assaulted and are harassed into submission. How can we produce a generation of young men and women who do not know dignity and respect, who have to surrender their rights and dignity to teachers so they can graduate? What rights do students have over their teachers in terms of performance? Elsewhere, students do have a say in the promotion of their teachers, but here in Nigeria too many evils are being committed.

Where are we going to look for the inspiration for Justices such as Earl Warren, who changed human rights in America? Or will our Supreme Court remain a special club of privilege? How can we have a Supreme Court that, with sufficient judicial activism and consciousness, can give life to the noble claims of the rights of citizens to live in dignity and freedom in the quest for happiness?

I have asked around and my knowledge is limited for those who can be our own local Justice Earl Warren, and it seems I hear only two names: the late Justices Kayode Esho and Chukwudifu Oputa of blessed memory. I know there are more, but clearly we need heroes and heroines.

Locally, on the issue of the likes of Thurgood Marshall, we must acknowledge the contributions of the likes of Gani Fawehinmi of blessed memory, Olisa Agbakoba, Clement Nwankwo, Chidi Odinkalu, Femi Falana and other budding lawyers. Law teachers must begin to recruit more and more young men and women who can confidently face the future and see law as a sharp instrument to help in our pursuit of happiness.

In the end, perhaps the pursuit of happiness is an elastic journey in the sense of the finitude of this mortal earth. However, the conditions can be provided for and ameliorated if we create a template that guarantees the celebration and appreciation of our common humanity. As Tolstoy said: "All unhappy families are unhappy differently".[4] Similarly, we will never pursue the same things in life, not even if we are identical twins. What is most important is the provision of the space that enables us to rise or fall at our own pace, to remove those obstacles that slow others down, and to provide those stepping stones that give others greater opportunity.

The pursuit of happiness cannot be given in incremental terms as tokens. Whenever the bar is lowered to anyone on the grounds of gender or disability, social class or status, we must all say, with Martin Luther King:

> No, no, we are not satisfied, and we will not be satisfied until Justice rolls down like waters and righteousness like a mighty stream. And when this happens, and when we allow freedom to ring, when we let it ring from every village and every hamlet, from every state and every city, we will be able to speed up that day when all of God's children, black men and white men, Jews and gentiles, Protestants and Catholics, will be able to join hands and sing in the words of the old Negro spiritual, "Free at last! Free at last! Thank God Almighty, we are free at last!"

Obafemi Owolowo University, Ife, 11th December 2015

---

[4] *Tolstoy, Anna Karenina, 1877*

CHAPTER SEVEN

Though Tribe and Tongue May Differ: Managing Diversity in Nigeria

Introduction

On January 20th, 2017, the world literally stood still as the Americans re-enacted their ritual of swearing in a new president. Against the backdrop of a giant American flag draped in the background, in an iconic metaphor of the intricate but seamless bond between faith and patriotism, a definitive pledge and allegiance of a people united under God, the new president raises his right hand, clutches a Holy Bible, and recites the pledge to the American people and to God. In that single moment, America and Americans celebrate the Pentecost, marking the greatest expression of diversity known to the human race. In the pulsating vitality of that moment, the past, present and future all melt into a single special moment.

In faraway Gambia, on the same date, a farce was being enacted. Instead of sharing a place in the sun with the world's greatest democracy, the new president of The Gambia was forced to take his oath in the country's embassy in another country. The tyrant within had decided that, like his counterparts elsewhere in Africa, he will defy the same process he had benefited from by staying on in power. Happily, unlike the other 'demi gods', he was quickly intimidated into silence and had to crawl out silently with his tail between his legs. It was a metaphor of the nature of Africa's democracy.

We in Nigeria have our own peculiar situation. Whereas Donald Trump will go down in history as the 45th American President, Nigeria suffers from an inability to chronicle its own leaders either by title or by numbers. We have had a prime minister, heads of state, and various presidents. We have also had a military president, and one who ran the country but only under the title of Head of Interim Government, a title previously unknown in the history of democracy!

Some, like General Obasanjo and Buhari, have governed as military men before proudly and happily returning as democrats to save a country that they could not save while they were in uniform. Both Generals Gowon and Babangida have tried but failed in their attempt also to salvage the country as democrats! General Abdulsalam is still young enough and, who knows, he too could still be called upon to rescue the country someday.

So, after over 50 years, the history of Nigeria's democracy has been the history of the size of the ambitions of the men in military uniform. In Nigeria, it is possible to earn retirement benefits as a military general, a former head of state and a democratically elected president. With the Senate becoming a place of refuge for former governors, one Nigerian earns retirement benefits as a former senior civil servant, minister, governor, and perhaps, senator. They could go all the way depending on the size of their ambition.

Students of presidential history in Nigeria would find the mutations quite curious and frustrating. For example, we have no common name for those who have governed us (whether we call them, Prime Minister, President, Head of State or Head of Interim Government). The presidency of Dr. Nnamdi Azikiwe was neither the same as that of Dr. Jonathan, nor that of General Babangida. Such is our state of confusion that even in the picture galleries of our former leaders, we still find the same man in different official attire appearing twice! We can locate part of the state of our confusion as a nation in the magnitude of the difference in tongue. But, let me turn my attention to the substance of my lecture today.

I have decided to title this lecture, *Though Tribe and Tongue May Differ*. As all of us here already know, this is one of the stanzas in the first national anthem that was composed by Ms. Lillian Jean Williams, a British woman. A second British woman, Frances Berda, composed the music ahead of our independence in 1960. When we consider the fact that the country was given its name by another British woman, we can see how much gratitude we owe to these three British women! We sang this anthem right up to 1978, when the military for some reason decided that we needed a different anthem. This was one of the demonstrations of Nigeria's impatience and strange belief that change of anthem was necessarily a sign of change of direction in the administration of the country.

Chapter Seven | Matthew Hassan Kukah

By definition, National Anthems are the highest expressions of the collective aspiration, vision, and dreams of a nation. They summon a nation to some form of secular worship; the words stir and strike the chord of patriotism in all citizens. The wordings of national anthems are often set against the backdrop of battle, in which the nation seeks God's intervention in vanquishing an enemy or enemies. The lines of a national anthem, often set in the tone of prayers, contain all their fears, hopes, and aspirations. The words often ring out, summoning an entire people to a triumphant parade of patriotism and sacrifice. Almost all anthems appeal to God for victory, and life is seen as a battle. To illustrate this point, let us look at a few anthems.

The British anthem, "God Save the Queen," set against the backdrop of monarchy, prays: "O Lord our God arise, Scatter her enemies, And make them fall: Confound their politics, Frustrate their knavish tricks, On Thee our hopes we fix: God save us all." The anthem of the United States of America, titled "The Star-Spangled Banner," was written in 1814 by Francis Scott Key, and echoes the same sentiments. It pitches the country against its enemy and foe and prays for victory in the words: "Their blood has wiped out their foul footstep's pollution. No refuge could save the hireling and slave from the terror of flight, or the gloom of the grave. And the Star-Spangled Banner in triumph doth wave, O'er the land of the free and the home of the brave." Freedom and bravery have come to define American life.

The South African national anthem, "Nkosi sikelel Afrika," which means "God Bless Africa," is an expression of the philosophy of the country itself: welding together an amalgam of groups, cultures, and faiths. The anthem therefore combines words from the Xhosa, Zulu, Sesotho, Afrikaans and English languages, in keeping with the rainbow hopes of the nation. The second stanza of the anthem appeals to God too: "Protect the nation by stopping wars and sufferings."

In other countries, almost every citizen from the cradle can sing their national anthem. Citizens also know a bit about the origins of the anthem, the composers, and some aspects of the history of the sentiments expressed. Not many countries have changed their anthems; the British still cling on to their anthem that was composed in 1745 by Thomas Arne. The Indians also still sing their "Jana Gana," composed by their favorite son, Rabindranath Tagore, who received the Nobel Prize in Literature in 1913. The anthem was first sung in 1911, celebrating India's pluralism, and summoning the Himalaya Mountains and Ganges River as witnesses. It acknowledges India's differences and concludes that: "the salvation of all peoples is in God's hands, thou dispenser of India's destiny."

Today, if I ask all of us here what the following have in common, say, Obasanjo, Buhari, Babangida or Gowon, we will all say: they were former soldiers who staged coups and became the head of state or president of Nigeria. If I ask what do Nwankwno Kanu, Daniel Amoakachi, Samson Siasia or Taribo West have in common, you will all say that they all played in the national team. But, let us stretch it further and ask what John A. Ilechukwu, Eme Etim Akpan, B. A. Ogunnaike, Sota Omoigui and P.O. Aderibigbe have in common. Can anyone attempt an answer? We might be lucky that a curious school child may be able to answer this question, but I doubt that past and serving presidents, governors, ministers, members of the National Assembly, and those who claim to be educated can offer a correct answer.

These people actually have only one thing in common: they wrote the final lyrics of our current National Anthem, drawing from the submissions made by different individuals when the military for some inexplicable reason decided that we needed a new anthem. If I ask what anyone remembers about a certain Benedict Odiase, many might just say, from the name, he must be a Bini man. In reality, he set the music for our national anthem and directed the Police Band in 1978. Sadly, with the nation no longer concerned with history, we can understand that nothing of this inspires us.

It is conceivable that when we decided on a new anthem, we had hoped that a new dawn awaited us. The old anthem had enjoined us to "stand in brotherhood even if tribe and tongue may differ," and called on us to "serve our motherland". We called upon God to help us to "build a nation where no man is oppressed". The second anthem enjoined Nigerians to rise and obey the nation's call. It hoped that "the labours of our heroes past, shall never be in vain". Notice that in the second anthem, fathers had taken over and "Motherland" had become "Fatherland". With a stained banner and oppression everywhere (military coups, blood, and civil war), we now only hope to "build a nation where peace and justice reign".

Perhaps, for General Obasanjo and his Supreme Military Council, a new anthem and a new Constitution were part of the efforts at putting the past behind us and asserting our independence as a nation. Who would have imagined that barely five years into the new anthem, during which we had been praying for God to "guide our leaders right" and to "help our youth the truth to know", that the military would destroy the foundations of these dreams by a coup and set the nation backwards again? Today, Nigerians merely sing the national anthem, but it would seem to have lost its flavor and appeal. Indeed, thanks to the police bands and our children, as otherwise, most of our citizens, from our presidents, professors, bishops, ambassadors, senators, and governors, cannot recite the words of our national anthem. The anthem is no longer a call to moral arms. It is a measure of how the milk of patriotism has been totally drained.

It is important to pose the question, where did we take the wrong turn? At what point did we lose the compass? This is the subject of many books, and I will not attempt to address all the issues in a short lecture such as this. I will simply identify some of the wrong turns I think we took and look at why and how tribe and tongue became weapons of war rather than of brotherhood.

Firstly, I will look at how and when we took the wrong turn. Secondly, I will look at how tribe and tongue began to differ, leading to the destruction of the foundation of our brotherhood and sisterhood. Thirdly, I will briefly look at diversity, and pose the question as to whether the differences in tribe and tongue by themselves account for our tragic history. I will briefly illustrate how others have managed these differences. By way of a conclusion, I will try to look at what challenges the new generation of Nigerians who are graduating today may face.

1. Nigeria and the Road Not Taken:

Let me start with the timeless poem, "The Road Not Taken," by the famous American poet Robert Frost (1874-1963). As almost every stanza speaks to our situation, please permit me to reproduce the words of the entire poem. It goes thus:

> Two roads diverged in a yellow wood,
> And sorry I could not travel both
> And be one traveler, long I stood
> And looked down one as far as I could
> To where it bent in the undergrowth;

Then took the other, as just as fair,
And having perhaps the better claim
Because it was grassy and wanted wear,
Though as for that the passing there
Had worn them really about the same,

And both that morning equally lay
In leaves no step had trodden black.
Oh, I kept the first for another day!
Yet knowing how way leads on to way
I doubted if I should ever come back.

I shall be telling this with a sigh
Somewhere ages and ages hence:
Two roads diverged in a wood, and I,
I took the one less traveled by,
And that has made all the difference

This poem has been subjected to different interpretations, and this is not the place to subject it to further interrogation or criticism. The lessons in the poem serve us whether as individuals, families, communities, or nations. First, life is about choices and these choices are never perfect; no one has the opportunity to see right up to the end of the road of his or her life. Frost was honest enough to know that, faced with a choice of two roads, he could not travel both. He looked far and he saw where the road bent in the undergrowth. He was honest enough to know that although the roads did look alike, there might never be only one bend on the road. He knew that in the end, each road has to have a bend, a signpost of uncertainty.

Frost sensed that this would be a long journey because, as he said, "way leads to way." Again, he is honest to know that as they say, you do not cross one river twice. So, he admits that much as he might dream, there is no guarantee that he would come back to the same road again. He summons history, knowing that its judgment would happen, long after he and the choice he made are gone. So, yes, he took a risk and was ready to live with the consequences. It was a decision based on courage, courage built on hope, and hope with faith as its foundation. It is not so much what history remembers, but for him, what is most important is that he took a decision and he took a turn.

What does this say to us today when we look back at Nigeria? We have lacked the courage to take some of the tough decisions that would have changed our country today. We found the discipline and demands of equality enshrined in our democracy difficult to uphold, and therefore we opted to cohabit with feudalism. The result is that we have constructed a rickety double decker identity vehicle whereby we inhabit one section as citizens and another as subjects. Government is unable to secure the loyalty of its citizens, who prefer to preserve their reverence and loyalties to their local communities. The consequences of our lack of clear choices now stare us in the face. We are unable to submit to a single loyalty code. The elites steal from government and return home to feather the local nest presided over by the local hegemon, before whom they prostrate as favourite sons and daughters adorned with feathers of recognition and appreciation.

Today, our youth face an uncertain future, one that is marked by the debris of broken dreams, journeys started but not completed or disrupted. We often fear to do something new because it has never been done before. The real reason why we stagnate is because we tend to say, this is how it has always been done, and our ancestors did it this way. In the name of culture, our development has continued to stagnate. In the name of cultural preservation, we are wearing beads we do not produce, turbans we do not weave, and pouring libation with cheap drinks we do not produce. It is of us that Gibran said: "Pity that nation that wears a cloth it does not weave, eats a bread it does not harvest, and drinks a wine that flows not from its own winepress." The consequences of the road not taken is what we are living with now; it has prepared the ground for why tribe and tongue now differ. It is to this that we shall now turn.

2. How Tribe and Tongue Began to Differ

It is not uncommon to hear Nigerians describe themselves or their heroes as being detribalized Nigerians. Although this is supposed to be a measure of how reliable or fit for public office these people are, in reality it says nothing about their character, patriotism, or degree of honesty. We are supposed to assume that for these people, ethnicity does not matter in the decisions that they take. This truism is popular but false because it is built on shallow sand. In reality, very often these so-called detribalized Nigerians are people who have a rather wide social circle or network of friends who could also be partners in crime, depending on the nature of the interests they pursue!

So, there are detribalized politicians, businessmen and women, as well as detribalized armed robbers and crooks in the system. For, when you probe them further, they are detribalized just because their drivers, cooks, stewards, mistresses, and girlfriends cover this wide social circle. For, in truth, if they were detribalized, they would put the nation first and not their selfish pursuits. When next you hear about a detribalized Nigerian, probe a little deeper because on Monday morning, the same man wears the garb of bigotry.

The first mistake we may make is to assume that ethnicity, tribe, or tongue do not matter. They all do. This has been the reality of human existence from the beginning of time. The challenge has been how to turn diversity into an asset, how to create a society where each citizen can have a sense of belonging and believe in fairness and justice. Cain and Abel were blood brothers and they spoke the same language, yet Cain murdered his brother. It is the institutions that we put on the ground, and as we see in the case of Cain, he had to face God's punishment after his crime. When people do not feel a sense of being equal before the law, then differences become manifest.

For example, it might be fair to say that the British did their best in Nigeria and left behind a structure and a bureaucracy that could have delivered on services and welfare. They laid the foundation for a pretty sound educational and economic base. Amidst the fears and anxieties of the minority ethnic groups about the prospects of domination by the dominant ethnic groups in the country, they at least set up the Willinks Commission in 1958 to listen to the fears of various groups across the country. This laid the foundation for managing the differences arising from the religious worldviews in the northern region of Nigeria by sending out a delegation to explore the best ways of managing Sharia Law and the British Common Law. They resolved this obvious conflict of laws by administering a penal code for the northern region.

Imperfect as this may have been, it did succeed in managing the differences among the peoples. They left us a regional political arrangement that took cognizance of our geopolitical and cultural differences by administering a provincial arrangement that has stood the test of time in almost every plural post-colonial state in Africa and Asia. While other nations of Africa and Asia have for the most part held on to these boundaries till date, it is the military in Nigeria that destroyed them by creating states.

It can be argued that the failure of the competing elites to manage diversity, marked by both ethnicity and regionalism, led to the first military coup. Indeed, managing the fallout of the coup tested the commitment of the competing elites. Nigeria could have survived both the coup and the civil war and still recovered to build a strong nation had the military not made several wrong choices. The first wrong choice in my view was the decision to create new states rather than carrying through the difficult negotiations from Aburi, no matter their consequences. For, as we know, rather than managing the challenges thrown up by the coup, the military government decided to create new states. The decision to create states was a reflex reaction to stop the ambitions of Colonel Ojukwu. As we know, the decision did not stop the war and the rest is history.

Notwithstanding the coups of 1966 and 1967, and the three-year civil war, the decision of the military to stay on in power was one of the worst decisions. The military had embarked on a scare mongering culture of fear that deepened the hostilities among our people and led to the distrust of politics and politicians. The military itself, which had the sole monopoly of violence and had used violence to secure power, widened the gap of confidence between the people and their politicians. Politics lost its glamour and politicians were projected as thieves and criminals, while the military deceived the people by presenting themselves as heroes, redeemers, and patriots.

As a result of this fear, politics and politicians were diminished as the military dug their heels into power. With limited maturity and experience, and lacking training and proper understanding of the texture of the country, the military turned the nation into a huge laboratory for experiment. Patriotic politicians with sound ideas and brains like Alhaji Tafawa Balewa, Alhaji Ahmadu Bello, and the Sarduana of Sokoto, who laid the foundation of our nation, fell by the bullets of military coup plotters. Those who survived, like Chief Obafemi Awolowo, Dr. Nnamdi Azikiwe, Sam Ikoku, Bola Ige, Sam Mbakwe, Abubakar Rimi, Solomon Lar, and a host of others, were subdued through imprisonment, intimidation, detention, trials, blackmail, and even murder. Politics became unattractive to men and women of honor and increasingly, it became a theatre for those who could swim in its shark-infested waters.

Seduced by the aura of power and in the heat of the oil boom, the military's appetite increased as it strengthened its grip on power by diminishing politics. Gradually, ethnic and regional politics began to destroy the cohesion of the military as an institution, and ethnic and regional interests subordinated national interests. With the erosion of their so-called esprit de corps and a high culture of coups and counter coups, the myth of the military collapsed and the system occasionally threw up men of questionable integrity and patriotism. All one needs to do is to look at some of the coup speeches of the time to see the perception these people had of Nigeria. These hurriedly written speeches suggested that even some of the coup plotters had no plan and no idea what they wanted to do. Do you recall that after those warped speeches, the last lines called on Nigerians to stay by their radios for further announcements? The bile, anger, frustration, and hate in those speeches are evidence of troubled minds with too many demons to fight.

Rather than build up institutions to encourage cohesion and progress, the military regimes continued to parcel out the country into more states and local government councils. Meanwhile, as the political space was opening up, the government had less and less resources to sustain the fiscal needs of new states and local government councils. States and local government councils reproduced the same characteristic of state capture, prebendalism, and clientelism as their masters and sponsors at the higher levels. This opening of the political space created a greater sense of ethno-regional and religious consciousness, with each state or local government creation marked by celebrations of independence. Yesterday's brothers and sisters became enemies, with the members of the new state or local government area celebrating their freedom from oppressive enemies. The new leaders of states and local governments often marked this independence by giving their kith and kin of yesterday short notice to pack and go. Allegations of domination versus marginalization filled the air as yesterday's oppressed became today's oppressors, thus renewing the circle of suspicion, fear, hatred, anxiety, and heightened sense of difference.

Another serious mistake that engendered a negative sense of difference in tribe and tongue was in the area of education. With power falling increasingly into the hands of armed men and their political counterparts, a culture of banditry and state capture destroyed the foundations of education; pillaging the resources of states became the end game. Military expenditure dwarfed expenditure in education, and with the intellectual class posing a serious threat, education took a lower rung in the ladder. Teaching became an exercise in drudgery and it attracted only those who had nowhere else to turn or were too old to compete elsewhere. Appointments of vice chancellors became an extension of state patronage, with vice chancellors and rectors becoming largely stooges to those in power. Despite the slight changes today, the universities of Nigeria are no longer seen as pivotal institutions for national development.

Over the years, a culture of the establishment of state universities has emerged to serve two purposes. First, in some cases, state universities were set up as a way of asserting independence from the Federal Government or addressing perceived federal neglect. Governors wanted to show how anxious they were to generate local manpower, often undermining the sense of national cohesion. Sadly, again, most of these state universities have reproduced the same contradictions faced by the federal universities. They have too often become theatres and battlegrounds for the local elite to angle for positions and appointments.

Today, both federal and state universities have gradually become hostages to the forces of ethnic, regional, and religious politics and power play. Our universities now have very little time and interest in serious academic activities and research. Cultism among students is merely a mirror reflection of the dirty power play at the higher levels of administration. Most federal universities, rather than reflect the aspiration of the nation, have become incubators of the worst form of ethnic or religious politics. Discrimination based on religion, ethnicity, and even political loyalties and other cleavages are rife in our universities.

In 2014, I delivered the convocation Lecture in the University of Uyo titled, "To Heal a Fractured Nation." In it, I argued that the federal government laid the foundation for the emergence of this distortion of our national identity when it decided to name federal universities after their local heroes. In their heydays, the University of Ibadan, University of Nigeria, Nsukka, Ahmadu Bello University, University of Calabar, Lagos, and Port Harcourt, among others, were the theatres of intellectual excellence, attracting some of the best brains from across the world. I pointed out that it was a grave mistake for the federal government to have named universities in Ife, Kano, Sokoto, or Awka after such favourite sons as Obafemi Awolowo, Ado Bayero, Usman dan Fodio, and Nnamdi Azikiwe.

An imaginative government anxious for national cohesion could, for example, have distributed these great names across the country and enabled them to be celebrated and appreciated outside their immediate areas of birth. Imagine if Ahmadu Bello University had been in Ife, Obafemi Awolowo in Zaria, or Nnamdi Azikiwe in Kano, and so on. Now, it is too late because a grievous and divisive wound has been inflicted. It is a measure of how bad things have become that this would be an unthinkable thought today.

Today, this narrow mindedness is being exploited because these universities have been turned into fiefdoms, placing the interests of the local communities over and above those of the nation and other citizens. Only favourite sons and daughters often hold key management positions in these universities, with little attention paid to qualifications and quality. The National Universities Commission must look beyond regulating academic standards and turn attention to how much these universities reflect the aspirations of our nation and how much they create a sense of belonging to all citizens. In some of these federal universities, local customs trump national, constitutional rights in such areas as freedom of worship and religion. Despite federal funding, today, Christians are out rightly denied places of worship in most federal universities in northern Nigeria despite the ubiquity of mosques. If universities that should be the platform for preparing leaders of tomorrow exhibit this bigotry, what do we expect in Abuja?

The final mistake that has exacerbated the difference between tribe and tongue is in the area of the operations of the Nigerian bureaucracy. Successive military regimes sought to create the bureaucracy in the image and likeness of their visions. Over the years, as corruption buried its teeth into the entire fabric of the nation, the bureaucracy became consumed in corruption. Promotions in the bureaucracy became the stuff of politics, and merit gave way to patronage, often based on ethnic, religious, or even political affiliations. Promotions based on ethnicity or religion were common depending on the affiliations of those in power. Today, public officers pride themselves in how much they have recruited persons from their clans, communities, or faiths. Lift the veil after a senior officer has left his or her post today and you will see how an entire system has become domesticated to meet the narrow interests of a tribe, religion or region. From the Presidential Villa, State Government houses, Security agencies, Bureaucracy, Ministries, Departments and Agencies, the stories are the same.

Finally, the most dangerous area where the difference between tribe and tongue has been exacerbated is in the area of religion. Since the end of colonial rule, no single President of Nigeria has demonstrated a clear commitment to address the issue of the real role of religion in public life. Not one. In northern Nigeria, the government has continued to confuse feudalism with religion, with successive governments merely adopting the attitudes of appeasement. The gains made by the late Sardauna of Sokoto in collaboration with the colonial government in the area of defining the role and place of law and religion in Nigeria have been squandered. The vacuum has now been exploited by politicians who continue to manipulate the religion of Islam as a platform for political power while keeping millions of their people impoverished and ignorant.

For example, the so-called debate over the status of Sharia law remains an issue whenever Northern politicians feel that their power base is threatened. Defending religion has become the task of civil servants and public officials who angle for power. The federal and state governments, on the other hand, have come to see state patronage of religion through the sponsorship of Pilgrimages as a form of collaboration. The real role of traditional rulers in northern Nigeria remains confused with religion. This has only further deepened our problems and sense of division as citizens. Today, we all see ourselves as Christians or Muslims and not citizens of one nation. The list of confusion is long, but we must bring this conversation to a close.

By way of conclusion, what does the future look like and how is the new generation expected to face these challenges? What lessons can we draw from the experience of others?

3. Summary and Conclusion: Managing Tribe and Tongue

One of the greatest American spiritual writers and public speakers of all time, the late Bishop Fulton Sheen, once stated that in life we have only two choices: "Never forget that there are only two philosophies to rule your life: the one of the cross, which starts with the fast and ends with the feast. The other of Satan, which starts with the feast and ends with the headache." Basically, he is telling us that either we fast now and have the feast later, or we have the feast now and the fast later. These choices are not different from the choices put before us by the poet Robert Frost, above. If we follow Archbishop Sheen's analogy, it seems safe to say that the Nigerian political elite chose the feast first, rather than the fast. The facts now stare us in the face: a country in total decay and disarray, a nation with no moral compass and no clear navigational aids, a people severely fractured and disoriented. Nigeria shows no sign of direction in any shape or form. Everywhere you turn, the faces are forlorn, with citizens looking as if they are on their way back from a funeral.

Hundreds of billions of naira and dollars and over fifty years later, the nation has barely 3,000 megawatts of power. Hundreds of billions and over fifty years later, there are no federal highways to be proud of, no railways, no water, no food. Everywhere you turn, shame stares us in the face. Does this look like a nation that can fight and win a war against corruption? I am not sure, because the lack of all the above listed items is corruption in capital letters.

President Buhari was right when he said: "If we do not kill corruption, corruption will kill us." The All People's Congress, APC, government has continued to lament about corruption, but they themselves keep playing politics and rejecting history. We are told that the corruption we now face is a product of the last 16 years of the malfeasance of the Peoples' Democratic Party, PDP. No one doubts that the PDP did a lot of horrible things, and not many of them have stopped. But up till three years ago, didn't most of the key actors today cut their teeth in the PDP? But can we really speak of corruption in Nigeria without a sense of history and how the military, by its culture of coups and counter coups, sowed the seeds for what we are reaping today? The immobility in the fight against corruption has made a pantomime.

Technically, the war against corruption is unwinnable if we imagine that one day we shall have a corrupt free society. Corruption is another word for poverty, injustice, insecurity, nepotism, a culture of might is right, a feeling of emptiness and helplessness. Corruption is not a disease from which we can be cured. Corruption can only be contained by development and strong institutions that serve as vehicles of restraint against human greed and infringement. President Buhari should have been more honest in admitting that he and his fellow military men laid the foundations for the tragedy that has befallen the nation. The PDP may have become a willing undertaker, but the patient was poisoned a long time ago. Fighting corruption is beyond politics.

Like fighting drugs, fighting corruption is not measured by enthusiasm or patriotism. Like our President, President Rodrigo Duterte of the Philippines, came with guns blazing to fight drugs in his country, despite seeming mentally unstable. He adopted the most unorthodox methods, and when the Catholic Church called his attention to his thuggish methods, he resorted to abuse and insults. He arrested, tortured, and murdered thousands of his citizens. In less than one year, he has become exhausted and suspended the war, he himself coming down with a disease resulting from his years of smoking. He has suddenly discovered his problem is the police, not the drug barons. Now, he has decided to take up the police. The former President of Colombia, the haven of drug barons himself, warned Mr. Duterte that he could never win the drug war if he treated it as merely a law and order matter. He argued that the drug problem, like corruption, is a social problem requiring social solutions. There is a clear lesson here for those who boast about a war against corruption in Nigeria but apply the wrong diagnosis of seeing it as a law and order matter.

One day I accidentally stumbled on some information about "The Ten Best, Worst, Most Educated and the Least Educated Leaders in Africa." To my greatest surprise, Nigeria did not feature in any of the lists. On the scale of leadership, sadly we have never produced the best, and happily we have not produced the worst. However, it is clear that education is a necessary but not sufficient condition for leadership.

Against the backdrop of this gloomy picture, you might ask, where is the hope? Well, some of my critics have said that when I speak, I leave the windows open and that I do not draw lessons or conclusions, and that I do not tell people what to do. Whenever I hear these criticisms, I am actually happy because that is what I want to convey; namely, the fact that I am also a foreign traveler searching for knowledge. My job is to offer you a fruit and not to masticate it for you. After all, I am just lucky to have this platform. Most of you here are far better qualified than me to speak to the issues.

However, what should we say to young people as they step into public life today in Nigeria? Sadly, but understandably, young people do not see much to be enthusiastic about. There are stories of many young men and women who have finished the National Youth Service and decided they would rather repeat it. Those leaders ahead of them have either continued to change their ages, refuse to retire, or fill up the spaces with their kith and kin. But is all lost? By no means at all. Amidst the circling gloom, there is hope in the air.

I do not believe that the problem with our country is necessarily about bad leadership, or that too many bad people have governed us. It is fair to say that we have had some really fine gentlemen and gentlewomen at the helm of affairs in our country, men and women who truly love the country and wanted to do good. The problem is that their good intentions were not enough, because nations do not run on good intentions or claims of patriotism. The most important thing that has been missing has been the lack of a clear programme of recruitment to public life. Too many people stumbled into power by accident and quick fixes. A coup culture has continued to trail our politics, which is expressed in the constant subversion of due process by those seeking public office. The nation has lacked men and women seeking power by the most decent means. Political platforms founded on deceit and bereft of moral standards cannot produce leaders with high moral standards. It is a culture of military coups that sowed volatility into the polity.

Diversity can and should be a great national asset if, like an orchestra, a country has visionary leaders who can harmonize the gifts and talents of its people into a beautiful music of unity. Diversity will remain a liability if every citizen, perhaps frustrated by poor leadership, decides to do their own thing, or survive on their own devices, whims, and caprices, as is the case now. It is institutions that regulate and ensure the proper management of diversity. Such institutions include effective Constitutions, a culture of discipline and submission to the rule of law, and a deliberate pursuit of the common good of each citizen. No matter the range of talents, no team can succeed if every player decides to rely on his or her own skills. Victory is the result of the co-ordination, co-operation, and collaboration of all the members of the team. This is the stuff of leadership.

A system with no succession plan is bound to suffer the malfunction that the Nigerian state has been subjected to. A situation where presidents and governors, not the electorate, decide who will succeed them is an abuse of democracy and process. It is a reflex of the inferiority complex that our so-called elected officials suffer. They fear an open process that will allow our people to freely choose. Today, as the late Professor Claude Ake said, our people are merely voting without choosing their leaders.

Although we have such bodies as the National Human Rights Commission, Public Complaints Commission, and the National Legal Aid Council, the lofty ideals of these institutions have been weighed down by bureaucratization, lack of adequate funding, and government interference. They have also become subject to state interference, cronyism, and patronage. Advocacy must become a tool for civil society groups, faith communities, and other platforms to confront the state. Here, there is almost no substitute to judicial activism.

For example, it was the Supreme Court of the United States that opened the gates of opportunity for black people through the landmark, epoch-making ruling that came to be known as Brown vs. Board of Education in 1954. The inspiring efforts of Presidents John F. Kennedy and Lyndon B. Johnson would finally find expression in the signing of the Civil Liberties Act in 1964. Most of these opportunities became possible through the sacrifices of people like Justice Thurgood Marshall, Rev. Martin Luther King, Malcolm X, Rosa Parks, and a host of others. There were also institutions like the National Association for the Advancement of Colored People (NAACP) and the Southern Baptist Leadership Convention (SBLC), among others. These individuals used these platforms to help America come to terms with laying the foundation for the management of diversity. It is on their shoulders that people like Barack Obama rose to his historic presidency.

By establishing the Commission for Racial Equality in 1976, the British Government sought to address issues of racial injustice that still existed among the citizens. The government knew that mere declarations of good intentions were not enough to ensure justice and equity. Thus, for the lofty prayers in our national anthems to be answered, or for the letter and spirits of our Constitutions to become real, governments must ensure that these institutions work for the benefit of the weak in society. Citizens must also develop the courage to stand together in solidarity. There is no substitute for judicial activism and a dynamic civil society teaming up with members of the faith community to celebrate our common humanity.

To our new graduates who are stepping into public life, prepare for both the best and the worst. I read somewhere that the Obamas had a peculiar way of bringing up their children. According to Mrs. Obama, she and her husband asked their children what sports they loved or hated the most. While they encouraged them to engage in the sports they loved, they also insisted that they learn the sports they hated. In their innocence, when the children asked why, the parents told them that life will never always offer you only what you want. Wherever you find yourself, know that God has put you there. I often tell the mostly Christian and southern Youth Corpers sent to Sokoto to get to know the language, make friends, love the people, and never seek an easy way out. You never know what the future will bring and whom you will need to rely on. I can tell because it has worked very well for me.

As for managing tribe and tongue, the first thing to acknowledge is that tribe and tongue are a gift of God. Like all gifts, it can be subject to abuse. What we face in Nigeria today is a series of consequences of wrong turns and wrong choices, whose negative impact has accumulated over the years. Rather than see diversity as an obstacle to development, what we need to aspire to and help to create is an environment where the energies of our diverse peoples can be properly channeled. This is a task to which each and every one must commit to. It is difficult to imagine how we might mend these broken tongues. With the right leadership and the right courage and vision, our tribe and tongue will continue to differ, but they will not necessarily become such deadly weapons of war. Things might get progressively worse if Nigeria does not take a turn earlier rather than later.

As you step into the future, remember that your life is a gift from God with a purpose and a mission. Happiness will not lie in what you acquire, what positions you hold, or how much money you make. True happiness will lie in discovering your mission, your vocation in life, and fulfilling it. Happiness will depend on your understanding that God has written your name in the palm of His hand and that He is with you. I read a strange story in the Daily Trust Newspaper of February 15th, 2017. A young lady, Jane Park, won the sum of one million pounds (some N382m) in the lottery with her first ticket in 2013. Today, barely three years later, she says she feels empty. According to her: "At times, I feel like winning the lottery has ruined my life. I thought it would make it ten times better but it has made it ten times worse. I have material things but apart from that, my life is empty."

Money is good, and without it life could be miserable. However, it is not everything. What are most important are the choices we make in life. One of Mahatma Gandhi's friends, to taunt him, asked: "If you saw two bags, one full of money and the other full of wisdom, which would you choose?" Gandhi said: "I would take the money of course." Knowing him for his disciplined and frugal life, his friend was shocked and derided him saying, Personally, I would take the bag of wisdom. But, Gandhi said to him: "Each one should take only what he does not have." Do you know what you do not have? Ask God to help you to choose well.

Finally, the challenges envisioned by those who composed our first national anthem are still with us, but they are indeed worthy aspirations. We must seek to mend the fractures in our society by looking out for the other. All our religions and cultures teach us about the need to stand together in love. Life is hard, but we cannot surrender to selfishness. Learning to stand in solidarity and seeing God in one another is the essence of our being human. We all have opportunities every day to live out these realities. We are all where we are today because we stood on the shoulders of others. Let us not hesitate to offer others a shoulder to lean on.

I want to leave you with something that I stumbled across some time ago. I do not remember even where I found it, but it is a very useful lesson for you as you step into the future. It is titled, "It Is in Your Hands." It goes thus:

A tennis racket is useless in my hands. But a tennis racket in Ms. Serena William's hands is worth billions of Naira. Remember:
It depends whose hands it is in.
A rod in my hands will keep an angry dog away. But a rod in Moses' hands parted the mighty Red Sea.
Remember: It depends whose hands it is in.
A catapult in my hand is a toy and it might manage to kill a bird. But a catapult in David's hand was a mighty weapon that fell the all mighty Goliath.
Remember: It depends whose hands it is in.
Two fishes and 5 loaves of bread in my hand are just enough for breakfast for my family.
But two fishes and 5 loaves of bread in my Lord Jesus' hands fed thousands.
Remember: It depends whose hands it is in.

A certificate from this university is a stepping stone to greatness.
Remember: It depends whose hands it is in.

My dear friends, the choice is yours. The keys to the doors of your future are in your hands. Please make the right choices and may God accompany you. Thank you for your patience.

21st Convocation Lecture, University of Abuja, Feb 24: 2017

CHAPTER EIGHT

Broken Truths: Nigeria's Elusive Quest for National Cohesion

1. Introduction: The Truth of our Nigerian Story?

Let me start with a conceptual clarification regarding the title and topic of this lecture. Not unexpectedly, my first reaction is to ask, what is a broken truth? What does an unbroken truth look like? When we speak of truth, we immediately recall the trial of Jesus before Pilate: When Jesus said to Pilate that he had come to bear witness to the truth, Pilate replied, "Truth, what is that?" (Jn.18: 38). Truth has been and remains a contested concept precisely because it's very veracity depends on a range of other options.

Today in the court room, an accused person takes the witness stand with a holy book in one hand, and promises to tell the truth, the whole truth, and nothing but the truth. Sadly, even up to the completion of the hearing of the case, we are often not sure which truth has been told; we are unsure what part, version, or fraction of the truth the judge or the jury may have heard. It is often said that to get to the truth, it is important to hear both sides of the story. Yet, even after both sides have told their story, we do not necessarily get to the so-called truth. There are often at least three sides of a truth: his/her side, the other side, and "the" truth!

We will all agree that knowing or finding the truth is integral to the attainment of justice. Justice Chukwudifu Oputa, the legal legend of blessed memory, came up with the dictum that justice is a three-way street: justice for the perpetrator, justice for the victim, and justice for the larger society. I remember saying to him once that I thought there should be a fourth leg of justice: justice before God. Of course, since we believe that only God is Truth, one would hope that the quest for justice on earth would be guided by and therefore somehow reflect God's Justice. But, let me here return sharply to the substance of this lecture— I have undertaken this philosophical excursion merely to serve the fact (truth) that this is a multifaceted conversation, which can only be enriched by a multiplicity of views.

As I was reflecting on what to speak on, this title came to my mind. I thought it would be a useful guide to help me address the issues concerning the collective sense of cynicism and anomie that has gripped our land and indeed our world today. We are surrounded by walls of lies, half-truths, and innuendos, which have become woven into the tapestry of our national history. I dare anyone to try to present one definitive narrative about any of the epochal events in our nation's history.

We have no comprehensive history of the civil war. We have no exhaustive history of the various coups that took place in our country. We have no complete narrative of the history of political formations and culture in Nigeria. Every phase of our recorded national history is a mish-mash of half-truths, stratagems, and incomplete stories, drawn from rumor, allegations, and outright lies fed to the public, as well as the fact that each of us sees reality from our diverse perspectives. Indeed, as Napoleon Bonaparte stated, "History is a set of lies agreed upon".

But where are the truth-tellers? How did all the mighty citadels of learning in our country, along with their theatre departments, parks, gardens and staff clubs suddenly become abandoned wastelands overrun by cultists, drug peddlers, and rodents? Who can forget the Faculty of Social Sciences in Ahmadu Bello University, Zaria, and other Marxist havens in the Universities of Port Harcourt, Calabar or Ife? Where are the colleagues, students, and successors of the likes of the late Professors Bala Usman, Patrick Wilmot, Mike and George Kwanashie, Eskor Toyo, Monday Mwangvat, Claude Ake, Sam Oyobvaire, and Adele Jinadu? Where is the generation whose intense scholarship gave us the phenomenal work, "The Kaduna Mafia"?

Today, to survey the intellectual landscape in Nigeria, is to see stalks cut low by the scythe of the grim reaper. After the hemorrhage of the generation that President Babangida accused of "teaching what they were not paid to teach" in the mid-1980s, the university environment became a conquered land of surrender where playing safe became the basis for survival. As military generals who themselves had no university education began to appoint vice chancellors—and even some from within their ranks—to administer the universities, so began our slouch towards Bethlehem, to quote Yeats.

Today, a band of illiterate so-called herdsmen have taken an entire nation hostage. A movement, Boko Haram, led by an illiterate, has taken on the entire security apparatus of the nation. How did we come to this sorry state? Will the next generation dream great dreams and hope they can be realized, or will they forever remain trapped in nightmares of the mass violence that has become their diet? What narrative shall the next generation inherit? Today, we rely on comedians for ephemeral comic relief. We have no Nobel Prize winning authors to celebrate in our universities, no academic feats worthy of international recognition. There is a need to interrogate the consequences of the choices we made or did not make and their impact on where we are today. To this I now turn.

2. Nigeria: The Road Not Taken

I have always loved to return to this great poem as a source of inspiration. It offers us an opportunity to speculate about what might have been had we made different choices. I will quote just the first and the last verses of Robert Frost's "The Road Not Taken":

> Two roads diverged in a yellow wood,
> And sorry I could not travel both
> And be one traveler, long I stood
> And looked down one as far as I could
> To where it bent in the undergrowth;
>
> I shall be telling this with a sigh
> Somewhere ages and ages hence:
> Two roads diverged in a wood, and I,
> I took the one less traveled by,
> And that has made all the difference

Even before independence, what would later become Nigeria had a rather distorted history cast in competing, even conflicting, narratives and experiences. A century before the invasions of the British, the peoples of most of what is now the Middle Belt had lived with the traumatic experiences of war, slavery, compulsory conversions to Islam, and the destruction of their cultures and habitats in the course of the establishment of the Sokoto Caliphate. The scars were deep, but not being a literate society, and with no written records about their own history and experiences, this subjugation had become embedded in the individual and collective psyche, surviving only in tales told by forebears. For instance, as children growing up, my siblings and cousins would gather around our grandmother at meal-time and whenever we seemed to be eating in a hurry, she would yell: "Why are you eating as if you are running away from Fulanis?" I had to wait for over forty years, going to the School of Oriental and African Studies in London, to stumble on the meaning of these words in the course of my research in the library. When I stumbled on a narrative of the days of slavery, it said that in the days of the Caliphate, communities to be invaded for slave raids could see the horses of the raiders by the dust they raised by day. As a result, the raiders took to raiding communities for slaves at night. They would often follow the direction of the cooking fires and strike at families in the middle of their meals. As such, families took to eating very quickly so they could put out the fires and go into hiding! Clearly, our grandmother knew we were too young to grasp the complexity of the history, but it was her life.

I am nostalgic about the days of Bala Usman and his radical movement, which enabled the generation of the time to address the primary contradictions and then set up a higher ideological platform that enabled scholars to unite and confront the secondary contradictions of a rogue state. The dreams of a non-sectarian society articulated by the Left have been replaced by the divisive rhetoric of those who now use religion and ethnicity to further divide our society.

As a rogue state continued to exploit its citizens, what we have had and still have is a nation too divided and distracted, a nation whose elite has been caught up in fighting so many little civil wars and squabbles that it has had no reserve energy to fight the larger war against the real enemy, the rogue state. As it rides rough-shod over its citizens, the Nigerian state leaves death and destruction in its wake. Rather than unite to confront it, its citizens continue to compose dirges in their vernaculars as they bury their dead, lamenting about marginalization. We now face the predicament of the axe and the forest trees, namely:

> The axe was felling the trees, and all the trees kept falling as the forest disappeared but the trees could not rebel against the man hewing them down because the trees said that the handle was one of them!

From independence till date, we have lived with horrible leadership, and we have excused the rogues on the grounds that they are our tribesmen, our fellow religionists, and that those who raise their voices are enemies of our tribe or religion. Unlike Frost's traveler, when we got to where the road diverged, we opted for the comfort of taking what seemed the easier road. Instead of the high road, in Michelle Obama's rendering, we took the low one. Choosing the road less travelled was too difficult. This is where we are now. So, what have been the consequences of these choices? It is to them that I now want to turn to very briefly.

The Colonial legacy and Independence

Before independence, the British tinkered with the system in a way and manner that literally sowed the seeds for our enduring conflict and convoluted history. We know of the anecdote that stated that had Nigerians disappeared, the colonial administrators in the north and south of Nigeria would have gone to war because of the intensity of their differences. We now know that the disparity in background, social status, and ideology meant that colonial administrators in the North and South had different and conflicting views about what the new nation would look like. It is clear that we became victims of these worldviews.

For example, in the area of education, the colonial officers in the North believed that education was meant to merely consolidate the stranglehold of the northern feudal classes over the masses of the people. Indeed, in 1922, when Barewa College was established, it was meant to educate those that the colonial administration considered would be the leaders of the north and Nigeria. Indirect rule as a system of government merely reinforced the powers of the Emirs, who appropriated residual powers from the colonial state especially in the areas of taxation, and used these to subjugate the non-Muslim communities.

In the South on the other hand, in 1834, almost one hundred years earlier, the Methodist Church established the first primary school in Badagry, and in 1859, the Church Missionary Society (CMS) established the first secondary school in Bariga, Lagos. Within that same period, inroads were being made in such areas of southern Nigeria as Efikland and Igboland. Thus, even before the British arrived, a local elite, primarily made up of descendants of the Liberian experiment, had emerged in the Lagos area. Missionary education, unlike the straitjacket impression that the colonial state sought to create in the North, had a more liberating, humanitarian, and egalitarian dimension. It was not only open to everyone, but was also presented as the means for breaking open the doors of the bastions of exclusion.

The British were determined to ensure the supremacy of the North in the new nation. They took three key steps to ensure that this happened. First, they decided on a regional system of government which was skewed to favour the North. Three quarters of the landmass was allocated to the areas of the northern part of the country that were coterminous with the boundaries of the Fulani caliphate, which the British themselves had overthrown. Second, the British closed their ears even to the realities of their own investigations through the 1958 Willinks Commission, and refused to acknowledge the loud cries from the minorities for the creation of a Middle Belt Region. Third, they offered independence, but only on the terms that were agreeable to the North. Thus, whereas the South, represented by the young Anthony Enahoro, wanted independence in 1956, the British opted to accept the proposition of the North, that independence would be, *as soon as it is feasible!* The agitations were renewed after independence. With the Tiv riots (1962), and the political crises in the western region (1965), the coups of 1966 and 1977 threw the country inexorably into the cauldron of a civil war whose details should be the subject of a different project. Was there another road to be taken? Well, the military thought so and it is to them that we shall now turn.

Enter the Military: Paradise Postponed

The wheels of the new nation had barely begun to turn when the vehicle hit a major gulley: the military coup of January 15th, 1966. The new nation would then go into a tailspin, dragged into a corrosive system that would prove to be worse than the colonial state it had just come out of. Military intervention coincided with the rise in the commercial value of oil, which had been discovered in the Niger Delta region of the country before independence. The sweet taste of crude money whetted the appetite of the military elite, who then proceeded to destroy the foundation of democracy and institutionalize a military command structure.

This is not the time or place to review the consequences and impact of military rule on the life of the nation. Seduced by the notion of the choice of a lesser evil, the military was often welcomed as heroes, messiahs that were praised for sacking a corrupt civilian administration. The accusations against the civilian regimes were often based on unproven claims of massive corruption, with the military promising to rid the country of the cancer of corruption. As it turned out, successive military regimes proved that their cure was worse than the disease they came to treat. The best place to look for the broken truths is in the speeches of the successive military coup plotters.

The speeches themselves illustrate very clearly a simplistic perception of changes in the society, a limited understanding of the complex issues of managing diversity and governance. What we find in the speeches is repetition of catalogues of the mess created either by their predecessors in the military or civilian governments. An exhausted citizenry, tired and pained by the chaotic state of things, would time and time again buy into these ill-thought-out speeches which promised social and welfare services, only to discover that they had been duped. Curiously, these speeches would all end with an appeal to the citizens to stay tuned to their radios for further announcements, showing clearly that the coup plotters had no agenda and no idea what they would do next. The motivation for coups was never as patriotic or as forward looking as the planners would make them out to be. They were largely cases of settling old scores or serving sectional class interests.

For example, when Major Nzeogwu came on January 15th, 1966, he said in his speech that he and his colleagues had come to "…get rid of those who took bribes and demand ten percent.…those who seek to keep the country permanently divided so that they can remain in office…we promise that you will no longer be ashamed to say that you are Nigerians". When a revenge coup was staged in 1967, it was to correct or avenge the severely strained events that had rocked the foundation of the country. In his speech of May 1967, General Gowon, the Head of State, decided on the creation of twelve states in order to avert a civil war. In his speech, Buhari stated that: "We have now reached a most critical phase where what is at stake is the very survival of Nigeria as one political and economic unit". His efforts towards saving the country as one unit did not succeed as the nation ended up in war.

Sadly, after the war, the military did not return to the barracks. Instead, an extensive economic development program was put in place, along with a post war rehabilitation program, which came to be known as the three Rs (*Reconstruction, Rehabilitation,* and *Reconciliation*) and which got buried in military ambition. The Gowon regime decided to shift the goal posts only to invite another coup, which came to correct the mistakes. The military dug in their heels.

When Buhari came in 1983, he said that the new government "…will not tolerate kickbacks, inflation of contracts and over invoicing of imports. It will not condone forgery, embezzlement, misuse and abuse of power". When he himself was overthrown, General Babangida lamented that, "it turned out that Major General Buhari was too rigid and uncompromising in his attitude to issues of national significance. Efforts to make him understand that a diverse polity like Nigeria required recognition and appreciation of differences in both cultural and individual perceptions, only served to aggravate these attitudes".

And on and on the military coup plotters went, telling tales to a naïve nation and citizens too dazed to see through the deceit. It is interesting that even by 1997 with the last coup that was foiled, the controversial Diya coup, a text of the proposed speech against the Abacha regime had planned to make the same claims to justify the reasons why the military had come again, reasons based on accusations against the Abacha government, and promises to do better.

Looking back, we can see that frustrations within the military had produced a culture of coups, intense infighting, and corruption within the institution. The more the coups were staged, the weaker and divided the military institution became. By way of counter-penetration, civilian influence began to play a significant role in military interventions. Regional, traditional, religious, economic, and social class interests held sway as these elite groups often funded military interventions to either forestall the erosion or the preservation of the influences of these groups. The end result was that a more divided, distracted, fractured, and confused military severely became a threat to national cohesion.

The sense of a national security apparatus was lost, thus opening the country up to the multiple stabs from aggrieved sectional, national, and international interests. More or less, this is the story of Nigeria today. As I said earlier, it is a sad story of an accumulation of lies, half-truths, and of subterfuge; of fractured hopes, like the jagged edges of broken bottles. The idea that today, semi illiterate and illiterate herdsmen have held the country to ransom under the Boko Haram insurgency and the endless killings across the country suggests how low we have sunk in the quality of our security systems and in terms of levels of cohesiveness in our society. An aggregate of these is what constitutes what I call "broken truths". By way of conclusion, let us look at the prospects of the future.

Democracy and the Return to Purgatory

Looking back, we must ask the question, what has happened or not happened to us? To attempt to answer these questions, I will have an eye to the future, and to that extent my attention will now turn to the young men and women who are our future, that is, our graduates on whose behalf we have all gathered here today. The younger generation must learn from our horrible mistakes—the hypocrisy, the deceit, and outright criminality—which has passed for governance in Nigeria.

With all its failures, our nation has survived three most critical threats to the very foundations of our Democracy. First was in 2000, when a few disgruntled Northern politicians took their hypocrisy to a very high level by declaring that they wanted the northern states to sign on to Islamic law.

Their hypocrisy was soon exposed, but not before it had produced all the ingredients of a military coup. The waywardness of that period merely validated what most Nigerians considered to be the misguided views expressed by Col. Gideon Orkar in 1990. As we recall, in his speech, Col. Orkar threatened to excise the core Muslim northern states from Nigeria, a move that Nigerians stood firmly against. Sadly, these hypocritical Northern Muslim governors and politicians exposed the limitations of the manipulation of religion. Happily, their political chivalry soon turned into a nightmare. Today, even in whispers, there is no mention of Sharia.

The second incident was after the death of Alhaji Umaru Yar'adua. The nation waited in bated breath for months, as we did not know whether the President was dead or alive. This period of uncertainty was a perfect excuse for a coup to protect Northern interests. Happily, the nation held on and the political class was able to find a solution to the problem.

Thirdly and finally was the election of 2015. There were many powerful forces that did not want President Jonathan to concede the elections. Again, it would have been easy to call in the military, but yet, our nation held on. So, on paper, we can say that Nigerians have signed on to the prospects of democracy as the best form of government to ensure national cohesion. The challenge is to accept its intricacies.

In her book, "Democracy: Stories from the Long Road to Freedom", Professor Condoleezza Rice, the former US Secretary of State, makes the point quite eloquently when she said: "Every Democracy is flawed at its inception. And, indeed, no Democracy ever becomes perfect. The question is not one of perfection but how an imperfect system can survive, move forward and grow stronger". The challenge for us, as I see it, is how to first appreciate that no system is perfect, and secondly find the way to best work through the challenges and improve the imperfections that are inherent in all human institutions.

3. The Road towards National Cohesion

So, how should imperfect mortals use an imperfect system to hold together and achieve national cohesion? I propose a few ideas that are not new.

First, if we accept that democracy is hard work on an imperfect system, then we need discipline and deep knowledge of what it is. So far, it seems that between the operators and the people, there is very little understanding of what democracy really is. A friend of mine who had served as a two-time governor of his state told me that in his view, and from interacting with his fellow governors, barely 30% of his colleagues had an idea about what their assignments were as governors. So, we must take very seriously the issue of the quality of people participating in this process and their pedigree.

Second, and arising from this, is the urgent need for us to create rules of engagement and a process of leadership recruitment. The literature on China, Europe and the United States of America, where democracy has matured, suggests that there is no way anyone can surprise the system. In China and all these Democracies, a certain degree of learning, experience and exposure are often basic requirements. Compare that with our system, where only the president or governor knows who among his cronies will succeed him.

Third, there is the need for a system that has what I will call, for want of a better expression, some level of ambiguity, tentativeness, and even uncertainty built into it. For example, one of the greatest sources of excitement for the FIFA World Cup is not so much the quality of play, though that is very important, but the uncertainty as to its final outcome. Our appetite is whetted by this uncertainty, and that is why we sit glued to the screens. Today, most coaches have learned to respect every team, saying there are no more small teams in the World Cup. Since it follows that only the best is good enough, everyone knows that it is hard work, not luck, connections, godfathers or prayer, which guarantees victory. Compare this with our Democracy, in which only those in power know whom they will rig into power to cover up their soiled footsteps.

Remember that General Babangida said that even though he did not know who would succeed them, he knew those who would not succeed them!

Imagine a young Nigerian seeking a job in an environment where every outcome is already predetermined. Today, recruitments and promotions in almost every spectrum of the public service under federal, state, and local governments, depend on whom you know not what you know. We claim to maintain high standards while ensuring everyone gets a chance in the society, but this cannot be practiced in such a morally despicable manner as we have in Nigeria. When access to the most sensitive positions in public life is based on family connections, outright barefaced and shameless nepotism, or religious and ethnic considerations, our nation is doomed. Loyalties in the security services, the bureaucracy, and so on are to those who got us in, not to the nation. You can understand why every nerve and bone of the nation is so weakened today.

Fourth, there is need for the university communities to become bastions of integrity. The university community must return to its preeminent high post of being the citadel of learning. Its prestige can only be returned if it focuses on research and academic excellence, rather than being distracted by the filthy lucre of politics and intrigues from politicians. To be sure, the academia must support politics, but this support must be based on its capacity to generate fresh ideas and to produce evidence-based research to assist policy makers. We need to identify, recruit, and retain the best. A culture of mentoring and raising the bar for intellectualism is an urgent proposition. This was the academic tradition before the military and politicians lured and lowered the bar for the primacy of academia.

Fifth, there is the dragon of corruption who has defied all the armies and the coup plots, who has subdued, converted, and tamed those who set out to conquer it. As we saw in the speeches of the coup plotters, fighting corruption has become the eternal vote catcher for Nigerian politicians, and the means of validating any military coup. However, the hard and sad fact is that corruption is everywhere and, like the mark of Cain, will remain with human systems always. There is no need for grand standing about ending corruption. The immune system of a giant can withstand a mosquito bite, but not that of a child. Corruption exists everywhere in the world and, sorry to say, in an invidious way, it is part and parcel of what drives development. At the White House, Downing Street, the Elysees Palace, Wall Street; everywhere, it lurks in the corner.

Chapter Eight | Matthew Hassan Kukah

It is just a question of the deodorant or pesticide that is used to control it and limit its extent and its effect.

Presidents Nixon, Hollande, Netanyahu, and Zuma, the whole lot, have had to deal with corruption allegations in various ways. And the deodorant used is a functional system that works and has enough mechanisms of restraint. The strategy for fighting corruption is not erected on the altars of high moral exhortations, but on the laboratory of scientific discoveries where technology provides the structures that are no respecters of persons or classes. This is where the academic community must take the lead by massive scientific research.

Finally, to return to where we started, we have expressed concerns over the fabrication of lies and half-truths that have characterized leadership in Nigeria by way of speeches and promises. Today, this country is on a moral free fall because no institution or instrument seems to command overarching loyalty: the Constitution does not; the courts do not; the security agencies do not; the bureaucracy does not; and citizens do not trust their leaders to act on their behalf. What we have is a nation where institutions which command loyalty elsewhere have been reduced to empty shells. An aggregate of these doubts make national cohesion impossible and unachievable.

4. Conclusion: The Seed of the Future is You

To end, let me refer you back to the beginning of my address. You will remember I mentioned broken truths, and then lamented how the truth-tellers were withered and their vines with them. And how a professional military turned cancer and began to feast on the carcass it had made of what was its mission to protect, splintering even further notions of truth and cohesiveness. You will also remember that I adduced some steps to redressing this monstrous effect.

Only one thing is left to say: to the young women and men of the University of Jos graduating class of 2018, I would like to congratulate every single one of you, God's children all of you, whether male or female, Muslim or Christian, whether Berom, Anaguta, Angas, Fulani, Junkun, Igbo, Ikulu, Yoruba or any of the 500 tribes and languages in our great country. And I leave you with a question and a message.

The question is this: Who will write the truth of this great country as well as right the wrongs of its past leaders? Who, please, tell me? Is she here? Is he present?

As for the message—you have worked hard and long and done what was required of you by the school and its administrators, and that is why you are here today, dressed in gown and mortarboard. You have done what is expected of you, but sometimes it looks like your country and its leaders do not do what you expect of them. You believe in your hearts and minds that the future is yours, just as this country is, although they don't act like they know it, and although you don't act like you know it either. And so, you are timid, and you whisper among yourselves, or you are excited at the passing of a "Not too Young to Run" Bill. I remember the late great Fela Anikulapo Kuti singing, 'Human rights na my property; So therefore, you can't dash me my property".

But I know the future is yours, and this country also, and that is the most pertinent thing I am here to tell you today. And I know something else: the leaders of today dominated and ruled the affairs of this country in their time, and it seems that they seek to dominate and rule the affairs of this country in your time also. It seems that they have forgotten that you exist, or even that the country they supposedly serve is yours. They seem to have buried you and deprived you of a mouth, a mind, and a future. The frustration of it is enough to want to swallow you whole or make you despair; but do not lose hope, and do not despair.

Decades ago, a Greek poet named Dinos Christianopoulos wrote a line, which resonates today still: "What didn't you do to bury me, but you forgot I was a seed".

On this note, I want to end with a little bit of history. Scripture says, "unless a seed falls and dies, it cannot bear fruit". During the First World War (1914-1918), between 20 and 30 million lives were lost. Two years later, the world powers created the League of Nations on January 10th, 1920. The Second World War (1939-1945) claimed between 80 and 100 million people. Barely one month after it ended, the United Nations was born on October 24th, 1945. By December 10th, 1948, in Paris, the world powers officially ratified the Universal Human Rights Declaration, a life changing decision that acknowledges the equality of *all* of God's children.

My dear graduates, you are stepping into a country that is at war with itself. However, reconstructing that world is your challenge, and each of you here has the right weapons to bring about that change. Your certificate is more than a thousand armoured tanks. A single one of you with a certificate is worth more than a thousand bandits, murderers, and assassins, by whatever name they are called.

Let me paraphrase some wise words I stumbled upon a long time ago:

A catapult and a stone in my hands can only frighten a little bird. But in the hands of Moses, it killed Goliath. It depends on whose hands it is in.

A tennis racquet in my hands might hit a ball across a net. But, a tennis racquet in the hands of Serena Williams is worth millions of dollars. It depends on whose hands it is in.

A soccer ball before me is nothing more than an inflated leather. But, in the feet of Ronaldo or Messi, it is worth millions of dollars. It depends on whose feet it is before.

A certificate from the University of Jos is perhaps just a piece of paper. But with it, Yakubu Dogara is now the Speaker of the Federal Republic of Nigeria.

It depends on whose hands it is in.

So, my friends, let your certificates be your road map. With them, you can form the strongest army in the world and conquer all the herdsmen and women in the world. With it, you can defeat their sponsors. With your certificate, you can cross any ocean, climb any mountain and make the sky only a stepping-stone to your dreams. The future is before you, a wide-open frontier of possibilities. Go ahead, conquer it, and create a new, peaceful, and just Nigeria. Fear not, the good Lord is ahead of you. God bless you. Help create a new, united, just, and strong Nigeria where no broken truths exist. Thank you very much for your attention.

Convocation Lecture, University of Jos, June 22, 2018

CHAPTER NINE

Some Reasons Why Nigeria Has Failed To Achieve Greatness

Foundations once destroyed, what can the righteous do? (Ps. 11: 3)

Let me first congratulate Dr. Bode Ayorinde, Pro-Chancellor and Chairman of Council of this august university and thank you immensely for the honor of being invited to give the convocation lecture and to also receive an Honorary Doctorate Degree from your institution. I was pleased to note that the University grew out of the frustration of the people of Owo on being bypassed on four different occasions when federal and state universities were cited in parts of the South-west way back in 1962. I also noted that even when Owo's favorite son, the late Chief Adekunle Ajasin, founded the first state university in Nigeria, very much against the run of play he did not locate it in his hometown. We are therefore thankful to God that Dr. Bode Ayorinde seized the initiative and has accomplished what both the Federal and State Governments were unable to do for the people of Owo. I join my other awardees in advance to congratulate him and, as I said when I wrote a tribute to Aare Afe Babalola, just next door in Ekiti, it is true that with the right nutrients, one tree can really make a forest!

You stated in your letter of invitation that my nomination was born out of what you called my commitment to societal ideals, leadership qualities, and my contributions towards peaceful co-existence and national cohesion. On this, you scored a bull's eye because I am ideologically convinced that the fight against corruption, building infrastructure, trying to take our people out of poverty, and a range of other government ideals, would all amount to what the lawyers refer to as placing something on nothing if there is not a united country!

The theme of national cohesion has run through many of my lectures. I went back and looked at a few titles of my previous convocation lectures across Nigerian universities and I will cite just three to illustrate my point. At the convocation lecture in the University of Nigeria, Nsukka, the title of my lecture was: "After the Insurgency: Some Thoughts on National Cohesion" (March 27th, 2014). On

February 24th, 2017, my convocation lecture for the University of Abuja was entitled: "Though Tribe and Tongue May Differ: Managing Diversity in Nigeria". Only last year, on June 22nd, 2018, at the University of Jos, my convocation lecture was entitled: "Broken Truths: Nigeria's Illusive Quest for National Cohesion".

Strange as it may sound, I have never felt the need to correct or change my reflections expressed in those previous lectures and, therefore, I am not sure whether I should feel a sense of vindication or am a victim of repetition. However, I strongly believe that the problems of Nigeria will, in the final analysis, be resolved within the Nigerian University System. In other words, if we lose the intellectual argument, we cannot hope to build a country. It is my belief that statecraft lies within the realm of ideas generated by intellectuals and not by vendors of moral claims.

When I accepted to deliver today's lecture, I reflected and concluded that I would like to examine the theme of Nigeria's low level of performance. My intention in this lecture is to identify only five out of the hundreds of reasons why our country has not achieved greatness. I wish to speak briefly about each of these five reasons, not by order of any importance. I am hopeful that I will simply generate ideas and hope that the lecturers and students can continue the debate in the lecture and seminar halls of the University.

1. Fractured Tongues and Broken Memories

To be sure, a lot of Nigerians have attributed our problems to what they call the "mistake of 1914", or the idea that Nigeria was a mere geographical expression. As such, in moments of frustration and anger, people have tended to simply say, well, let every group go its way because we were never meant to be one country in the first place.

On this matter, which I refer to as "fractured tongues", I argue that our differences should be an asset not a liability. Rather than work to pull these threads of differences into a beautiful mosaic, our leaders have often sought halfhearted solutions, more out of ignorance than malice. Lacking in the art of statecraft, at the level of geopolitics, we have been set against one another, divided into factions and fractions, through the creation of new states, Local Councils, and new cultural spaces (Chieftaincies). Thus, wherever the pieces fell from this balkanization, new identities and new animosities that emerged as yesterday's victims became today's oppressors. Many great Nigerians grew up, attended the same institutions with people of other tribes and religions, and had big dreams for our country, but found themselves forced to retreat to the womb of ethnicity, religion or region. Today, national cohesion is in retreat, as every community is now a nation with its own anthem and flag.

Every country in the world is a work in progress, and if border issues are still not on the table, new identities based on economics, history, or culture emerge that are daily being contested. Those who created Nigeria did not foresee globalisation in the shape and form of competing, counter penetrating, and contending identities as we have today. The challenge today is not the boundaries of geography but the spread of ideas and knowledge, and of course memory is a source of knowledge.

On the issue of broken memories, I remind us that history is about memory, and we all remember even the same incidents differently depending on experiences and circumstances. In 2018, our internationally renowned historian, Professor Obaro Ikime, emeritus Professor of History, University of Ibadan, called attention to this dilemma with a publication provocatively titled: "Can Anything Good Come out of History?" He rang the alarm bells by recalling that as far back as 1987, he had chaired a team of moderators who looked at the questions set for the Joint Admission Matriculation Examinations in 1987, and discovered that right across the entire country, only 8,000 candidates had offered History!

Our situation got progressively worse when the government itself decided to remove History from the syllabus. Strange as it may sound, I do not recall that the Historical Society of Nigeria rose up against this decision nor did it seriously consider putting down tools in protest. Today, we have paid the supreme price; even as the subject has crawled back, it is not getting the attention it deserves.

This is not the time or place to examine when or where we took the wrong turn. Before the novelists came to the fore, our Historians were at the forefront of putting out some of the most distinguished accounts, interpretations, and re-interpretations of the cultures, histories, and legacies of our people. They gave us a new way of looking at ourselves. How could we have forgotten that this country holds the record for churning out some of the most brilliant historians on the African continent? Who can forget the extraordinary scholarship of people like Professors Dike, JF Ayandele, Tekena Tamuno, Nzimiro, Eskor Toyo, Obaro Ikime, Bala Usman, Mahmud Tukur, Monday Mwangvat, EJ Alagoa, Anthony Asiwaju, Elizabeth Isichei, B. Barkindo and perhaps, the greatest of them all, my dear friend, Professor Toyin Falola. Had there been a Nobel Prize for History, Professor Falola should have taken it a long time ago.

Without History, a nation navigates without a compass and memory becomes subjective. Today, Nigerian youth are total strangers to their own local, cultural, or national history. Ask a young person where they come from and they say, "Daddy said we are from Owo". Too many of our youth have no sense of ownership of their narratives. No nation can develop in ignorance of its past.

2. Multiple Colonialisms and Consequences

Citizens of what is now modern Nigeria carry the burdens of the legacies of multiple colonialisms, namely feudal colonialism (e.g., the Sokoto caliphate, Benin or Oyo empires), British colonialism, and military colonialism. All these forms of colonialisms were characterized by force, violence, domination, and the imposition of new cultures, altered identities, and legacies. An appreciation of this is fundamental to appreciating Nigeria's state of stasis, anomie, and stagnation, and why national cohesion remains so elusive. Very little has been done to purify memory and create a united narrative for our people. The result is that we remain victims, creating counter narratives of historical injustices etc. The legacies of ethnic hegemonies arising from the Benin or Oyo Empires, for example, are extant and, in some cases, still culturally felt. The same cannot be said of the Sokoto caliphate, British colonialism and military rule, whose scars are still visible. Whereas the impact and influence of secular and ethnic empires tended to be largely cultural, the Sokoto caliphate and British colonialism combined religion, state capture, power, and domination. Their impact and dominance still hover over the polity.

While the British oversaw the growth and development of their empire through resource extraction, forced labor and extreme taxation, the Fulanis as junior partners had their Emirate system adopted as a form of administration across the north while deriving economic benefits to run their Emirates. Immediately after independence, confronting this injustice would form the bedrock of the politics of, for example, Mallam Aminu Kano's Northern Elements' Progressive Union (NEPU), framed around the theme of liberation of the oppressed, Talakawa. This resistance and contestation laid the foundation for the development of the radical tradition in Northern Nigeria. Students of

Nigerian politics might recall that the first thing that the two states of Kano and Kaduna did under NEPU was to abolish the *Jangali* cattle tax across the two states!

The succeeding elite had barely settled down when the military struck. That single event set a chain reaction across the new country. The ripple effects have not died down till date, not to mention the fact that we still have military presidents in power! The military that staged coups was not a foreign army. Tragically, thoroughly ill equipped to govern, having no ideological slant towards negotiation and consensus, the military soon threw the country into a civil war. Even after war, the military dug its heels into politics and destroyed the foundations of law and order. Till date, this legacy still accounts for the deep fractures and fissures on the polity. Digging deep into these legacies and their consequences is fundamental to understanding our state of disequilibrium.

3. The De-legitimation of Democracy

Military rule bred uncertainty and indiscipline because there were no term limits, no training, no transparency, and no institutions of accountability or clear process of recruitment. Whoever pulled the gun first qualified to take over the reins of power. The coup culture institutionalized opportunism and subversion of process, thus constituting the worst form of corruption. No qualification was required for any office including that of the President or Head of State. We may recall, even though Col Dimka did not seem to know the difference between times of the day (remember the coup speech that suspended movement from dawn to dusk!), he could still have become our head of state. The legacy explains why our elections are often a coup by other means (recall the heavy military presence on election days or the remaking of the judiciary).

It is important, therefore, that we understand why our journey from military rule to democracy has been such a herculean task. Whereas democracy sees opposition as a value, an asset, the military sees it as an evil, an enemy to be destroyed. Democracy is about process, discipline, order, education, vision, freedom, values, and accountability. Democracy is about consensus, persuasion, appeal to reason, and managing diversity of expression and association for individuals and groups. This is why, even with its imperfections, democracy is seen as the best system of government for ensuring equitable development.

Chapter Nine | Matthew Hassan Kukah

When Nigerians say that corruption is killing us, they are mistaking the symptom for the disease. The lack of openness and freedom during military rule or any dictatorship severely compromises governance. As the world-renowned Indian scholar and winner of the Nobel Prize in Economics (1998), Professor Amartya Sen, would say, without freedom there can be no development for individuals and community. The inability in Nigeria to allow the free flow of ideas and channel individual and collective efforts, creates a culture of selfish pursuit and monopoly of power without responsibility. In response, the citizens succumb to the philosophy of "Everyone for himself and God for us all". This is why corruption is ubiquitous and now, strangely, seems to be the only thing that works in Nigeria. This is why we cannot summon enough moral courage to end it. When Mr. or Mrs. Integrity is wheeled to power by the proceeds of corruption or the corrupt, Mr. or Mrs. Integrity is corrupt by association! All he or she has done is to outsource corruption to a third party.

4. Lack of Political Culture, Vision and Goals

Nigerians continue to wonder why it is that all governments over time have continued to look the same, and why they leave us the same legacy of frustration and regret. For example, in the heat of the collective national euphoria that greeted his coup on December 31st, 1981, Ghanaians baptized Flt. Lt. JJ Rawlings as "Junior Jesus". Midway, in their frustration when they discovered he was not the Messiah, they renamed him "Junior Judas"!

Why do we followers succumb to what I call the disease of Israel? You recall that when faced with the hardships in the desert, the people of Israel became nostalgic of their chains of slavery in Egypt. Reminiscing about Egypt, they said: "We sat around pots of meat and ate bread to the full...We remember the fish and the cucumbers, leeks, onions and garlic" (Ex. 16:3, Numb. 11:5). In our case in Nigeria, how often do we hear, "Oh, under Abacha, the Naira was stable, under Obasanjo, we knew where we stood, or under Jonathan, a bag of rice was 9,000 naira at least". So, what shall we say tomorrow when President Buhari is gone? The delusion of our messianic search is part of our frustration.

Military coups disrupted and destroyed the basis for the emergence of political culture. A political culture is a set of more or less immutable laws even if un-written; they guide conduct and behavior in the political arena. Political culture relates to processes, rules of engagement and fair play, bilateral expectations that all actors play by the same rules. When imbibed, political culture guides our expectations and prepares us to access that there is another day, that only one person can win, that we must live to fight again without bitterness, and that elections are not a war and politics is a game. The do or die in our politics are clear indicators of the death of political culture.

The lack of a political culture sows the seeds for prebendalism and clientelism, where godfathers make their own rules or seek to compromise existing institutions like the Judiciary, the Electoral Body or the security agencies. Politicians with no political culture see politics as a distribution agency. They hide their incapacity, incompetence, and inefficiency under the table by appealing to ethnic, regional, and religious evangelism, thus further dividing our people along these lines. This is one of the reasons why, for us in Nigeria, national cohesion and development have become dreams deferred.

5. Lack of National Monument-Heroes-Totem-Constitution

Ours is a nation with no national heroes. Our heroes are unable to cross the boundaries of our ethnicity, regionalism, or religion. The nation has no Fidel Castro, no Nelson Mandela, no Abraham Lincoln, no Pandit Nehru, no Mahatma Gandhi, and no Winston Churchill. A culture of relativism means if you call the name of prominent Nigerians, they will have to go back to their region or ethnic enclave to command respect. Thus, Awolowo is leader of the Yoruba, Azikiwe for the Igbos, Sardauna for the Hausa-Fulani North, Tarka for the Tiv, and so on down the line. Often, a leader is hoisted on a national pole by party fanatics, hypocrites, and sycophants with the sobriquet of *Baba*, as long as they are on the throne. No sooner do their tenures end than they are sent back home with no more title of reverence.

As a corollary, Nigeria has no monuments, no totems and its Constitution still remains suspect and inspires little confidence even from those who operate it. The Constitution should be our sacred secular text and should command awe. We see executive lawlessness at the highest level with disobedience of court orders and appointment to the Judiciary the subject of political maneuver.

Today, what would have passed even as national or regional monuments are all in various stages of decomposition: Tafawa Balewa and Tinubu Squares, the National Theatre, the National Stadia across the country, the Niger Bridge, Cocoa House etc. The country has no sacred spaces which can metaphorically serve as places where citizens can mourn, celebrate or look back and ask if the dreams of the nation have been sustained or betrayed.

In the United Kingdom, they have Hyde Park Corner, Big Ben, Tower Bridge, the London Eye etc. In the United States of America, the Lincoln Memorial and Arlington Memorials, the Statue of Liberty, the Washington Monument and a host of iconic institutions command the awe and respect of citizens. In China, they have the Great Wall, the Terra Cotta Warriors, The Forbidden City, The Guangzhou Tower, and China's incredible bridges spanning over so many miles. In Paris, France, you can see the Louvre Museum, the Eiffel Tower and so on. The Vatican has St. Peter's Basilica and Square, the Museum, or the Sistine Chapel.

Apart from being imprinted in the minds of the young and inspiring citizens to greatness, or serving as places of cohesion, can you imagine the billions of dollars that these countries have continued to reap from these monuments and the millions of citizens from around the world who troop to these countries every year as tourists? Can you think of a single place in Nigeria where the Local, State, or Federal Government collects a single Naira, not to talk of dollars, from tourists – even enough to buy a generator? In contrast, the Vatican Museum attracts over 20,000 visitors on a daily basis, every day of the year.

A history of the triumph and sacrifices of the military in American life is celebrated through the Arlington Memorial. Built in 1864, it has a total of almost 500,000 graves. The Memorial is one of the most beautiful, scenic, picturesque, breathtaking sights I have ever seen. It conjures up emotions even for the stranger and visitor to the United States by the sheer idyllic architecture and layout. It is a piece of history in memory of those who have, over the years, from the War of Independence, died in the cause of wars across the world. Every year on May 25th, America marks Memorial Day and evokes memories of pain, sorrow, joy and hope, and the knowledge that it is the sacrifices of those buried there that has kept the country strong. America uses this history to romanticize valor and patriotism. This is what has inspired them to the feeling of invincibility.

Think about us in Nigeria. Where is the nation's military cemetery and who remembers anything about it? Nigeria has no memory. Apart from the tomb of the so-called "unknown soldier", which only appears on television when the president of the day is laying a wreath, I am not aware of anything that the Nigerian government, despite being ruled by military heads of state and presidents, has done to evoke emotions in Nigerians regarding the sacrifices of those who have given or risked their lives for our nation. National cohesion arises from deep, intangible emotional symbols that inspire us.

6. The Power of One

I want to end by reflecting on what I call the "Power of One". How many people do we need to effect change in a society? How do the great men or women of history come about? What inspired them? Was it in the genes or by divine providence? History is replete with men and women who have risen to prominence and have assumed a larger than life stature in our memories. Very often, we marvel, we believe that God made them special and that their greatness is one of those things that happen only to a few selected ones.

Yes, our lives are a vocation and yes, like little Samuel, we get a call and we often refer an Eli to guide, one who can interpret God's will to us by directing us to say, "Speak Lord, your servant is listening". However, the Bible tells us that God has no photocopies and that we are therefore all originals, made in the image and likeness of God. We will not all be Martin Luther King, Nelson Mandela, Pope John Paul II, or Mother Theresa. There will only be one Mohammed Ali, one Pele, Lionel Messi, or one Abraham Lincoln. Some will be great composers while others will be great listeners or dancers.

God created us for a purpose and a meaning in life. He is the Lord of History and time. However, for us Nigerians, God has become the greatest excuse for the inefficiency, corruption, and shameful degrading life of our people today. We are over 90% Christians and Muslims in Nigeria, but there is nowhere in the world where religion has become an incubus, a burden, and a source of dreadful violence as it has in Nigeria. Our leaders are constantly kneeling before pastors and imams seeking blessings while the rest of the world is moving on, drawing inspiration from sweat, brains, and brawn without evoking God. We, on the other hand, evoke God to witness to our corruption and outright larceny.

In Nigeria, government is the major source of wealth and power. Someone undertook an analysis of the billionaires of Nigeria. Surveying 47 billionaires, the study shows that the source of wealth of Group One, made up of 24 members of the list, made their money from using public office. Group Two is made up of 10 members who made their money from being close to those in power (beneficiaries of humungous contracts, oil deals, subsidies etc.). Group Three is made up of those who made their money from industrial activities and run real businesses with no obvious linkage to those in power. Group Four is made up of those who are smart but whose source of wealth is said to be hazy, grey, and undefined.

Today, Africa has over 400 million young people whose futures seem to hang on a balance. There are over 700 million people out of Africa's 1.2 billion people who have no access to electricity, water, or food. Africa is full of challenges and too many stories of tears and pain. However, as the Holy Book says of Esther, perhaps it was for a time like this that we have prophets for the future like the founder of your university, Chief Ayo Ayorinde. Nations are built on the shoulders and visions of great men or women like him. What has held Nigeria down has been the strong power grip that the center has had on the resources of Nigeria, a hold that those who run our country have used rather irresponsibly.

Yes, it is important that our country opens up to business. However, it seems to me that so much effort is being made to make Nigeria an attractive bride often to the detriment of our local professionals and contractors. We have remained on the same spot of potentiality for too long, with a landscape littered with thousands of abandoned projects. Some parts of the country often look like a post war environment with the litter of abandoned projects. Surely, Aliko Dangote and Tony Elumelu must have junior brothers or cousins. The gap is far too wide for smaller competitors. Most of this is because the adrenalin of the politicians is often high when it comes to serving as middlemen and fixers, often sabotaging their countries in the name of oversight.

We seem to have outsourced the development of our country to foreign partners. Yesterday we were in China looking for help, today we are in Russia and Saudi Arabia. I stumbled on a list of activities by foreign countries and companies, thus raising the question as to what the future of our local industries and businesses is in the eyes of the federal government. It reads thus:

Russia is to build rail tracks for Nigeria. China is to build roads and bridges. India is to help Nigeria with its ICT. Germany is to build new power plants. The US is to provide Nigeria with vaccines. The UNDP is providing grants to farmers and improved seedlings. Bill and Melinda Gates are helping us fight malaria. President Jimmy Carter helped us to dig latrines and fight hookworms. Turkey is planning to build a garment factory in Nigeria. The UK wants to build a new terminal in the Niger Delta. So, what are we doing for ourselves? Where do our thousands of excellent engineers fit in designing our future?

Finally, on your behalf, and on behalf of your parents, we thank Chief Ayorinde and all those he inspired to invest in this university. I salute all those great individuals across Nigeria who are daily investing in education and other areas of life. The honor you graduates owe your parents and the founders of this university is hard work and achievement.

As Nigerians, we are not made up of only *Muslims* or *Christians, Men* or *Women, Rich* or *Poor, Happy* or *Sad, Young* or *Old.* We are citizens with different tastes and different convictions even within these same categories. There is so much more to define each one of us. What matters is not who your parents or your tribe are, or where your town is, but what you can make out of the talents God has given you. Your name is already written on God's palm (Is. 49:16). Don't try to cut corners. The road to success is often long and hard. It is often the road less travelled, but it is the most rewarding one.

My dear graduates, I appeal to you, throw away the oppressive and tyrannical yoke and petard hung around your necks by our generation. Being an alumnus of Achievers University is the surest way to enable you swim successfully in the ocean of life. The choice is yours; remain locked in the dark abyss of ethnicity and religion or liberate yourself. Armed with your certificate, listen to what the Holy Book says: "Stand at the crossroads and look, ask for the ancient paths, ask where the good way is, walk in it" (Jer. 6: 16). And, as Rumi said: "It's your road and yours alone. Others may walk with you, but no one can walk it for you". God bless you.

8th & 9th Convocation Lecture, Achievers University, Owo, Ondo State, 8 November 2019

CHAPTER TEN

Nigeria: What Time Is It & Where Are We?

Introduction

P ressure from the Vice Chancellor made me hurriedly come up with a title as strange as this! However, it is a title that gives rise to many thoughts, particularly so as we look at our world, and more specifically, our nation, today.

The notion of time is philosophy or sociology. Time naturally means different things to different people. It generates different levels of adrenalin in each of us depending on the occasion. A long time with a loved one can seem so short. A short time with an enemy could seem like eternity. A winning team would wish to bring the time to an end, a losing team on the other hand would wish to borrow more time. Time generates different levels of anxiety for the hanged man or for the man waiting to hear the cry of his first baby. Perhaps in the end, the greatest definition of time is what the holy Bible said, that for everything, there is a time.

Julius Sevilla, an inspirational speaker on leadership, says that: "Time waits for no one, stops for no one. Excuses will not slow down time. Indecision will not slow down time. Complaints will not stall time. Regret will not turn back time. Don't waste your time in anger, regrets, worries or hate. Time will not turn around and cry along with you. It's time to let go of the past and stop worrying about the future. Your only time is now. So, make sure you spend your time with the right purpose, right deeds, right emotions, right thoughts and the right people. Time flies: You can. You will not pass this way again. Do what time does, keep moving."[62]

---

[62] https://www.youtube.com/watch?v=hOro8zP7sIY

I believe that a reflection on time is pertinent for a gathering such as this. For the graduates, your performance may have much to do with how well you used your time. For those who used it well, stay on that path because the future is waiting for you. For those who may not have done so well, remember that you still have time to re-set your clock if you want a happy life. For those just getting started, you have a chance to reflect on the road that lies ahead of you. How you use and manage your time will largely determine whether the investment being made by your parents pays off or not.

I use the concept of time largely as a metaphor for defining both identity and vision. Players and their team members must have a common sense and understanding of time. Equally so with actors in a film or play. Similarly, students and the university staff know that all things being equal, if you register for this or that course, both sides know when you should graduate. Imagine what chaos there would be if each student, department or faculty considered time differently from the university authorities. Imagine what would happen if passengers had a different understanding of time to the managers of the flight or train.

In the drama of life, each and every one of us is allotted time, and our ability to make or not make any contribution in life depends on how we manage this gift, this investment. Every individual, every generation, every society must appreciate what time it is, the challenges of the time, and figure out how to use it well. Today we reflect on what we did with the time of yesterday. Tomorrow will depend on what we make of today's time. Time is another word for the gift of life, an investment. The bank of time neither grants loans nor cancels debts. So, management of time is so central and critical that literally everything, success or failure in life, depends on its use.

In the next few minutes, I will not dwell on the philosophy of time, but reflect on how our country has used its own time. This of course sounds very ambitious. I wish to briefly look at what has happened to our own time, how is it that our dreams of yesterday seem to have turned into nightmares. I will argue that our inability to manage time is another word for what Onyeka Onwenu referred to a *squandering of riches*.[63] It is also almost akin to what the American intellectual referred to

---

[63] Onyeka Onwenu. (2018). *A Squandering of Riches*. Keni St George; British Broadcasting Corporation. Television Service.; Pennsylvania State University. Audio-Visual Services.

as scoundrel time, and Scripture refers to as the years consumed by the locusts. Whether we can salvage something out of all this, and pull out a few chestnuts from today's inferno, remains the challenge for our future.

1. Time, Moments for Nations: How telling Time became difficult in Nigeria

I believe that the first signs of our confusion with time arose from the synchronization of our African time with a new clock. To be sure, before colonialism, we can argue that we all had different clocks and used them differently as communities. We had no sense of urgency because everyone, individuals or communities, had their time and managed it as they wished. Traditional societies relied on a crystallization and interpretation of the intersection between terrestrial elements such as the state and position of the sun, moon, stars, shadows, or such neighbours as the cock.

There were no bells announcing that it was time for the farmer to head to his farm, nor was there a time for any farmer to return home. Communities however had an agreement on the times for the community festivals, market days, or meetings at the village square, for example. Community cohesion depended on a common understanding of duties and responsibilities of members of the community on the major issues.

However, the emergence of the modern state compelled us all to submit to a new sense of time with the emergence of the clock and calendar. The new clock now became the center and means of regulating all activities for the individual and his/her community. Metaphorically, and for nation building and progress, to attain a common sense of cohesion and act as a community, our nation's Constitution, our national anthem, and our common currency could now be referred to as some form of a clock, marking our sense of common purpose.

In other words, looking at the same clock and holding on to the same time on the clock, you could be punished or rewarded based on how each fulfilled or failed to fulfil their obligation to the rules surrounding time and its management. As we will see, confusion later set in because just after the British left, we all seem to have reacted differently to the concept of time. Goals, vision and a sense of national unity and common purpose began to change as different persons, groups, and institutions began to react differently to the dictates of a common clock. Even the titles of our novels would gradually suggest this: *Things Fall Apart, My Mercedes is Bigger than Yours, Born without a Silver Spoon, or The Famished Road.* In my view, the confusion we find ourselves in now is the visible manifestation of the fact that perhaps we may not all have had, or indeed still have, a common understanding of the clock and time.

We may recall the famous anecdote about how our founding fathers, the famous three, Nnamdi Azikiwe, Ahmadu Bello and Chief Awolowo, saw the future of the country after independence, namely, their sense of time. We tend to refer to the first generation of the political class as *founding fathers*, and I think this reads too much into our history. You cannot found what was already there. You can only found something whose vision only you possess. The British had founded and named what would later become Nigeria; they designed a political, social, and economic map for it. What those we call the founding fathers sought to do, and did, was to put pressure on the British to step aside and the British did that, not by conquest but on their own will and at their own time. As we all know, there was even no agreement among the three 'founding fathers' as to when the British should step aside.

Let me turn briefly to the story of the United States of America as a way of illustrating what founding fathers should look like. What today we call the American founding fathers were preceded by the Pilgrim Fathers, who set out from Europe in search of a new land to practice their faiths; a new land away from the oppression and persecution that they had experienced in Europe. In other words, they were looking for a place to *feel at home*, practice their faith freely, and live their lives as they believed. The settlers would later decide to bring an end to British colonial rule by way of war. They would still fight another war to decide what manner of country they would bring about, one that would enable them to live according to their convictions and principles. This is why the country would later be known as the *land of the brave and the free!* These founding fathers were culturally of the same world view. They were White, Anglo Saxon, and Protestant. These identities would later coalesce to become the categories of power in America captured in the acronym WASP (White Anglo Saxon Protestant).

If you compare this with our situation, the confusion begins to show very clearly why it is more important for us to be modest in our application of this term for our situation in Nigeria. Yes, like the American founding fathers, we were colonized, but unlike them, the colonized already had a solid ideological basis for being in the new lands which they had also taken over by conquering others. They had come to find and extract minerals and make profit. Theirs was an economic adventure that came when slavery ended. In the American case, the founding fathers raised a superior force, built an army, economy, and ideology that would surpass that of their colonizers. They conquered their oppressors and laid the foundation for a new and free nation based on its own new principles and ideology of freedom.

In our own case, our so-called founding fathers were hurriedly brought together, taken outside their own country and participated in a debate that they did not frame about the future of their country. They had no common vision of a country because their views were the views designed by the colonizers. Both Nnamdi Azikiwe and Awolowo had been exposed to the secular democracy of the West, whereas Ahmadu Bello had just come out of the womb of feudalism and an Islam inspired by the Arab world. Ahmadu Bello was a proud prince of the over one-hundred-year-old Caliphate which had been overthrown by the British. He was proud of his ancestry and unwilling to trade its values for the new values espoused by the British. Azikiwe and Awolowo, on the other hand, looked into a future framed through the lenses of a Western liberal worldview of modernity, individualism, progress, and freedom. Whereas Ahmadu Bello was no stranger to privilege, having come from an environment of slave holders, his counterparts came from a background that celebrated egalitarianism, success, and struggle.

On a broader note, Chief Awolowo's exposure to Fabianism and Azikiwe's exposure to the liberal culture of American democracy ensured a coincidence in their world view, but the same could not be said of the Sardauna. Hence, according to the famous anecdote, when Azikiwe suggested that they should *forget* their differences and unite to move the new nation forward towards a liberal Western worldview, the Sardauna suggested rather that they should *understand* these differences with his own face of Janus facing the opposite direction. The inability of these fathers to synchronise their clocks and agree on what time it was has haunted us and accounts for our seeming immobility.

It has led us to an internecine war and back. It has led us to several Constitutional Conferences. Despite all these initiatives we have not been brought together, but instead we have been inundated with the threatening clouds of fear, anxiety, suspicion, self-doubt, self-abnegation, lassitude, ennui, exhaustion, and despair. With these twisted hands of the clock, we have been unable to tell what time it is. Today, by whatever name our confusion is called, whether we call it the quest for *true federalism, resource control,* or *restructuring,* the essence is the same: we have one clock but no common agreement as to what time it is.

2. Lessons from the American Experience

Let me now turn our attention to briefly look at the American experience, with all its imperfections, and see what lessons we can draw from it today.

The American story of democracy is not perfect, but I believe no other country in the world has made such great sacrifices to institutionalize this system of governance than that country. They have since outclassed and outlived those from whom they borrowed the system, from the Greeks to the French. They received the statue of Liberty as a present from the French on October 28, 1886. The timeless and most inspiring words of the poet Emma Lazarus, summoning all to freedom, have the power of a sacred text: "Give me your tired, your poor, your huddled masses yearning to breathe free, The wretched refuse of your teeming shore, Send these, the homeless, tempest-tost to me, I lift my lamp beside the golden door." It can certainly be argued that America has sought to remain faithful to these goals and aspirations.

The very successful story of the United States of America illustrates what human beings, collaborating with the grace of God, can achieve when they work together. Do not get me wrong. I am not naïve to think that the United States does not have its own problems. We can remember the struggle of Martin Luther King for equality of the black race, a struggle that continues today. We can recall the struggle of women to have their equality as citizens recognized. We can also afford to quarrel with the new restrictions imposed by the Trump administration today, whether on border walls, immigrants, visas, or how much you need to have to get their visa. But in whichever way we look at things, every struggle there still finds it legitimacy in the vision of the founding fathers of that country.

In 1776 after they won their war against Britain, the founding fathers of America set about laying down the moral basis for what they had done. After the holy Bible, the Declaration of Independence can be considered the most powerful source from where the United States has continued to draw its moral authority. The writers (Thomas Jefferson, John Adams, Benjamin Franklin, Robert Livingston and Robert Sherman) stated very clearly the reason why they had fought a war and what kind of society they wanted to live in. They stated: "When in the course of human events, it becomes necessary for one people to dissolve the political bands which have connected them with another, and to assume among the powers of the earth, the separate and equal station to which the Laws of Nature and of Nature's God entitle them, a decent respect to the opinions of mankind requires that they should declare the causes which impel them to the separation. We hold these truths to be self-evident, that all men are created equal, that they are endowed by their Creator with certain unalienable Rights, that among these are Life, Liberty and the pursuit of Happiness. - That to secure these rights, Governments are instituted among Men, deriving their just powers from the consent of the governed, That whenever any Form of Government becomes destructive of these ends, it is the Right of the People to alter or to abolish it, and to institute new Government, laying its foundation on such principles and organizing its powers in such form, as to them shall seem most likely to affect their Safety and Happiness. Prudence, indeed, will dictate that Governments long established should not be changed for light and transient causes."

Who would imagine that these words, written over three hundred years ago, are still so inspiring? They could pass for a text of agitation from any of the angry, frustrated and militant separatist groups spread around every nook and cranny of Nigeria today. So, what time is it for Nigeria? How does it happen that we have not been able to resolve problems whose solutions were offered over three hundred years ago by men and women of vision? How could we have offered to sit for their examination, and over forty years later are still unable to graduate?

The founding fathers of America drew their strength from the Christian faith, calling their nation a "City on a hill, a Nation under God and God's country". The inscription on their currency reads, "In God we trust". Today, these appellations have paid off because faith, including today greater respect for all faiths, has remained the rallying cry for the people. Thus, we can all agree that America may sway, but it remains a worthy reference point for how democracy should be.

Apart from the Declaration of Independence, two other speeches are important for understanding why American democracy has stood the test of time and why honoring the time-tested principles laid down by the founding fathers has conferred a form of secular sacredness to these texts. The first is the Gettysburg Speech, which Abraham Lincoln delivered at the dedication of the cemetery at Gettysburg in Pennsylvania on November 19th, 1863, after the war. It is one of the shortest but most memorable speeches. The entire speech is less than 300 hundred words.

Among other things, Lincoln said:

> But, in a larger sense, we cannot dedicate–we cannot consecrate– we cannot hallow–this ground. The brave men, living and dead, who struggled here, have consecrated it, far above our poor power to add or detract. The world will little note, nor long remember, what we say here, but it can never forget what they did here. It is for us the living, rather, to be dedicated here to the unfinished work which they who fought here have thus far so nobly advanced. It is rather for us to be here dedicated to the great task remaining before us – that from these honored dead take increased devotion to that cause for which they gave the last full measure of devotion – that we here highly resolve that these dead shall not have died in vain – that this nation, under God, shall have a new birth of freedom – and that government of the people, by the people, for the people, shall not perish from the earth.

This speech reflects the consistency in the mind of Abraham Lincoln. On June 16th, 1858, Mr. Lincoln had just been nominated to contest for the position of senator for the state of Illinois. His acceptance speech which has gone down in history is a most remarkable speech. It has come to be known as the House Divided Speech. Although Mr. Lincoln lost that election, the contents of the speech show an ideological consistency that would run through his life. His entire political life would hang around the themes of this speech. Among other things, he said:

> A house divided against itself cannot stand. I believe this government cannot endure, permanently half slave and half free. I do not expect the Union to be dissolved - I do not expect the house to fall - but I do expect it will cease to be divided. It will become all one thing, or all the other. Either the opponents of slavery will arrest the further spread of it, and place it where the public mind shall rest in the belief that it is in course of ultimate extinction; or its advocates will push it forward till it shall become alike lawful in all the States, old as well as new - North as well as South.

America has continued to use the Constitution as a moral foundation for its politics and life. The Constitution has been placed at the center of American life as the totem, a kind of a sacred political text. For example, it has become the Bible of Democracy, and while other crimes can be tolerated in the politics of the United States, any sign of a breach of the Constitution, real or imagined, can attract a political death sentence for the offender. It is a measure of how absolute compliance with the Constitution has been strictly adhered to, that in the over 200-year history of American democracy, only three Presidents (Andrew Johnson in 1868, Bill Clinton in 1998, and Donald Trump in 2019) have so far been impeached by Congress. It is significant to note that all were subsequently acquitted in the course of trials in the Senate. Richard Nixon had the wisdom to resign (on August 9th, 1974) before the Senate trials could commence.

After writing their Constitution in 1787, it became clear to the founding fathers of America that individual freedom was very important. As such, the first Ten Amendments, known now as the Bill of Rights, focused largely on promoting individual freedom against the excesses of the state. It is significant to note that the First Amendment focused on freedom of religion, speech, and press. It addressed the issues of the rights of citizens to free assembly, and also the right to petition government. This is significant because coming out of the tyrannical rule of colonialism, the founding fathers sought first to establish the fact that the government has to earn the trust of citizens as opposed to those rights being taken for granted. They had experienced abuse of power and knew the consequences of unchecked power.

Here, the issues of the legitimacy of government are based on a convergence between the ideals of the Constitution and the state's capacity to enforce them. The 13th, 14th and 15th Amendments addressed the very controversial issues of abolition of slavery. Since the fate of black people and women had not been anticipated in the Constitution, it became clear that securing these rights was fundamental to legitimizing and ensuring the sacredness of the Constitution.

The 13th Amendment abolished slavery and any form of servitude (December 6, 1865). The 14th Amendment (July 14, 1868) defined citizenship and inserted a protection clause for all citizens, while the 15th Amendment (February 3, 1870) granted all male citizens the right to vote. It would take till the passage of the 19th Amendment on August 18, 1920, for all white women to get the right to vote, and the Voting Rights Act in 1965 before all women could vote!

We see here a consistency in goals and objectives of the founding fathers, the framers of the Constitution, and the goals of liberty and the pursuit of happiness in the declaration of independence. In keeping with the goals and ideals captured in the Declaration of Independence, the Gettysburg speech, and the Constitution, we see that the totality of the American dream is nailed firmly on the mast of democracy, with the pursuit of happiness and human freedom as the basis for the creation of an egalitarian and prosperous society. It is to be assumed that based on their experience with their past, America's commitment to democracy would remain resolute, but only to the extent that it is the guarantee for the realisation of the goals of their society. And, as I have said, future politics and politicians will be measured by how far or close they are to the principles of the founding fathers of the nation.

Against this backdrop, the question to ask is, what time is it in Nigeria? To get a sense of where we are or where we have come from, we will have to attempt to trace the story of our wanderings and meanderings on the terrains of democracy. We will have to address the issues around the undulating contours that is Nigeria's severely fractured landscape.

Today, growing education, increasing political consciousness, and upward economic and social mobility, have all combined to make Nigeria a cauldron of competing, conflicting, and bubbling nationalisms. We are all wrapped in one torn blanket of frustration and near despair. No state, ethnic group, or community can agree about their future in the union. Everyone is in revolt mode and most Nigerians believe they would rather be anywhere but in the country itself. Nigerians have continued to demand, with increasing aggressiveness, a more rugged political space to contain their energies. Sadly, we are all coming to terms with the fact that our efforts at Constitution making have largely been desultory.

This is neither the place nor time to review Nigeria's Constitutional history, for I will be venturing into an area that I am least qualified. However, to understand our country's convoluted Constitutional history is to appreciate the nature of our colonial history. Unlike the United States of America, we did not defeat the British and therefore did not possess the requisite moral authority to draw a distinct line between the ugly past and the future. What we had was an inchoate amalgam of concessionary initiatives that upended the interest of the British and made Nigeria's interests subordinate while the political class and bureaucracy acted as junior partners. Unlike the Americans, it was the colonial state which made our various laws ranging from those laws which legitimized trade and coincided with the period of their occupation, through amalgamation to independence. Military rule, coming on the heels of the colonial state, further deepened the culture of servitude and subordination of human rights under the jack boot of militarism.

Constitution making in Nigeria has continued to be a cat and mouse game, pitching the conservative statist interests of those in power with the wishes of the ordinary citizens. This legal puppetry would gradually suffer diminished legitimacy as the process deteriorated to the abyss and became a tool in the hands of despots seeking illegal processes of breaking the rules of the game. Thus, between 1914, 1922, 1946, 1951, 1954, 1960, 1963, 1979 and 1999, the list may be long, but the journey towards Constitutionalism hardly ever got started.

Almost every attempt at reviewing the Constitution has been an ambush against the wishes of the people by a rampaging political elite who often turned the platform into a theatre for unsavory political gymnastics. Fora for these reviews of the Constitution are often crowded by shady conspirators and carpet baggers who, on behalf of the dark interests of the day, turn the exercise into a bazaar for political horse trading. So-called Constitution Review Assemblies or Conferences become victims and instruments of state capture. Does it not sound strange that from 1914 till date, we still have not been able to agree on a Constitution? Right now, the 8th Assembly is in the process of embarking on another of these wild goose chases, not to talk of the Political Reform Conferences of 2005 and 2014 which were of limited mandates but seen as attempts to manipulate the Constitution!

In these platforms, politicians often deploy pseudo nationalistic platitudes as application of *Sharia law, true federalism,* or *resource control,* to appeal to their bedraggled and traumatised constituents. They cast the others as enemies of their constituents and by the time these events are over, the centrifugal elements have weakened our common sense of nationhood, and politics becomes a war of Us against Them. The exploitation of these sentiments by a crooked political class is largely responsible for the mess we find ourselves in now. From Boko Haram to banditry and kidnapping, the logic is the same: how can politicians who themselves kidnap the political process and the machinery of power find the moral authority to ask for anything different? Those in the bush are largely just adopting less civilized methods than their uncles and brothers in the political field!

3. What Time is it, Nigeria?

To answer this question and by way of concluding this lecture, I can only say that sadly, there is still no agreement over an answer to that question. I have tried to argue that the United States of America, with all its imperfections, has demonstrated to us that the resilience of any nation, its capacity to meet the needs of its people, cannot be undertaken outside a set of ideals, principles, and vision of a future anchored on Constitutionalism and shared values. Thus, close to two hundred and fifty years after the Declaration of Independence, the United States has had a total of 45 presidents, from President George Washington (inaugurated April 30, 1789) to Donald Trump (inaugurated January 20, 2017).

Compare this with Nigeria which, after just 60 years of independence has produced a total of a hotchpotch of 15 individuals who defy nomenclatural logic. Apart from the fact that two have come back after changing their uniform as military heads of state, one was a Head of Interim Government, a position unknown in any system of government anywhere in the world. Or, take Anambra, your state. Although it was created only in 1991, it has had 20 governors! Nigeria has not had an aggregate of shared values hewn and crafted into a Constitution to inspire the reverence and awe of its citizens and has no process in leadership recruitment. This is the vacuum that the political elite has exploited by turning the country into a jungle where the rule of men has replaced the rule of law and mere human instincts have become substitutes for Constitutionalism.

It is time to take stock. Chinua Achebe had warned that it was still *"morning yet on creation day"*. Perhaps we should have listened to Wole Soyinka and *"set forth at dawn"*. Had we done so, as Ben Okri said, perhaps, just perhaps, we would not have been on this *"famished road"* festooned with the debris of our broken dreams and nightmares. Nigeria and Nigerians, what time is it? Where are we? The enemies of Nigeria know what time it is, but do we Nigerians know what time it is? For Boko Haram, they are reaping the harvest of a war they started. For the bandits, Ali Baba and his forty thieves, it is harvest time.

For these young men and women who are graduating today, for the university community, what time is it? For the graduates, it is important to remember the sacrifices made by your family to get you to where you are. You are bearers of visions and dreams. Although it seems to be a time of despair, I agree with the Vice President, Professor Yemi

Osinbajo, who warned in his lecture at the Federal University in Dutse last month that your generation should not dwell on those who tell you that the days of yesterday were better. The best days are ahead of us because the days of the godfatherism are over. The days of the stranglehold of feudalism are coming to a close. The birth of a new Nigeria is a possibility, but it will depend on so many factors. We will look at only a few.

4. Factors that make a New Nigeria Possible

Education & Knowledge

As a matter of urgency, the Nigerian elite must wake up to the fact that in history, there has been a correlation between civilization, modernity, statecraft, and power, with education and knowledge. Therefore, the educated elite in Nigeria must take full responsibility for the mess that we have now found ourselves in, where the national clock is now broken and threatened with destruction by those who believe time is a waste and an irritant. The forces of darkness have seen democracy, transparency, freedom, and individual rights as irritants. Today, we are reaping the fruits of the consequences of intellectual retreat.

Some years back, I followed with interest a debate between Igbo and Yoruba elite in diaspora over which group was most educated and who got what degree first. The debate was quite enlightening. However, how did we come to the point in Nigeria where, whereas elsewhere, democracy, state craft and modernity are driven by men and women of knowledge who draw the lines between antiquity, feudalism and modernity, in Nigeria, the intellectuals have been reduced to spectators of the process of statecraft? Unless this is reversed, we will continue to reap the fruits of those men and women who, Janus faced, want to drag us into the furnace of darkness and death.

The foundations and operations of British colonialism across the world were driven by Oxford and Cambridge graduates. It is not surprising that British Prime Ministers have been of the Oxbridge hew, nor are we surprised by the fact that the Ivy League Universities have been the laboratories for leadership in that United States. Leading nations is not a game of chance. Nigeria has a choice: either the elite, that is the educated such as you, take up the lead, or we will perish in the face of those who do not know how to tell time.

Igbo and Yoruba 'elite' must unite

Following closely, the burden now falls on the Igbo and Yoruba elites to lead the charge by identifying their colleagues across the entire country. Let us look at the spread of universities in the country and appreciate why both the Yoruba and the Igbo elite must unite to offer this country a scientific understanding of how countries grow. So far, we have been victims of the blind trying to lead a country and a people that they are intellectually not equipped to lead. Elitism, not in its abstract form, is a desirable and noble virtue to the extent that it dreams, envisions, and imagines a good society and then lays down the scaffolding to hold those dreams. Once the elite renounces its obligations, the mobocracy in its raw form takes over and this is what we have today in Nigeria.

Young Graduands, make a difference!

Thirdly and finally, to you the graduates, dreamers, and visionaries of tomorrow, I throw you the challenge: take a dive, take the risk and make a difference. The future lies before you and it is yours to conquer. The era of glorified feudalism is gradually coming to an end. What we need now is a secular society that can embrace modernity, not one that uses religion to mask the fear of change and progress. What you need is what God has already given you, a good brain. Use it well. Don't ask what time it is. The clock is in your hands. Thank you and God bless you all.

10th Chukwuemeka Odumegwu Ojukwu University Convocation Lecture
March 20, 2020

CHAPTER ELEVEN

The Just War Theory and the Morality of the Iraq War

Introduction

Personally, I have never really been convinced about the propriety of recourse to the *Just war Tradition* as a means of gauging the quality of the moral decisions to go to war. Any war. I know that Pacifism has a bad name as an option for the faint hearted in a world suffused with the braggadocio and machismo of the powerful. I do not think I qualify to be called a pacifist. Although I hover on the borderline I do lean heavily on the side of Pacifism. I have been asked by the organisers of this event to try and answer the question as to whether the decision to go to war in Iraq was morally right. To make matters worse, I have been asked to examine the issues of the moral justification of this war at a time when even the greatest war mongers and sabre rattlers are now busy eating humble pie, no thanks to the tragedy that has been unfolding regarding the excesses of the forces of the so called *coalition of the willing* and the torture chambers that are now symbolised by Abu Gharaib prison and Guantanamo Bay detention centre. This war is therefore the worst advertisement for any attempt to apply the just war theory in defence of modern wars.

My task in this paper is to go beyond merely saying that the war is not morally right to trying to explain why this is so. To do this, I will divide this paper into five sections. Section 1 will attempt to merely restate the main arguments of the Just War theory. Section 2 will try to examine the arguments that the proponents of this war have advanced to support going to war in Iraq. In doing this, I will highlight some of the arguments advanced by **George Weigel,** Pope John Paul 11's biographer and one of the leading Catholic theologians in the United States today. I will then briefly critique his arguments in support of the war, using the responses of the Vatican and the Archbishop of

Canterbury, **Dr. Rowan Williams** as starting points. Section 3 will review the United Nation's position and argue that in the final analysis, that organisation's final decision should determine the legitimacy or otherwise of any war today. Section 4 will advance the arguments for the *presumption against war*, as my personal philosophical position. Finally, in section 5, using the world's experience in the last 50 years, I will argue that the experiences of the world with wars should be the best advertisement for the *presumption against war*.

1: The Just War theory and the Morality of War

The original theory of the theology of a just war is often attributed to St Augustine and Thomas Aquinas, the two leading theologians of the Catholic Church. And rightly so. However, both theologians drew their inspiration from the ancient philosophical thoughts of people like Aristotle and Cicero, the great thinkers before them. The teachings of both Augustine and Aquinas were naturally based on Catholic theology. With time, Augustine's original theories have been amplified by other theologians and scholars of the just war theory[1]. Today, the conditions for the just war have expanded from three, four and now six. They are presented as follows:

* **Just Cause**: That there has to be evidence that the cause for going to war is a just one, not just the result of the thirst and lust for power by some lunatic leader. Thus, in the case of this war, the central question then is, was there a just cause for going to war? If so, were there other alternative routes that could have been taken and were not explored? Indeed, what cause was the United States and those who supported the war fighting? These are questions that must be answered before the just cause condition can be accepted.

---

[1] The names of Francisco de Vitoria and Francisco Suarez are often cited.

* Legitimate authority: Here, the issue of legitimate authority means that the President and the Commander in Chief who declares war must possess that legitimate authority. As everyone now knows, the issue of the legitimacy of the elections that brought George Bush to power remained an issue well after the President had been sworn in. When I realised from his accent that the taxi driver bringing me to the airport was from Haiti, I asked him about his country. He obviously was an Aristide supporter. He said to me:

> Well, the Americans have taken our President away and we do not know where they have put him. At least, we know that he was elected by us. But, Mr George Bush who took him away was not elected. He was merely given a job by his father's friends in the Supreme Court!

* Last resort: This implies that all other forms of a peaceful resolution to the conflict have failed and war is the only last option left to remove the aggressor or repel and attack.

* Proportionality between offence and Response: Here, under the theory, a justification for going to war would imply that in undertaking the war, all attention must be paid to the fact that the wound or damage to be inflicted in the cause of the war must be in direct proportion to the injury inflicted by the aggressor. Or, that enough care is taken to ensure the limitation of collateral harm on non-combatants along with the belief that the benefit of going to war will outweigh the harm that may follow from the war. This is the protection valve enshrined in the sentiments captured by the Geneva Convention.

* Reasonable chance of Success: Here, the one going to war must ensure that in assessing his chances, he assures himself that by leading his country to war, he has chances of winning the war.

* Right Intentions: The intentions to go to war must be right and that means that the one going to war must ensure that he has all the facts at hand. Now, when we reflect on the war in Iraq, can we say that the American President and his advisers had all the facts before them? If the President knew then what he knows now, would he have still gone to war? And, if the Secretary of State knew then what he knows now, would he have made the gung-ho speech at the United Nations, a presentation that it is now realised was full of doctored and questionable intelligence?

By merely looking at these so-called justifications for war, it is clear that they are literally impossible for us to meet. It is important to state that the idea of the just war theory arose largely because Christianity found itself dealing with the problems of empire building and the attendant requirements characterised by war and conquest. It is important to state that the principles of the just war theory developed not because Christians were seeking to justify war. On the contrary, a proper interpretation of the spirit of the philosophy shows very clearly that St. Augustine had a *presumption against war* at the back of his mind. The idea of going to war was more a search how to make the best out of a very bad situation. St. Augustine himself admitted that the *law of Love* prohibits any Christian from killing or wounding another. The *law of Love* obliges a Christian to come to the defence of the other, and in the process, giving one's life is to be seen within the context that one is fulfilling the Scriptural injunction that reminds Christians that there is no greater love than to lay down one's life for the sake of another [2].

Let me state from the very beginning that I believe that a presumption against war is the most sensible option to take in discussing the issue of the just war theory and whether or not it can be used to justify any war, no least the current war in Iraq is another matter altogether. Indeed, the realities that stare us in the face impose on us a serious need to rethink all the assumptions that we have often had about war and how best it can be fought. My presumption against war is based on the following reasons:

- I believe that war, any war is a mortal sin and I do not see how any sin can become acceptable. St James makes the point very well: Where do all these wars and battles among you come from? Is it not precisely in the desires fighting inside your own selves? You want something you lack so you are prepared to kill. You have an ambition you cannot satisfy, so you fight to get your way by force (James, 4: 1-2)

---

[2] This text, has become the favourite in all war memorial speeches. President's Bush's speech on V-Day on Sunday June 6th was laced with these quotations.

- War is a human invention, the mere extension of human greed and it must never be presented as if it were some biological necessity.
- From history and with the benefit of hindsight, it is clear to us that every war in human history could have been avoided.
- Again, from history, it is now clear to us that no single war has offered solutions to the problems it sought to cure.
- Nearly every war has been the failure of human Prudence and humility.
- No war has ever been fought with all the facts available to the combatants. In almost every case, allegations, spurious intelligence reports, claims and counter claims of enemy superiority and evil intentions have been hoisted as a basis for going to war. And, in the end, as it is with the weapons of mass destruction, we have always tended to realise that the facts we thought we had, were not really the facts.
- All the variables for a Just war conditions are unrealisable almost in the same way as Shylock's pound of flesh became impossible.

This brings us to the real question that I have been asked to address, namely, is the war with Iraq morally justifiable? From some of the above observations, it is clear that I am of course against this war and I do not see what moral justification we can find for it. I was against it for all the reasons I have mentioned above and of course, there was the more difficult situation created by the decision of the United States to isolate the rest of the world and then present the war as a settling of scores between the Bush family and the people of the United States. Broadly, President George Bush said that he had to go to war with Iraq for, among others, the following reasons:

- That he considered September 11th a declaration of War by Al Qaeda against the Government and people of the United States.
- He linked the war to both the pursuit of Al Qaeda and government of Saddam Hussein who was credited then with supporting and having links with Al Qaeda.
- President Bush then gave the axis of evil speech, arguing that war was necessary because, as he argued, there were ticking time bombs out there and Iraq had a stash of dangerous weapons.
- He argued that there was evidence that Saddam Hussein had Weapons of Mass Destruction, (WmD) which could be deployed at

short notice.

- George Bush also stated that the people of Iraq had suffered untold hardship under Saddam Hussein and that the same Saddam had used nerve gas against his own people as well as the Kurds (The United States had used similar dangerous weapons in Vietnam and it had also urged the Kurds to rise against the regime of Saddam Hussein and then backed out of helping them at the last minute[3].
- President Bush claimed that the United States of America had to fight to war so as to give the people of Iraq democracy and freedom which they had been denied.
- America's manifest destiny means that it has the duty to save the world and so this war was in pursuit of some military missionary mission.

So, when we put some of these reasons together, is there anything that brings us closer to accepting that there was a moral basis for this war? To answer this and other questions that arise from this, let me turn to the debate between Dr. George Weigel, the Republican theoretician who seemed to have provided the rationale for Bush's war, and the more reasoned and humane approach canvassed by Dr. Rowan Williams, the Archbishop of Canterbury.

George Weigel hinged his argument for the war on the following reasons:

- That it is possible to use proportionate and discriminate military force to moral and worthy political ends.
- That the just war theory is a theory of statecraft. Thus, **Bellum, i.e.,** use of armed conflict for public good is an acceptable option. It is **Duelum**, that is, the use of armed conflict for private ends by private individuals that is morally wrong.
- Presumption against war leads to dubious moral judgements and distorted perceptions of political reality.
- There is a moral obligation to rid the world of this threat to peace and security for all[4].

3

[4] George Weigel: *Moral Clarity in a Time of War.* (First Things, January, 2003).

Weigel went on to argue that America's fight was both in defence of itself and also in fulfilment of its moral obligation to the rest of the world. This moral obligation makes America what is today known as the world's Globocop[5]! And, he reasoned, since America had been attacked on the 11th September, it had no obligation to wait for anyone to determine when it could seek vengeance. Therefore, America was right in acting alone because the responsibility of self-defence can be exercised unilaterally. In fairness to both Bush and Weigel, America had been attacked, but surely, that was beside the point. If America was going to war to avenge September 11th, it ought to have known that hundreds of others had died in Africa (Kenya and Tanzania) well before September 11th. The nature of the victims of September 11th and the realisation that terrorism was a global phenomenon meant that the problem could not be solved unilaterally and that is precisely why the matter went to the United Nations.

Dr. Rowan Williams on other hand presented a different argument, challenging some of the assumptions made by Dr Weigel. His thesis seemed to be based on what I can say is a *presumption against war.* According to him:

- Rather than adopt the sweeping arguments against terrorism, it is important to seek an understanding of the moral objectives of the terrorist without in any way approving of the goals and means employed by the terrorist.
- Rather than adopt the unilateralist position on the basis of strength, there is need for the United States to bring more people and interests on the table.
- By acting unilaterally, the United States was seeking to be a judge in its own case.
- By taking the law into its hands, the United States was engaged in **Duellum** and not **Bellum**. In this case, it was acting as a private person seeking private gain and pursuit by the employment of violent force.

---

[5] America's perceived role as the Global Cop of the world arose immediately after the collapse of the Berlin wall.

It is evident from these arguments that if we were merely to deploy this theory, then as we can see from these positions, the argument cuts both ways. But, as I have noted above, these moral conditions for the just war have now been transferred to a secular authority as the legitimating authority. That authority is the United Nations. Let us now turn our attention to that world body.

3: The UN and Moral Authority: Some Lessons

According to the just war theory, in the event that the decision to go to war has been taken, the legitimate authority must ensure three conditions, namely;

- ***Jus Bellum***. Justice at the beginning of the war.
- ***Jus in bello***. Conduct of war.
- ***Jus ad Pacem***. surviving the peace.

However, we tend to forget that the debate about the Just war theory came about also at a time when God Himself was the Sovereign. But, with the changes in the nation state occurring especially after the French revolution and the ouster of the Church from the public sphere, sovereignty became a geopolitical and human form of expression. There was talk about the sovereign as a ruler and the sovereignty of the nation-state. The emergence of the nation state led to the quest for peace and security for individual states and neighbours. The issue of how best to deal with war became very important. The first world war (1914-1918) forced the world to face the challenges of war. Thus, the founding of the League of Nations in 1920 was aimed at creating conditions for unity among nations as an antidote to war. The United States never really joined the League because domestic opinion was against American involvement with wars beyond its borders. When the Second World War broke out, the League of Nations was rendered impotent and it was formally dissolved in 1946 to make way for the United Nations. That is why, the United Nations framed its moral duty to end war and seek peace by stating that: ***We the peoples of the United Nations, determined:*** *To save succeeding generations from the scourge of war, which twice in our life time has brought untold sorrow to mankind, and reaffirm our faith in fundamental human rights, in dignity and worth of the human person....establish* *conditions under which justice and respect for the obligations arising from treaties and other sources of international law can be maintained………… To practice tolerance and live together in peace with one another as good neighbours and to unite our strength to maintain international peace and security and to ensure by the practice and acceptance of principles and the institution of methods, that armed force shall not be used save in the common interest [6].* Realising its imperfections as a human institution, the United Nations noted that in the unlikely event that war broke out, its aim has to be: ……*to maintain international peace and security and to further cooperation in solving international problems and to be the centre of harmonising the actions of nations in the attainment of common ends [7].*

From here, we can glean two very important issues. First is the fact that there is also a sense in which the states that had signed on to the United Nations had, by that act more or less surrendered their sovereignty to that body in dealing with matters of international peace and security within its members. The powers of the United Nations to decide on issues of war rest with the Security Council. In the years of the cold war especially, the Security Council was very cautious in holding the balance between the super powers. It can be argued that at the heart of the United Nations and the Security Council there is a philosophy of a *presumption against war.*

Therefore, in arguing that there is no moral basis for this war, I progress from two positions. First of all, my personal belief that war is a moral failure and should be avoided at all cost as a means of resolving human problems. I also base my arguments on the fact that since death, torture and other humanly degrading actions form the basis of war, it is impossible for us to find a moral basis for it. Human life and its preservation are at the heart of human civilisation and God's plans for creation. Thus, even to the unbeliever in God, the centrality of human life and its nurture remains at the heart of every human endeavour. The first and the last rules of war are Death. Yet, despite this presumption against war, we have to take cognisance of certain evils that distort and threaten the lives of individuals, communities and the world at large.

---

[7] *United Nations Human Rights Declaration, 1948,* Art 4

Chapter Eleven | Matthew Hassan Kukah

However, if, in the final analysis, the case is made for repelling aggression, or removing a threat to human life and civilisation, then, it is the United Nations through the Security Council that should provide a moral basis for that war. Here, I use the word morality more to explain the legitimacy of the action more than morality in its theological context. As a result, many of the arguments against the Iraq war, whether moral or ideological hinge on the fact that the United Nations, the body into whose hands the nations of the world have handed over sovereignty did not play a central role in authorising the war. Thus, it is here that the moral, ideological and legal arguments against the war all conflate.

4: A Moral Presumption Against War

Clearly, had the United Nations approved the decision to go to war, the rest of the world would have more or less be left with nothing much to argue against beyond the usual moral appeals against war. At this point, our debates would have centred around ensuring the proportionality argument. Beyond the moral appeals to caution, the rest of the world would have had very little to quarrel with the United States because at that level, it would have been the rest of the world acting in unison to destroy Saddam Hussein's dangerous war arsenal or his links with terrorism. After all, before the Iraq war, there were both the wars in the Gulf (1990) and Afghanistan (1994). In both cases, the anti war protests were moderated by the nature of the circumstances. Indeed, in a letter to the President George Bush, in the run up to the war, the President of the United States Bishops Conference, Archbishop Wilton Gregory reminded the President that the Catholic Bishops Conference shared the concerns of the President about terrorism, the pains of September 11th and so on. But, he argued, their objection to the war was among other things based on the fact that the war did not have a United Nations mandate. We had, he said supported the war in Afghanistan and Bosnia on the grounds that it had a UN mandate. The moral position, based on a presumption against war was however taken by the Holy Father.

Right from the beginning the Holy Father, Pope John Paul 11, had in the tradition of the Catholic Church consistently appealed to the world to avoid war. His various addresses to the United Nations had always focused on the need for that august body to keep the world free from war. Since the beginning of his Papacy, the Holy Father, Pope John Paul has consistently kept the **World Day of Peace** as a very important day to draw the world's attention to the possibilities and the hopes a just world order based on equity. After September 11, the Holy Father condemned that act as inhuman. He had stated that: *The 20th century bequeaths to us above all else, a warning: Wars are often the cause of further wars because they fuel deep hatreds, create situations of injustice and trample upon people's dignity and rights. Wars generally do not resolve the problems for which they are fought and therefore, in addition to causing horrendous damage, they prove ultimately futile. War is a defeat for humanity. Only in peace and through peace can respect for human dignity and inalienable rights be guaranteed*[8]. Again, in his Encyclical, *Sollitudo Rei Socialis*, the Holy Father had drawn attention for the need of the world to focus on human dignity. *What is at stake*, he had warned, *is the dignity of the human person, whose defence and promotion have been entrusted to us by the creator, and to whom the men and women at every moment of history are strictly and responsibly in debt*[9].

This teaching was following directly in the footsteps of his predecessors. The Papacy of Pope John xxiii more than any other really broke the grounds for the enunciation of the theory of the *presumption against war*. The Catholic Church began its trenchant criticism of war right from the time the super powers began to toy with weapons of war by the development of atomic power. In the Encyclical **Pacem In Terris**, the Pope stated that recourse to atomic power would pose a serious danger to the world[10]. Following very closely at the Second Vatican Council, in the document, **Gaudium et Spes**, Catholic Church warned that: *The arms race is an utterly treacherous trap for humanity and one which injures the poor to an intolerable degree. It must be feared that if this race persists, it will spawn all the lethal ruin whose path it is now making ready*[11].

In its teaching, the Catholic Church has sought to urge the leaders of the powerful nations of the world to replace the arrogance of power with humility and service for the good of humanity. The Catholic Church has developed these principles over the years by focusing on three main principles which it has taught over the ages. The sources of these teachings are the various Encyclicals, Pastoral Letters, the

---

[8] Maryknoll Magazine, May/June 2004, p2
[9] *Sollitudo Rei Sociallis*, par 47
[10] *Pacem In Terris*, n127
[11] *Gaudium et Spes*, no 80-1

Documents of the Second Vatican Council and recently, the very elaborate New Catholic Catechism. The principles in question are the **Common Good,** the principle of **Subsidiarity** and the gospel of **Solidarity**. Rather than recourse to war as a means of resolving the problems of the world, the Catholic Church has consistently taught that a clear understanding of these principles is a greater guarantee to a just world order, rather than war.

By the **Common good** is to be understood the sum total of social conditions which allow people, either as groups or as individuals, to reach their fulfilment more fully and easily. The common good concerns the life of all. It calls for prudence from each, and even more from those who exercise the office of authority. It consists in three elements: *respect of person, social well being, and peace.* These principles are interconnected because it is clear that respect for the human person as the child of God leads to social well being and an effective programme of social well being naturally leads to peace. The Catholic Catechism for example states that: **Peace** *is the security of a just order... it presupposes that the authority should ensure by morally acceptable means, the security of society and its members. It is the basis of the right to legitimate personal and collective defence*[12]. The Catechism further warns that: *Excessive economic and social disparity between individuals and peoples of the one human race is a source of scandal and militates against social justice, equity, human dignity, as well as social and international peace*[13]. Again, the Church explains the context of **Solidarity** when it warns that: *Socio-economic problems can be resolved only with the help of all forms of solidarity, solidarity of the poor among themselves, between rich and poor, of workers among themselves between employers and employees in a business, solidarity among the nations and peoples. International solidarity is a requirement of the* **moral order***, world peace depends in part upon this*[14].

In teaching the world these lessons about the centrality of the human person, the Catholic Church is emphasising the need for the world to move away from the belief that on his own and through the exercise of power through war, the human person can become the architect of the kind of world that St Augustine aspired to when he

---

[12] *Catholic Catechism*, n1905-1910.
[13] *Catholic Catechism*, n1955, GS, 28, (3)
[14] *Catholic Catechism*, n1941.

preached for the attainment of Peace as, *Tranquilitas ordinis.* The achievement of *Tranquilitas ordinis*, had some basic assumptions as to what it was and the conditions for its realisation. In any case, its conceptualisation assumed either the supremacy of the Catholic doctrine or at least a Christian basis for the laws of society. But things have changed so drastically in two distinct ways which now challenge both the theory and the basis of identifying how a society might gauge a state of *Tranquilitas ordinis.* First of all, we can neither assume the supremacy of Catholic doctrine nor the dominance of Christian thought, philosophy and doctrine. The world is now inhabited by contending ideologies and philosophies, many of them, at best un-Christian or at worst, outrightly anti-Christian, not to even talk the now diminishing role of the Catholic Church and Christianity in world affairs. The debate about whether there is a Christian legacy in the formulation of the Constitution of the European Union is one clear example. Secondly, is the Evangelical rhetoric of a George Bush in appealing to the just war theory an appropriation of this doctrine or does it derive from an acceptance of Catholic social teaching? How might the just war theory affect China's decision to go to war for example, or to what extent can it inform Iran or Saudi Arabia's decisions to got to war? These to my mind are the realities of the present world and they are important in our assessment of the relevance of the just war theory as the quest for world domination masquerades as the wish to establish a *tranquilitas ordinis.*

5: So called Just War vs. Children of a Lesser God

As we have noted above, Aristotle and Cicero influenced both Augustine and Aquinas. However, both Aristotle and Cicero believed primarily in the superiority of their local civilisations, cultures and cities. Thus, there was something racist in what drove their philosophies. Both men were clear about the fact that what they and their civilisations were superior to any other. Thus, war was one way of incorporating lesser mortals into a world that already had both a superior citizenry and civilisation.

For example, when Aristotle speaks about the *just ordering of the state*, he is speaking of the Greek city-state, not just any state. He was neither concerned about devising a programme for the international relations of Greece and other cities, nor was he really concerned about the equality of others with Greece. Aristotle believed that any Constitution that focused on war, like the Spartan Constitution did, ran the risk of losing the *raison detre* for its existence, since the attainment of order and justice were at the heart of every city-state. Indeed, for him, any city-state whose Constitution trained its people for war faced imminent danger because it was nobler to seek to govern free people and not subjects. Just as an individual sought peace and happiness internally, so should a city.

Cicero on the other hand believed that except wars that were meant to repel evil or for punishment, no other reason was justified forever going to war. If a superior people like the Romans rule over the uncultured people, they were doing a favour to the uncultured people. So, the uncultured people are better off subdued for they are worse off if not subdued. Thus, Roman rule was justified because of the opportunities it brought to those whom it governed.

A conflation of these contradictions led to the collapse of the Roman Empire. Thus, Augustine's writing of the just war theory must be understood within the context of the circumstances that led to the writing of his magnus opus, The City of God. Essentially, this book, written over a period of a period of 13 years, set to answer some very profound questions about history and the will of God. The Goths had ransacked Rome in 410 and there arose some profound questions: why had Rome, the epicentre of world civilisation fallen? And why did Rome fall at a time when Christianity was on the rise? The Roman emperors believed that it was the Christians whose subversion led to the fall of the empire. This subversion was manifested in their reluctance to serve the Roman gods. Augustine argued that the Roman Empire had been caught in the contradictions of its own fractured world and he believed that rather than blame the Christians, it was more appropriate for the Romans to blame their gods! This is what provided the backdrop for understanding the just war theory. But, now that the idea has been co-opted by the strong, how might we assess its relevance especially given the new geopolitical calculations that under gird world politics.

It seems clear to me that the warmongers of today base their quest for war not on the superficial need to *do good* but their national self-interest. Tied to this is the belief in racial, cultural and ideological superiority of some races and classes. When we reflect on the claims made by the Bush administration in its decision to go to war, these realities begin to emerge. The decision to go to war was based on the assumption by the Bush government that America had a moral claim to change Iraq into the image and likeness of itself. But, so much has happened now that even the greatest supporters of the Bush administration are now left with a feeling of total shame at the barefaced lies and fabrications that preceded the decision to go to war.

What is more, the culture of torture that has emerged from the war, other preoccupations with economic interests all now show that the United States' mission to Iraq was founded on nothing other than its quest for conquest, resource accumulation and control as a means of not only consolidating its own gains and power, but its mission of empire building.

The war against terrorism is a matter of legitimate concern to the world in general. However, the United States has decided to use that war as a cover for its other personal missions. Thus, as one of Tony Blair's advisers has argued, the world is apparently divided between **Chaos** and **Order**.

Robert Cooper, one of Prime Minister Tony Blair's Senior advisers has argued that: *We may not be interested in chaos, but chaos is interested in us. In fact, chaos or at least the crime that lives within it, needs the civilised world and preys upon it. At its worst, in the form of terrorism, chaos can become a serious threat to the whole international order. Terrorism represents the privatisation of war, the pre-modern with teeth* [15]. What is most interesting in the position canvassed by the likes of Cooper is that they cut off substantial swaths of the colonial banditry that enabled those who lived in chaos yesterday to transmute into those who live in Order today. It is this deception that hurts the struggle for a just world and that is why, in discussing the conditions for a just war, we must focus more on where these wars will be fought and by whom.

This war has thrown up new challenges and it is evident that the United States will neither win the battle nor the war. The lesson here is two fold. First of all, again, a presumption against war must become the norm and secondly, as history has shown, war will always prove to worse than the disease it seeks to cure. British colonialism and America's later day quest for glory and dominance account for the problems of the

---

[15] Robert Cooper: The Breaking of Nations: Order and Chaos in the 21st Century (Atlantic Books. London. 2003) p70

Chapter Eleven | Matthew Hassan Kukah

world today. And it is an open question whether, having caused the problems in not only the Middle East but also the rest of the world, the same style of banditry, exploitation and war can cure the problems of the past. As it is now clear, Osama Bin Laden's driving philosophy is the quest for the purification of the holy land of Islam. By accommodation and compromise with the Kings and Princes in the Arab world, the United States and its business surrogates had continued to exploit the resources of these countries for itself and to build these dubious empires of so called **Order**. The result is that the source of their **Order** is the source of our **Chaos**. As long as these tensions continue, the ordinary people were further and further away from a *Tranquilitas ordinis.*

If we look at what has happened in post colonial Asia, Africa and Latin America, what we see is the devastation that has led to what the likes of Cooper now hypocritically refer to as Chaos, from which they now recoil. The developing world is unable to chart its course of development because multinational corporations, Oil companies, Construction companies and mineral development conglomerates are engaged in scotch earth wars for resources across Africa, Asia and parts of Latin America. Governments continue to rise and fall, rebels groups spring up all over Africa sponsored by foreign interests who are determined to corner resources beyond their borders.

The Marxists do have a point in explaining human greed and irrational delusions of grandeur as propelling forces to the world's mindless empire building projects. The Portuguese remained in Angola and Mozambique and left behind barely any educated elite. They had to be routed by a protracted struggle characterised by blood and tears. The Belgians were in Zaire, a country which King Leopold turned into his private estate. An Arab Muslim elite holds Sudan hostage and now over 2m are dead. The world has looked the other way until recently. The new interest in securing peace in Sudan is due to the fact that Sudan now has Oil deposits! The Portuguese were in East Timor for 400 years and left hardly any educated human beings. All they left were claims of adherence to Catholicism from Angola to Zaire.

To put what I am saying in context, a glimpse of the effect of wars in developing countries from in the wake of the end of colonial rule will show the seriousness of what we face today. It will also help the developing world to realise the futility of the claims that the just war theory makes any sense. What the rest of the world hypocritically talks about when it employs the just war theory is the quest for the most strategic means of the continuous exploitation of resources outside their boundaries, so called boundaries of **Order**. It is those caught in this tragic time warp that I call children of a lesser god! The diagram below tells the story of wars that are connected with colonial heritage of the various developing nations in the world today.

Post colonial wars around the World.

Country	Years of War	Deaths	Debt	Comments
Angola	36	1.5m	$9.6b	Liberation war
Burundi	10	300,000	$1.1b	Hutu-Tutsi war
Cambodia	30	1.85m	$2.7b	Khmer Rouge war
Lebanon	25	170,000	$12.5b	Civil war ended '91
Liberia	14	250,000	$2	Ethnic war, .6m ref
Guatemala	36	200,000	$5b	War ended '96
Haiti	14	na	$1.25b	Aristide removed
DR Congo	5	5m	$11.4b	Post Mobutu
Sierra Leone	11	200,000	$1.2b	Ethnic war
Nepal	6	10,000	$2.7m	Maoist vs Feudalism
Somalia	13	500,000	$2.5b	Clan wars
Sri Lanka	19	150,000	$8.5b	Tamil -Singhalese
Sudan	35	2m	$20b	Ethno-Rel: 4.4 IDPs
Rwanda	1	800,000	$1.3b	Hutu-Tutsi
Afghanistan	24	1m	$2.4b	5.4m refugees.

Source: The Daily Express, (London) May 31st, 2004

It is a realisation of this accumulation of injustice that has now led to the moral revulsion which drives the young men and women who make up Al Qaeda today. When Osama Bin Laden says he wants Americans and other foreign troops out of Saudi Arabia, who will deny him that right in this age of sovereignty? Who will deny this when it is clear that the presence of the foreign troops is merely consolidating the power of tiny elite while the majority of the population wallow in poverty? This is the foil that Osama Bin Laden and his millions of supporters have used to wrap his discontentment. Three points are worthy of consideration here.

First of all, as is now clear, no one really knows for sure who has what weapons of mass destruction and when they might be used. The recent drama in Pakistan and the humiliation of Dr. Abdulkader Khan are part of the theatre, but this did not come close to addressing the real issues of the proliferation of nuclear weapons in the world today. Acquisition of these weapons was facilitated by the same contradictions what under girded the cold war. Financial resources were all that one required having access to these weapons and, as it is now clear, the end of the cold war left so much uranium that was unaccounted for. But what is even more important is that there will always be enough greedy people in Europe who will do anything for anyone that has the big cheque. Thus, as long as the terrorists have the money, so long will they continue to acquire these weapons.

What is more, neither the United States nor any other European power has the moral authority because through the CIA and other agencies, the United States Government has moved around in the shadows of the capitals of the developing world from Addis Ababa, Kabul, Karachi, Kinshasa to Tehran in search of recruits for its dirty jobs in overthrowing governments and so on. Closely related to this is the level of sophistication of those whom the world simply dubs terrorists. A certain level of racist arrogance refuses to understand why anyone who has had access to the values of the west and has a good western education can turn against this wonderful civilisation.

This is the first major mistake because it means that the west continues to think that those who are today's martyrs are some illiterate and frustrated young people under the seduction of some bearded, tea drinking and drug induced mullahs in some caves. This is why there has been an attempt to present Osama Bin Laden not only as a nut case, but also as one whose actions can be framed within the context of some form of psychological deviance[16]. The result is that many westerners remain confused as to why and how anyone in their right senses who has imbibed the values of the west through the indoctrination of education and so on could suddenly go back to the old ways of what they see as primitive Islam.

Even the prestigious *Financial Times* of London editorialised in this regard when it argued for example that: *One of the biggest shocks since the terrorist attack on America of September 11th 2001 has been the revelation that the young, western educated men from well to do families have provided some of Osama Bin Laden's most dedicated operatives. Those under investigation for the Madrid bombing last month include Moroccans who had appeared to their neighbours as westernised and middle class[17].* This devaluation of the **Other** seems to be a

---

[16] *Michael Post argues that Osama's frustration lay in the fact that his father had divorced his mother.*
[17] Financial Times, April 1, 2004, p13

precondition for justifying the war but it does not bring us any closer to finding a solution to this problem.

Secondly, there is the problem of the changing demography and its implications for the west and Islam. As it is, demography is on the side of the non-western world, not only in this war but also beyond. There is enough evidence to support the fact that the United States runs the risk of suffering more demoralisation than the Al Qaeda Army. Osama bin Laden himself made this point a long time ago when he mocked America thus: *We have seen in the last decade, the decline of American government and the weakness of the American soldier, who is ready to wage cold wars and unprepared to fight long wars. This was proven in Beirut when the Marines fled after two explosions. It also proves that they can run in less than twenty-four hours and this was also repeated in Somalia..... After a few blows, they ran in defeat. They forgot about being the world leader and the leader of the world order. They left, dragging their corpses and their shameful defeat, and stopped using such titles*[18].

The rise in the level of recruitment and the fact that there are hundreds of what Al Qaeda itself refers to as **Sleeping cells** [19], means that there are still hundred of thousands out there who are lining up for martyrdom. What is very interesting in all this is the fact that for a people who have grown to worship the *American dream* and the material comforts that have come to define western life, it is impossible to sell the idea that for the youth in the Arab world, the *dream of martyrdom* is the ultimate dream! Unless we grasp why it is that makes these young men and women to surrender the ideals of today for the martyrdom of today, fighting terrorism will fail to understand that terror is merely a strategy for a much deeper war that is a conflation of so many historical, religious, cultural and philosophical quests for freedom and justice.

Thirdly, there is what I call the **culture of counter-penetration**. From Osama Bin Laden to those young men who flew those planes, it is clear that Al Qaeda adopted what I will call counter-penetration as a

---

[18] Osama Bin Lade, Interview with John Miller, ABC News, May 28th, 1998. Quoted in Bernard Lewis, *The Revolt of Islam*. The New Yorker, November 19th, 2001. p62

[19] **Sleeping Cells** are made up of those who cut their teeth during the days of the Mujahedeen in Afghanistan. These recruits went back home after their training armed with the Manuals of instructions on Al Qaeda philosophy. With no direct contact with Osama Bin Laden, *Sleeping cells* can **wake** up any time they are ready to inflict any havoc (as in Kenya and Tanzania).

Chapter Eleven | Matthew Hassan Kukah

strategy. By counter-penetration, I mean the ability of these young Arabs to acquire the *resources* of the west and then turn those resources around against the west. This ranges from education, culture, financial institution, science and technology. What would Al Qaeda have done without the ***Internet***, the ability to fly planes, or to move huge sums of money using the thoroughly corrupt international financial systems? This counter-penetration makes Al Qaeda a cancer cell that might be almost impossible to weed out by the kind of tactics that the west has employed. Against this background, what lessons should the world learn from this war?

It is clear to me that the issue is not so much the question of who wins this war. If anything, this war is the greatest justification if ever there was any, of the spuriousness of those who reject the presumption against war and argue that this war met the standards of the just war theory. Even if this war proves President Bush right in the end, that is, that they find the weapons of mass destruction or that it is discovered that Saddam Hussein really had connections with Al Qaeda, it does not detract from the fact that the Government adopted lies and subterfuge as a strategy, a questionable strategy which has put not only the lives of thousands of innocent citizens in jeopardy, but a strategy that has brought the world closer to a brink from where it will take generations to pull back, recover and stabilise. What is more, with the Americans poised to stay on interminably in Iraq (they have built the biggest embassy anywhere in the world in Baghdad, it is clear that return of sovereignty, especially teleguided by the Americans will only secure a short reprieve. The challenge now is how to stop Iraq from sliding into war in the short or long term. By way of Conclusion therefore, I want us to review what the world has lost to war as a means of showing the hopelessness of contemplating the adoption of the just war theory as a legitimating for war.

6: Conclusion: Beyond the Fog of War, a Rainbow:

I have tried to argue in this paper that *a presumption against war* is a plausible proposition in discussing the just war theory. I take case of the position of presumption against war based on my belief that war is a human invention and not a biological or necessity and that there must be more humane ways of resolving conflicts than resort to war. Beyond the fact that new developments and attitudes towards religion have changed, there is no consensus as to what might constitute what Augustine and the fathers of the just war theory had in mind when they thought that war could form a basis for the establishment of a *tranquillitas ordinis*. The two cities that Augustine visualised were the *Earthly city* is the city where: *all the righteous, wherever they may be in the Universe, the fallen angels, the souls of the unrighteous, the unrighteous who are living on earth dwell* and the *City of God* which is: *a city of the righteous, a city pervaded by a system of right relations which unites God and his angels and saints in heaven with the righteous on earth*[20].

In the mind of St Augustine, the two worlds that constituted the *City of God* and the *Earthly city* had their distinct characteristics. However, in reflecting on the morality of the war, I have tried to show that in the history of the world, all wars have proved to be worse than the diseases they sought to cure and that gradually, precious, God given human life is being subordinated to the whims and capricious quest for power of the new empire builders. I have shown that the attempt to rationalise the just war theory today is untenable largely because western powers have build their lives on the sweat and tears of colonised countries of the world. What the modern day empire builders are trying to do now is to find a moral basis for the continued exploitation of the resources of the developing world and reduce life to a contestation around the Oil wells and minerals in these countries. Let us therefore by way of conclusion turn our light to the United States which has now assigned itself what it sees as a God given *missionary* right to make the rest of the world in its image and likeness.

If anyone is well placed to deal with the issues we have been trying to articulate, I think it is Robert McNamara. He was the Secretary of State for Defence during the Vietnam War. It is also interesting that even though President John Kennedy and Robert McNamara were both Catholics, his warmongers did not push the just war theory to push him into war during the Cuban missile crisis. What is more, Robert McNamara realised more than anyone else the futility of war because he lost his job during the war with Vietnam. He also realised along with the

---

[20] Ernest Barker: Introduction to City of God
(London: JM Dent and Sons. 1945)px vii

President how much the war with Vietnam incapacitated the President's lofty quest for a great social programme to lift up the lives of poor people. Two films have tried to capture these realities. The first, *A Path To War*, traces the nature of the gathering storms that led the United States into Vietnam. The new film, *The Fog of War*, is McNamara's attempts on celluloid to clarify his vision after with hindsight. Looking back, McNamara has highlighted the following lessons:

1: The human race will not eliminate war in this century, but we can reduce the brutality of war, the level of killing by adhering to the principles of the just war theory in particular the principles of proportionality.
2: The indefinite combination of human fallibility and nuclear weapons will lead to the destruction of nations
3: We the richest nation in the world, have failed in our responsibility to our own poor and to the disadvantages across the world, to help them advance their welfare in the most fundamental terms of nutrition, literacy, health and employment.
4: President Kennedy believed that the primary responsibility of a President is to keep the nation out of war if at all possible.
5: War is a blunt instrument by which to settle disputes between or within nations
6: We fail to recognise that in the international affairs, as in other aspects of life, there may be problems for which there are no immediate solutions and certainly non-military solutions. At times we may have to live with an imperfect, untidy world.

The lessons of war have always been clear to the world and its leaders. For example, in 1945, at the end of the Second World War, Franklin Roosevelt stated that: *The work my friend, is peace. More than an end to war, we want an end to the beginning of all wars, yes, an end to this brutal, inhuman, and thoroughly impractical method of settling differences between governments*[21]. The sheer amount of wastage and devaluation of human life which is the consequence of war makes war unjustifiable. What is more, post war reconstruction is fraught with difficulties because more often than not, the nation's resources would have been diverted to the war. As it is with

---

[21] Quoted in *Peace Flier*, nd.

the case of the war with Iraq, we know that the United Government has approached the war mainly as job creating, moneymaking business. It is reckoned that in the war with Afghanistan, the United States ratio of civilian contractors to military personnel was 1:60 and now, in the war with Iraq, that ratio is now 1: 6^{22}.

Apart from the huge volume of resources already cornered by such business behemoths like *Halliburton*[23], the employment of civilian contractors to undertake prison interrogations and other security related duties seems to fly in the face of what a war is and the commitment of civilians. But, again, here we come face to face with the reality of why it is impossible to simply agree that the common good is what propels nations to war. Clearly, economic considerations are now major drivers of war especially in the United States. This was the philosophy behind the concept of the military-industrial complex. The stunning film, *JFK* argues that the late Kennedy was a victim of the interests shrouded in the military industrial complex framework and that he had to go because placed those interests in jeopardy by trying to end the war. Below is a table of the United States tale of engagement with wars in the last two hundred or so years. What we present here is the list of casualties as far as the Americans are concerned. But the low level of American lives can be explained by the superiority of their weapons and the fact that all these wars have been fought outside their shores. But, the losses suffered by the either enemy countries and the rest of the world compounds the problems. For example, during the First World War (1914-18), 8.5m soldiers died while 28m civilians lost their lives leaving 7.75m missing and 21m wounded[24]. Subsequent wars have similarly led to the deaths of millions of civilians, soldiers and the destruction of civilisations and added to human suffering.

---

[22] National programme on public radio, Saturday, June 5th, 2004.
[23] For a comprehensive account of the politics of Halliburton and the US military see, Jane Mayer: *Contract Sport: What Did Dick Cheyney Do for Halliburton?* The New Yorker Magazine. February 16th, 2004, p80-92
[24] Richard Regan: Just War: Principles and Cases. (The Catholic University of America. Washington. 1966) p132.

Chapter Eleven | Matthew Hassan Kukah

American involvements in Wars from 1775-2004

Wars	1. Years	Deaths	Costs	Comments
Revolutionary war	1775-1783	25,000	$101,100,000	
War of 1812	1812-1875	2,260	$90,000,000	
Mexican War	1846-1848	13,283	$71,400,000	Territory
Civil War	1861-1865	360,222	$3, 183,000,000	Union forces
Civil war	1861-1865	260,000	$2,000,000,000	*Confederates*
Spanish-American	1898-1898	2,446	$283,200,000	Territory
World War 1	1914-1918	116,516	$78,676,000,000	
World War 2	1939-1945	405,399	$263,259,000,000	Nazism
Korean War	1950-1953	36,516	$67, 386,000,000	Cold war
Vietnam War	1957-1975	58,000	$150,000,000,000	Cold war
Gulf War	1991-1991	305	$61,000,000,000	Agnst Hussein
Afghan War	2001-2001		Na	Taliban rule
Iraq War	2003-?		$87,000,000,000	

7.*Source: World Book, 2003*

The just war theory is neither a doctrine nor a dogma. Time has since changed so decisively as to render some of the assumptions untenable. As I have stated, the so-called civilised world has spent the dawn of human civilisation rampaging the rest of the world. In the process, civilisations have been destroyed. The experience of the United States with this war is again a further validation of what I have tried to say in this paper. The tragic events and revelations of America's resort to immoral and underhand tactics in its fight for what it claims was a just war have depleted its moral capital seriously. The public hearings over the real events that led to the tortures in the Iraqi prisons are more a symptom than the disease. Even the most well intentioned could never have believed it would come to this, and yet, for anyone who supported this war to turn around and shed crocodile tears, is to assume that there is such a thing as a good war. To imagine that there can ever be a good war is the same as saying that there can be rules guiding what can constitute a good rape. Even the ardent supporters of the war who thought that Israel might end up as a springboard for democracy in the Middle East are now eating humble pie. Today, Friedman, the influential foreign

Affairs Editor of the New York Times who supported the war has come to the conclusion that President Bush has *a moral vision, but he has no moral influence* in the world[25]. These scars are the realities of war. And that is why the world must turn away from war and look to a future

---

[25] Thomas Friedman: *Dancing Alone*, New York Times, May 15 n[th], 2004, pA27.

where we can build and sustain a world that is based on shared values of our common humanity, equality and justice. In my view nothing else will do. I thank you very much.

(Paper presented at a Conference on the War in Iraq and the UN at the House of Lords, London, May 19, 2004).

Index

257

www.ingramcontent.com/pod-product-compliance
Lightning Source LLC
Chambersburg PA
CBHW020344270326
41926CB00007B/311